TEMPLE BETH SHOLOM
Stratford, CT

This Book has been donated

by

The Sorhaindo/Levi Family

Rituals of Childhood

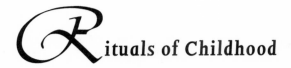

Rituals of Childhood

Jewish Acculturation in Medieval Europe

Ivan G. Marcus

Yale University Press   New Haven and London

Frontispiece: Detail of school initiation scene from *Leipzig Maḥzor* (see p. 82).

"Honey" is excerpted from the book-length poem *Claims* by Shirley Kaufman.
© 1984 The Sheep Meadow Press. Reprinted by permission.

Designed by Deborah Dutton.
Set in Postscript Monotype Joanna type by Tseng Information Systems, Inc., Durham,
North Carolina.
Printed in the United States of America by BookCrafters, Inc., Chelsea, Michigan.

Library of Congress Cataloging-in-Publication Data
Marcus, Ivan G.
Rituals of childhood : Jewish culture and acculturation in the Middle Ages / Ivan G. Marcus.
p.   cm.
Includes bibliographical references and index.
ISBN 0-300-05998-1 (alk. paper)
1. Jewish religious education of preschool children—Germany—History.   2. Initiation
rites—Religious aspects—Judaism—History.   3. Judaism—History—Medieval and early
modern period, 425–1789.   I. Title.
BM85.G4M37   1996
296.4'42—dc20   95-24663
                                                                              CIP

A catalogue record for this book is available from the British Library.

The paper in this book meets the guidelines for permanence and durability of the
Committee on Production Guidelines for Book Longevity of the Council on Library
Resources.

10   9   8   7   6   5   4   3   2   1

To Judy

Contents

Acknowledgments

This book has been gestating for many years. Parts of it were offered as lectures at the invitation of the Friends of the Library of the Jewish Theological Seminary of America, Dropsie College, the annual meeting of the Association for Jewish Studies, and the World Congress of Jewish Studies in Jerusalem.

Many colleagues read all or part of the manuscript, discussed specific points with me along the way, offered important suggestions and alternative readings and interpretations, or gave me references I had not seen before. It is a great pleasure to acknowledge the help of Shalom Bar-Asher, Sebastian Brock, Evelyn Cohen, Jeremy Cohen, Mark R. Cohen, Shaye J. D. Cohen, Giles Constable, Joseph Dan, Howard Eilberg-Schwartz, Shamma Friedman, Isaiah Gafni, Avraham Grossman, Itamar Gruenwald, Joseph Hacker, Elliott Horowitz, Moshe Idel, William C. Jordan, Elaine Morris, Miri Rubin, David Ruderman, Peter Schäfer, Raymond P. Scheindlin, Annemarie Schimmel, Menahem Schmelzer, Robert Stacey, Regina Stein, Kenneth R. Stow, Michael Swartz, Israel Ta-Shema, Eli Yassif, Israel Yuval, Yitzhaq (Eric) Zimmer, and the anonymous reader for Yale University Press.

I wish to express my appreciation to Professor Menahem Schmelzer, former Librarian, and Professor Mayer Rabinowitz, Librarian of the Jewish Theological Seminary Library. Over the years, they and Rabbi Jerry Schwarzbard and their assistants made the rich treasures of that unique library available to me with unfailing patience and resourcefulness.

The manuscript of this book was also improved by enthusiastic early editing from Judy Goldberg and my son Magen D. Marcus.

Robert Bonfil and Harvey Goldberg, both of the Hebrew University of Jerusalem, went out of their way to devote much time and thought to the entire manuscript. I am very grateful to them for their probing written comments and electronic and face-to-face conversations.

The completion of this book was encouraged at a critical time by my editor at Yale University Press, Charles Grench, to whom I am especially thankful.

Material support for the publication of this book has been provided by a publication grant from the Lucius N. Littauer Foundation, and it is also published with the assistance of the Louis and Minna Epstein Fund of the American Academy for Jewish Research.

It is appropriate that I dedicate this book about children to my wife, Judy, who as a pediatric hematologist and oncologist draws on her abundant energy, talent, and optimism to initiate her patients and their families into the mysteries that lie before them, and who, as my best friend since we were teenagers, has enabled us to initiate our four sons into schooling and adult life.

Rituals of Childhood

He said to me, "Mortal, eat what is offered you; eat this scroll, and go speak to the House of Israel." So I opened my mouth, and He gave me this scroll to eat, as He said to me, "Mortal, feed your stomach and fill your belly with this scroll that I give you." I ate it, and it tasted sweet as honey to me.
Ezekiel 3 : 1–3

Oh Book! infinite sweetness! let my heart
Suck every letter, and a honey gain,
Precious for any grief in any part;
To clear the breast, to mollify all pain.
"The H. Scriptures I," George Herbert

Fridays my father came home
for the weekend smelling of damp wool.

He knew there were things more lavish
than his Morris chair, but he sank into it
loosening his tie, and letting me
smooth the fur of his eyebrows
with my doll's comb.

He told me his mother put honey
on his tongue the first day at heder
to sweeten his whole life. . . .
"Honey," Shirley Kaufman

Chapter One

Introduction: Ritual and Medieval Jewish Cultural History

At age five or six, a Jewish boy living in medieval Germany or France might begin his formal schooling by participating in a special ritual initiation ceremony.[1] Early on the morning of the spring festival of Shavuot (Pentecost), someone wraps him in a coat or *talit* (prayer shawl) and carries him from his house to the teacher.[2] The boy is seated on the teacher's lap, and the teacher shows him a tablet on which the Hebrew alphabet has been written. The teacher reads the letters first forwards, then backwards, and finally in symmetrically paired combinations, and he encourages the boy to repeat each sequence aloud. The teacher smears honey over the letters on the tablet and tells the child to lick it off.

Cakes on which biblical verses have been written are brought in. They must be baked by virgins from flour, honey, oil, and milk. Next come shelled hard-boiled eggs on which more verses have been inscribed. The teacher reads the words written on the cakes and eggs, and the boy imitates what he hears and then eats them both.

The teacher next asks the child to recite an incantation adjuring POTAḤ, the prince of forgetfulness (*sar ha-shikheḥah*), to go far away and not block the boy's heart (*lev*; i.e., mind). The teacher also instructs the boy to sway back and forth when studying and to sing his lessons out loud.

As a reward, the child gets to eat fruit, nuts, and other delicacies. At the conclusion of the rite, the teacher leads the boy down to the riverbank and tells him that his future study of Torah, like the rushing water in the river, will never end. Doing all of these acts, we are told, will "expand the (child's) heart."[3]

This book is a study of the history and interpretations of the medieval Jewish initiation ritual by means of which a northern European or Ashkenazic Jewish boy began his religious studies. It illustrates how an anthropological historical approach to the history of medieval Jewish ritual can contribute to a new cultural history of medieval European Jews viewed as a distinctive culture. Understanding medieval European Judaism as a culture, in turn, suggests a new model for thinking about Jewish acculturation in medieval Europe, the interactions that occurred between Jews and Christians in the larger society in which both were actively present. By analyzing rituals, gestures, narratives, and pictorial representations, we will see how ancient Jewish traditions were remembered and reconfigured, often as part of a polemical response to contemporary Christian symbols.

A variety of verbal and pictorial sources may be read as expressions of social polemics, a category of interactive cultural history which Natalie Zemon Davis applied to the Protestant and Catholic conflicts in sixteenth-century France. Living apart and yet together in Latin Christendom, Jews and Christians celebrated their religious cultures in public ceremonies which the members of the other saw and which helped shape their own way of making sense of the world. This cultural feedback was a central feature of the culture of Ashkenaz.[4]

The symbolic analysis of rituals and other reflections of Jewish-Christian social polemics offer us a different perspective from studies of Jewish-Christian interaction based, for example, on developments in Jewish law or on formal written disputations, which are usually called polemics.[5] Moreover, an anthropological history of medieval Jewish culture attempts to get beyond the distinction between elite and popular culture even in their "reciprocal influence," and to reach a more comprehensive understanding of the culture as a whole.[6]

European and American historians,[7] not only anthropologists and students of comparative religion, have studied rituals.[8] And although anthropological research is usually associated with doing field work on living cultures, important results can be obtained from a historical study that is based on written sources and ethnographic narratives and reports. James A. Boon, for one, has challenged the assumption in modern anthropology that privileges field work as immediate, in contrast to written or other sources not directly experienced by the participant-observer.[9] Field work is actually less immediate than it appears, Boon argues, because the researcher must always interpret data as they are gathered, noted down, and finally written up. Theory always plays a critical role in the interpreter's very act of observing and recording, procedures that are not prior to theory but are embedded in it. The distinction between direct observation and the interpretation of written sources or surviving material objects thus becomes blurred, and in the end all data are turned into literary texts that have to be interpreted.

Although historical anthropology is theoretically possible, we might still ask if it can be applied to religious cultures that are highly textual in character, in contrast to the nonliterate cultures for which it has traditionally been used. But to accord special standing to Judaism, Christianity, or Islam, for example, reflects a cultural bias.[10] Without presupposing the evolutionary schemes that make possible the invidious distinctions between higher and lower, civilized and primitive, researchers can apply to Judaism and other literate and literary cultures the same anthropological analysis they do to nonliterate ones.

The textual and highly literate character of Judaism in particular should not deter us from applying this perspective to studying it, if only because the history of the Jews is broader than the history of the literate males whose writings are usually studied. Not all Jews were rabbis who wrote books, and even those who did were social as well as intellectual beings. They were members of families and clans, made livings, wore clothing, ate meals, and marked life-cycle events with rituals that express specific patterns, sometimes as a result of interacting with the Christian culture in which they also lived. In short, the Jews of medieval Europe constituted a distinctive culture.

Anthropological inquiry has been applied to Jewish history, but mainly the ancient and modern periods.[11] Although S. D. Goitein was alert to ethnographic accounts and drew on his own firsthand field experience with recent Mediterranean Jewish immigrants to Palestine and Israel when he presented the Jews of *A Mediterranean Society*, until very recently this approach has not been applied to Ashkenazic Jewry in northern Europe during the central Middle Ages, and when it has, it has drawn more on narratives than on rituals.[12] A study based on rituals may make visible certain patterns that have been overlooked until now—in particular, cultural structures and core values that do not otherwise emerge clearly.[13]

For the most part, the study of the Jews in medieval Europe has focused on prescriptive written sources, especially rabbinic texts.[14] Among the fields covered are the political and legal status of the Jews, Jewish-Christian polemics, rabbinic legal culture and biography, Jewish communal governance, and the rabbinic genres of Talmud and Bible commentary, legal codes and responsa, liturgical and secular poetry, homilies, pietistic writings that make use of exempla, religious philosophy, mysticism, and story cycles and related narratives.[15] Given the tendency in medieval Jewish studies toward specialization and toward viewing Jewish culture as types of writings by genre, it has been difficult to find a vantage point from which to discover the mentality shared by the rabbinic elites and other Jewish men, women, and children.

But an anthropological historical perspective on the culture of the Jews in medieval Europe suggests ways to answer questions such as, How did medieval Jews make sense of the world in which they lived? To do this, we must redefine the subject at hand not as "the culture of the Jews," which generally tends to be male, rabbinic, and written, but "the Jews as a culture," which is more all-embracing. So understood, an anthropological historical investigation of the medieval Jewish culture may enable us to get beyond the limits posed by the study of certain genres of written sources and of the world shaped by the rabbinic elite alone.

Ritual and Medieval European Jewish History

The study of ritual in general offers a perspective from which to see how a culture looks at the world. Ritual includes not only religious rites performed in the home or in synagogues and churches, but all conventional gestures that are routinely expressed in the life of a particular group. For our purposes, the term *ritual* may be used interchangeably with *custom*, *rite*, and *ceremony*, and it can include words as well as gestures. It need not be restricted to the exotic because ritual encompasses most aspects of everyday life from birth to death throughout the calendar year.[16]

As the symbolic or evocative language of the body, ritual mediates between the unexpressed inner world of the self and "gestures forth the world as meaningful and ordered."[17] It is a visible expression of the individual's unseen values, beliefs, and attitudes, and is "a way of conceptualizing the world."[18] But it also offers a way of understanding the social implications of inner moods and thoughts. Since a culture is not simply an aggregate of its individual members but is a social construct, rituals also evoke shared values that are experienced in public. As a result of its public record, many of ritual's symbolic modes of action are traceable in historical reports and visual representations as well as in ethnographic records. And so if we would understand a culture as a whole, we should study its rituals, customs, and gestures in addition to its narratives and other types of collective expression.

Although ritual is a form of symbolic knowledge that is present everywhere in medieval Jewish culture, it has been relatively neglected both as a subject in its own right and as a key to understanding the culture of medieval European Jewry as a whole. For example, a subject as dramatic and performative as the Jewish liturgy has been studied until very recently as the history of the written prayers alone. But when Jews prayed they not only recited or read words; they also moved their bodies in specific ways. Ignored has been the history of the gestures involved in the performed rites that literally incorporate the words and physically express attitudes. Gestures such as bowing or kneeling, reciting the words in a low voice and moving the lips, holding hands together or raising them, lifting or lowering the eyes, among many others, are often dismissed as merely customs, on a lower plane than the texts. But there is no a priori reason why nonverbal aspects of the liturgy cannot be studied in texts and pictorial representations as much as the words of the prayers themselves.[19]

A vast amount of information about other rituals and ceremonies is also to be found in the sources that deal with different aspects of medieval Jewish life, including the study hall, family celebrations of Sabbath and festivals, everyday routines, life crises, and rites of passage. We see evidence of ritualized behavior in depictions of grooming and dress, manners, jokes, and games. And yet the history of Jewish gestures and rituals is still largely unwritten.[20]

Ashkenazic Culture and the Ritualization of Metaphors

Since ritual is a form of public symbolic expression that is reflected in collective actions, it is an especially appropriate way to examine the culture and history of medieval Ashkenaz. One of the features of medieval Ashkenaz is its tendency to generate many rituals and customs, at least some of which seem to exemplify a cultural process that the anthropologist James Fernandez has called "the ritualization of metaphors."[21] This is a cultural mechanism in which individuals take a metaphorical statement about themselves to be fundamentally true. Perhaps the most famous case in the anthropological literature is the claim of the Bororo from Brazil: "I am a parrot."[22]

A metaphor ultimately derived from late biblical religion illustrates the tendency in medieval Ashkenaz to act out textual metaphors ritually: the Jewish community is holy like the ancient Temple.[23] By ritualizing variations of this root metaphor, Ashkenazic Jewry generated many new customs and rituals. I am not suggesting that the Jews of ancient times or in Muslim Mediterranean lands did not create many customs and rites of their own, nor am I denying that they sometimes did so in the form of the ritualization of metaphors.[24] Most peoples do. But there seems to be a special propensity in Ashkenazic culture to do this in patterns of behavior that presuppose the Temple-like holiness of the community.

The tendency to generate new rituals grounded in metaphors, as well as the specific forms that this process takes, may reflect the influence of the surrounding medieval Christian culture, which was saturated with symbols and rites derived from sacred texts.[25] In resisting the powerful culture that surrounded them, the Jews of Ashkenaz polemically denied the central root metaphor of the sacrificed Jesus but at the same time internalized the process of generating new polemical rituals drawn from ancient themes and images that placed Israel, not Jesus, as the locus of the sacred and even of sacrificial martyrdom.

We see a dramatic example of the Ashkenazic pattern in the form of the sacrificial and self-sacrificial acts of martyrdom that some Jews acted out in the Rhineland in the spring of 1096 in the wake of Pope Urban II's call for an armed pilgrimage to Jerusalem — the First Crusade.[26] Faced with the prospect of death at the hands of Crusaders, Jewish men and women in the Rhenish towns of Mainz and Worms killed their families and then themselves.[27] Three Jewish narrators writing in the first half of the twelfth century in Germany described the riots and compared the martyrdom to Abraham's sacrifice of Isaac.[28] In Genesis, however, Isaac does not die but is saved from his father's hand by divine intervention. The metaphors that represent medieval Jewish martyrs as biblical Abrahams and Isaacs make sense in part in light of ancient literary traditions according to which Abraham actually did kill Isaac, who revived and was about to be killed a second time before an angel checked Abraham's hand (Gen. 22:15).[29] The metaphors represent an acting out of the central self-image in Ashkenaz of the holy people as Temple, according to which German Jews in 1096 acted both as Temple priests and as sacrifices.

This pattern, as I shall argue, also illustrates how much Jewish culture in Ashkenaz was deeply embedded in a Christian milieu. The ritualization of the specific metaphor that a Jewish community is collectively a sacrificed Isaac takes on special significance as an acted-out polemical riposte to Christian claims that Jesus's death was an atoning sacrifice. It also counters the ancient Christian assertion, found in the Epistle to the Hebrews, that Jesus represented a substitute for the Jerusalem Temple. The 1096 acts of ritual sacrifice and suicide express a medieval Ashkenazic mentality that resonates with ancient Jewish ascetic and Temple metaphors and an awareness of living in a contemporary Christian culture that was derived in part from the same reservoir of ancient Jewish lore. The issue of whether Jews who acted out the metaphor of a sacrificing Abraham and a sacrificed Isaac understood the literary tradition of Isaac's death and resurrection or whether this association was only in the minds of the later narrators is not clear. But in either case, the narratives illustrate how literary metaphors—Isaac as sacrifice, Abraham as priest—could be translated in Ashkenaz into the behavior of ritualized killings.

Although there are significant differences between the rituals of sacrifice and suicide attributed to the Jewish martyrs of 1096 and the child's school initiation rite, both are case studies of the same process of the ritualization of metaphors. When the boy eats sweetened letters of the Torah, he acts out the prophet Ezekiel's metaphorical vision of eating God's words, which he describes as "sweet as honey" (Ezek. 3:1–3). The foods the child eats are all traditionally equated with the Torah: flour, oil, milk, and honey. In addition to the metaphors of eating the Torah, the child is placed on the lap of the teacher who, like Moses, is compared to a nurturing mother (Num. 11:12). The conclusion of the ceremony, when the teacher leads the boy to the riverbank, is based on the metaphor that the Torah is like life-giving water (e.g., Ps. 1:3). As we shall see (in chapter 5), these metaphors all have a literary history from ancient Judaism, but they are acted out, ritualized, in the medieval Ashkenazic initiation ritual.

A Model of Ashkenazic Acculturation

The study of Jewish rituals in Ashkenaz not only enables us to understand better the deep structure or core values of the culture of Ashkenaz but
also permits us to reexamine how the Jewish minority in Christian Europe
acculturated in a special way to the environment of the Christian majority.
But to claim that Ashkenaz expressed itself in any form of acculturation is
contrary to the historical model of Ashkenaz proposed in the nineteenth century by such shapers of Jewish historiography as Heinrich Graetz, who cast
a long shadow over Jewish historiography to the present.[30] According to this
view, the rabbinic courtier elite of Muslim Baghdad and Cordova acculturated
to the cultural norms of the majority, but the rabbinic class of Ashkenaz was
not influenced by the dominant Christian culture of northern Europe in any
fundamental way.[31]

This negative conclusion is based on the unexamined assumption that
medieval Jewish acculturation is demonstrated to the degree that it follows the
same pattern of elite cultural borrowings that supposedly defined the Jewish
courtier class in Muslim Spain or Sepharad. According to the commonly accepted view, a few members of the Jewish minority in the Muslim East and
especially in Muslim Spain were highly acculturated in a symbiotic manner to
their Arabic milieu. They participated in the court life of Baghdad and Cordova
and later in the courts of the petty kingdoms in Andalusia from the mid-
tenth century until the Berber Almohad invasion, beginning in the mid-1140s.[32]
Among them, R. Samuel Ibn Nagrela (993–1056) was the military commander
of King Habbus of Granada and wrote secular Hebrew poems from the front.
But he also served the Jewish community as *nagid* or head of the Jews, mastered
Arabic verse, and was an authority on Jewish law.[33] R. Moses b. Maimon, Maimonides (1138–1204), the avatar of Arabic-Jewish symbiosis, combined being
a Jewish legal and communal authority with writing religious philosophy in
his synthesis of Neoplatonic Aristotelianism and Jewish revealed traditional
lore.[34] Both men were leaders of Jewish communities and also served Muslim authorities. This group is often pictured as living within two medieval
cultures.

In contrast, the elite Jews of northern Europe have generally been thought
of as rabbis who lived in relative cultural isolation from the culture of their
Christian environment.[35] Jewish religious figures in northern Europe such as

R. Gershom b. Judah of Mainz (d. 1028), Rashi, and Rashi's grandson R. Jacob b. R. Meir Tam (d. 1171), also of Champagne, are viewed as religious commentators, jurists, liturgical poets, and even communal leaders. But scholars have portrayed them as living in relative cultural and political isolation from neighboring Christian elites despite the fact that they resided in the same small towns.[36] Some have decried this situation, others have praised it, but most have taken it for granted.[37]

Before we can see how the culture of medieval Ashkenaz was related to the culture of Latin Christendom, we need to reexamine the meaning of the term *acculturation* and its use in premodern and modern settings. The issue is not whether Jews in Latin Christendom spoke the vernacular and picked up words or phrases from medieval Latin.[38] They did. But there has been resistance until now to the possibility that northern European rabbinic thinkers were deeply aware of and engaged by the central themes, values, and world picture of Christianity and that this awareness shaped medieval Jewish traditions as a counterweight or social polemical response to them.[39] Contact was limited, we are told, because most Christians were illiterate and were not candidates for the symbiotic exchange that obtained in Muslim lands between members of both elites. Or, the Christian elites were churchmen and Latin Christian culture was a hostile religious environment in which Jews could not participate, unlike in the Islamic lands, where the court was the scene of poetry contests about "wine, women and death."[40] There were no comparable courts in the north where Jews and Christians could meet, drink, and compete verbally as near equals.[41]

This contrasting picture of Muslim-Jewish acculturation and the absence of acculturation in Latin Christian Europe has persisted despite a new scholarly consensus that has been taking shape about the two subcultures of medieval Sepharad and Ashkenaz. What has not been sufficiently appreciated is that the very definition of Jewish acculturation as elitist and as borrowing and adapting genres foreign to Judaism from the host culture has been based on the Muslim–Spanish courtier example, which itself is assumed to be historically accurate. When it is then applied to the Ashkenazic case, it leads to the predictably negative result that the rabbis of Ashkenaz did not acculturate—in the specified sense—in Latin Christendom.

Accepting the accuracy of Jewish symbiotic acculturation in Muslim Spain, some students of Jewish history have even tried to find Ashkenazic analogues to the model of medieval Sephardic elite acculturation. This is reflected in the interest taken in hebraei, the Jewish scholars with whom French Christian exegetes spoke and exchanged views about the original meaning of the Hebrew Bible, which Christian scholars usually read in Latin. They are repeatedly cited as evidence of intellectual exchange between Jews and Christian exegetes such as the twelfth-century Victorines in Paris—an influence of Jews on Christians, to be sure, but one modeled on elite cultural exchange typical of the Muslim-Jewish culture.[42]

The application to Ashkenaz of the Sephardic model of elite acculturation is also reflected in the attention given to the field of Jewish-Christian formal polemics, those written and dramatized confrontations between Jewish leaders and Christians, the latter often apostate Jews, in which the Jew defends Judaism from an intellectual assault, sometimes in the court of a pope or Christian monarch. It too is elitist and emphasizes that the rabbis in the Christian north engaged with Christian culture in the court, as had other Jews in the Muslim south.[43]

Another instance of looking at Ashkenazic culture through a lens more appropriate for Spanish-Jewish culture is the disproportionate attention scholars have paid to those northern French Hebrew Bible commentators who emphasized the so-called plain or contextual meaning (peshaṭ) of the biblical text, rather than homiletical or numerological techniques.[44] The former is a characteristic feature of Spanish-Jewish Bible commentators who were influenced by Arabic grammarians and the Muslim interest in the language and literal meaning of the Qur'an. To assert, as some have, that the northern French interest in the literal meaning of the Hebrew Bible was motivated by a polemical agenda to deflect contemporary Christian arguments reinforces the perspective that acculturation in Ashkenaz, as in Spain, was elitist.[45]

And, to a limited extent, it was. But even if we grant, for the time being, the validity of the Sephardic model of elite symbiotic acculturation, we should realize the limitations of applying it to the Jewish culture of Germany and northern France. For the Sephardic model catches only the occasional encounter in Ashkenaz between a churchman and an Ashkenazic rabbi and misses the everyday interactions of ordinary Jews and Christians who lived in the same small towns and villages. Applying the Sephardic typology to Ashkenaz allows us to notice the rare occasions when a Jewish leader was forced to defend the faith in a public forum, but it cannot help us understand how most Jews viewed the Christian world in which they lived day in and day out. In short, holding up the Sephardic model of acculturation to Ashkenaz does not enable us to comprehend Ashkenaz as a whole, but only those aspects of Ashkenaz that resemble the culture of Sepharad.

But the Sephardic model of Jewish symbiotic acculturation itself is not without its problems despite its pedigree in the scholarly literature. The way the term *acculturation* is used in modern and premodern contexts needs to be clarified. To avoid the anachronism of imposing the modern meaning of the term on premodern Jewish societies, it is time to rethink the use of this term. As Robert Bonfil has argued in regard to the cases of the Jews in Muslim Spain and in Renaissance Italy, Jewish elites there did not acculturate in the modern sense of diluting their Judaism and collective identities as Jews by borrowing elements from the non-Jewish majority culture, thus drawing closer to that culture. Had they done so, Bonfil observes, the Jews would have converted to Islam or Christianity, as some undoubtedly did.[46]

Rather, we should understand premodern Jewish societies, not as the merging of Judaism into Christian or Muslim culture, but the reverse. Jews so interpreted their Judaism that they merged elements of Arabic or Christian Renaissance culture into Judaism. Thus, in Muslim Spain, Arabic cultural elements such as metrical court poetry or Aristotelian philosophy were integrated into Judaism: the Jews who were poets and philosophers thought of themselves as being no less Jewish than before. Calling this process of cultural openness and adaptation by the same term by which we refer to modern secularization is anachronistic and misleading.

I propose, then, that we distinguish between *modern* or *outward acculturation* and *premodern* or *inward acculturation*. The former refers to the blurring of individual and communal traditional Jewish identities and of the religious and cultural boundaries between Jews and modern societies. The processes of modernization and secularization during the last two centuries, in Western Europe and the United States, for example, are cases of modern acculturation. The latter refers to premodern cases, be it in the Ancient Near East, the Greco-Roman world, Muslim societies, Latin or Eastern Christendom, or Renaissance Italy, when Jews who did not assimilate or convert to the majority culture retained an unequivocal Jewish identity. Nevertheless, the writings of the articulate few or the customs of the ordinary many sometimes expressed elements of their Jewish religious cultural identity by internalizing and transforming various genres, motifs, terms, institutions, or rituals of the majority culture in a polemical, parodic, or neutralized manner.

Viewed this way, medieval Muslim and Renaissance Jewish acculturation did not, as Cecil Roth imagined,[47] anticipate modern acculturation or Jewish Westernization and secularization, when groups of Jews actually did exchange elements of their traditional Jewish religious culture for a more secular ideology and pattern of living. To view premodern Sephardic and Renaissance Italian Jewish acculturation as precursors of nineteenth-century secularization is yet another example of "the Whig interpretation of history,"[48] according to which the historical meaning of early phenomena is assumed to anticipate and lead to later developments.

We should view the process of premodern Jewish acculturation in Latin Christendom in a similar conceptual framework. There is only a difference of degree, not of kind, between Ashkenazic acculturation, on the one hand, and Muslim Sephardic and Renaissance Italian acculturation, on the other. In Latin Christendom, I will argue, Jews adapted Christian themes and iconography, which they saw all around them every day, and fused them — often in inverted and parodic ways — with ancient Jewish customs and traditions. In all three cases Jews absorbed into their Judaism aspects of the majority culture and understood the products to be part and parcel of their Judaism, and they continued to think of themselves as being completely Jewish. Modern Jewish acculturation is something new and altogether different.[49]

It is not a question of Jewish thinkers or groups adopting Christian patterns of behavior with the result that they somehow became less Jewish and more like the Christian majority. Only by converting did that happen. Rather, they managed to act out and reconstitute those combinations of Jewish and Christian traditions to fashion a parody and counterritual as a social polemic against the truth claims and values of the majority culture. The Jews in medieval Ashkenaz did not assimilate themselves into Muslim or Christian culture. Rather, they assimilated reworked aspects of Christian culture, in the form of a social polemical denial, into their Judaism.

Once we realize that the Sephardic model's preoccupation with elite symbiotic acculturation is an artifact of earlier scholarship, we no longer have to contrast the Ashkenazic case to it and are free to consider both from a perspective grounded in a more empirically based model of Jewish culture and inward acculturation in both Muslim and Christian lands. Such a model would posit as its subject Jewish and Christian cultures, not only elites, that coexisted in the same society. Ignoring the loaded and correlated categories of elite symbiosis or isolation, we would define culture not only as the world of the elites but also as the rest of society, which embraces all members of each community or sets of subcommunities, however large or limited in size. Relying on the theoretical underpinnings of a new understanding of Jewish acculturation, we are able to explore the dynamics of the ways the Jews of Latin Christendom remained Jewish but also remained aware of their Christian surroundings in a profound way.[50]

Ashkenazic Rites of Passage

Among the rituals that are especially suited to reveal deep cultural patterns in medieval Judaism are those publicly observed life-cycle rites which Arnold van Gennep called *rites de passage*. Although in late antiquity Jewish ceremonies such as circumcision, marriage, and mourning the dead had been performed at home, during the Middle Ages they increasingly moved into the public arena of the community's synagogue and thereby became shared public celebrations. Because they were celebrated in public, they reveal core features and assumptions embedded in the Ashkenazic culture and society that celebrated them.[51]

Among the other Jewish life-cycle events of childhood, no special ritual to mark a person's attainment of religious majority existed in late antiquity, either in the home or in the synagogue. When a ceremony did emerge in the late Middle Ages, it was in the synagogue, not in the home. In ancient Judaism, what later was called *bar mitzvah* and referred to the chronological event of a boy's reaching the age of thirteen years and a day was not marked by a special ceremony.[52] Girls reached their age of majority a year earlier, but neither gender marked the occasion with the celebrations and public rites that came to define it for boys in the late Middle Ages in central Europe and for girls in more recent times.

The way a small boy began his formal Jewish education also reflects this shift from domestic to more formal and public events. Although rabbinic sources do not treat early childhood education in a systematic way, the earliest age at which a child was given any kind of instruction was when he was able to talk, and then it was his father, not a teacher, who gave him his first phrases to memorize. Providing a son with his religious education was, like circumcision, a father's religious obligation, and like circumcision it could be delegated to the father's agent.

The change in the male child's status from being a small boy at home, where he might pick up various customs and even occasional snatches of sacred learning from his parents, to being a pupil in the more public space of the synagogue and school already began in the rabbinic period, but it remained a family event. No elaborate public rite to mark this occasion has been preserved from late antiquity. Nor was it associated then with any special time of the calendar year when the rest of the community celebrated a public festival. Only in medieval Ashkenaz do we first get such a ceremony to mark the formal transition from home to school during the festival of Shavuot, and it is the public character of this ceremony that permits us to see in it reflections of the culture of Latin Christendom within Ashkenaz.

In one way, the history of the school initiation ceremony is different from the history of circumcision, bar mitzvah, marriage, and mourning. It has not only a beginning but also an end: at some point it was discontinued, and only traces persisted, such as giving small schoolchildren a piece of honey cake or candy. Thus it constitutes a self-contained unit of study for us to trace the rise and fall of a Jewish children's ritual. These shifts, in turn, offer the historian opportunities to explore changes in the culture in which they occurred. By examining closely the elements that make up the boy's initiation into schooling, a child's rite of passage celebrated in public, I will seek to uncover fundamental values and ways of looking at the world that are at work in the culture of Ashkenaz in its European Christian setting.

The Child's Initiation and Its Meanings

After defining the Ashkenazic ceremony by contrasting it to related medieval variations and folk traditions and presenting its various versions and contemporary contexts (chapter 2), I turn to two traditions from late antiquity and the early Middle Ages that were combined and transformed in the medieval European rite. First, elements from ancient Jewish schooling that themselves reflect Greco-Roman pagan practices are discussed (chapter 3). The

medieval ritual derives in part from ancient Jewish customs that introduced a
child to formal schooling when he was a certain age or when he was ready,
but not at any special holiday or time of the calendar year.

A very different set of customs was integrated into the medieval ritual
from ancient and early medieval traditions of adult magical mnemonics and
mystical Torah study. Unlike the ancient pedagogic practices, the elements discussed in chapter 4 are related not only to age but also to the spring festival of
Shavuot, when some adult Jews studied the Torah in special ways. The child's
pedagogic regimen from late antiquity, based only on his age or readiness,
and the practices of adult magic and mystical learning attached to the Shavuot
holiday were combined in the different versions of the medieval initiation
ceremony.

In Chapter 5, I interpret the ceremony as a whole in different ways and
offer evidence from Hebrew and Latin manuscript illuminations that complement texts drawn from a variety of genres. Different readings converge to
suggest that the child is a symbol for the collectivity of Israel, that is, the Jewish
people. The individual Jewish child's personal "entry into Torah study" symbolically recapitulates the paradigmatic biblical story of Israel's journey from
Egypt to Sinai. At another level, the child's rite of passage merges with the local
Jewish community's own remembering of the biblical narrative during the
spring holiday cycle from Passover to Shavuot that describes the formation of
the Jewish people and its arrival at Mount Sinai. In this way, the child's public
gestures mimic the community's celebration of a remembered sacred past.

These overlapping circles of meaning present the small child as a symbol
of the Jewish people at its formation or cultural birth as a Torah community.
Superimposed on that symbol is another. The child leaves his natural mother
at home and enters the culture of a new symbolic mother—the male Torah
teacher, who is portrayed as the nurturing mother of a newborn child. The
female image of the Torah teacher is based on rabbinic glosses on the Song of
Songs and ultimately on the metaphor of Moses as the nursing mother of the
Jewish people, in Numbers 11:12: "Did I conceive all this people, did I bear
them that You should say to me, 'Carry them in your bosom as a nurse carries
an infant . . .'?" In the Leipzig Maḥzor the portrayal of the male Torah teacher
holding the boy on his lap resembles in form a particular type of Madonna
and Child.

A third metaphor envisions the small child who labors to study Torah as a pure sacrifice whose efforts bring vicarious atonement to the rest of the Jewish community. This motif is especially pronounced in the version of the ceremony in the *Maḥzor Vitry* from northern France. A similar metaphor about the Torah as a child sacrifice is found in a contemporary Hebrew text, possibly also from northern France, known as *Ḥuqqei ha-Torah ha-Qadmonim* (The Ancient Rules of the Torah). Like a Temple sacrifice, the child must be pure and protected from sources of pollution. I compare these representations of the Jewish child — as reborn individual, as nursing infant, as sacrifice — to a contemporary Christian religious vocabulary that focuses on the image of the Christ Child in new ways — as a symbol of rebirth, as the nursing infant with his mother Mary, and as an emblem of salvation in the eucharistic wafer.

In Chapter 6, I examine the Jewish child's rite of passage historically against the backdrop of contemporary Christian rituals of initiation and other Jewish rites of passage, especially the late medieval innovation of bar mitzvah. The diachronic or historical analysis complements the synchronic or interpretive approach. A cross-cultural context enables us to understand better how the Jewish initiation rite emerged when it did and why it eventually disappeared, yielding its place to the bar mitzvah ceremony as a Jewish boy's second initiation after circumcision.

The school ritual emerged as a response to changing circumstances both in the Jewish culture of Ashkenaz and in the host culture of Latin Christendom in the twelfth and thirteenth centuries. The new scholastic textuality of the northern French Talmud glossators, the Tosafists, part of the renewal of the twelfth century, advocated the privileged authority of written texts, one of which claimed that age alone determined when a child should begin his studies. This claim, in turn, provoked rabbis from German Ashkenaz to articulate and defend for the first time in writing their ancient and early medieval customs, one of which was the child's Shavuot Torah initiation rite that combined ancient schoolchildren's traditions with mnemonic practices of adult food and verbal magic.[53]

Though prompted by a shift in Jewish culture, the ritual was articulated in the "grammar of perception" of contemporary Jewish-Christian cultural polemics.[54] The symbolic act of ingesting sanctified bread (the honey cake), itself a symbol for the Torah, is a response to the eucharistic devotion; the ways the teacher and child are portrayed make sense especially in light of the imagery of the Christ Child and the Madonna; and the idea that the father who brings his son to school offers him as a sacrifice competes with the contemporary image of the Christ Child in the eucharist as a sacrifice.

The disappearance of the school initiation and its eventual replacement in the late Middle Ages by the new rite of passage, bar mitzvah, reflects a culmination in the development of a new attitude in Jewish and Christian cultures toward children. In the late twelfth and thirteenth centuries preliminary signs of a new awareness developed not only of childhood per se but also of the relation between a child's age and consent to his assuming full religious responsibility. Leaders of Christian religious communities found fault with the ancient practice of infant and child oblation into monasteries, the Christian equivalent of a Jew's entry into the adult religious life of the synagogue community. The newly organized Cistercians banned oblation before the ages of twelve for girls and fourteen for boys.

We see a similar pattern in late medieval Judaism. Whereas the Talmud and early Ashkenazic custom permitted a boy well before the rabbinic age of religious majority to observe many adult religious rites, later Ashkenazic authorities objected to this practice. They insisted that full participation in adult religious life should wait until age thirteen or even until physical signs of puberty appeared. They insisted that children act like children, not little adults, as they had in the school initiation ceremony.

Both religious cultures defined majority, then, as a necessary condition before letting children enter the religious life and set up a new boundary between childhood and adulthood at a specific age. In Judaism, the age of thirteen generally became that new boundary. The Jewish reformers' distinction between childhood and religious adulthood after age thirteen eventually won out. The small child's school initiation rite disappeared, and by the fifteenth or sixteenth century at least preliminary forms of bar mitzvah had taken its place.

The story of the child's initiation ceremony illustrates a complex pattern of Jewish culture and inward acculturation that is typical of medieval Ashkenaz and suggests new directions for historical research grounded in an anthropological historical methodology and perspective. I begin with the ceremony itself in all of its diversity as preserved in texts and representational images.

Chapter Two

The Initiation Rite

The school initiation ceremony seems to be a simple Jewish folk custom, traces of which survived in the nineteenth-century East European ḥeder, or Jewish primary school. As documented in the film *Hester Street*, which portrays Jewish immigrant life in New York City at the turn of the twentieth century, the rite followed Russian-Jewish immigrants to America. In one scene, a small boy studies the Hebrew alphabet for the first time. Standing behind the seated child, the teacher drops candies on the book and says in Yiddish, "Look what an angel has thrown down from heaven!" This expression is visually represented already in Italian-Jewish elementary school wall charts as an angel dropping something from above (figure 1).[1]

Some Jewish communities still mark the day when a young child receives his or her first *ḥumash* (Pentateuch) or *siddur* (prayer book) by giving out honey cakes, candies, and other treats. Similarly, Germans give new schoolchildren a horn filled with sweets (*Zuckertüte*);[2] American children eat sweetened Alpha-Bits as a breakfast cereal, and American and Israeli parents give their children chicken soup combined with English or Hebrew alphabet noodles. Perhaps the ceremony is just an example of the familiar custom of giving children sweets or other foods, including edible alphabets, to encourage them to start school or to learn their ABC's.[3]

In fact, we find reference to this general custom in medieval Jewish sources. For instance, Maimonides introduces the following parable in his *Peirush ha-Mishnah* (Commentary on the Mishnah):

Imagine that a little boy is brought to a Torah teacher. This is a great benefit to him in light of the education that he will ultimately acquire. But because of his age and ignorance, he understands neither the benefit

1. Detail of Hebrew letters wall chart, Venice 1656. New York, Library of the Jewish Theological Seminary of America, NS E88, Drawer 8, L19. Reprinted courtesy of the Library of the Jewish Theological Seminary of America.

nor the education that (the teacher) will help him acquire. Of necessity, the teacher, who is more educated than he, will motivate him to study by using something which the young child already desires. (The teacher) should say to him: "Study and I will give you nuts or figs or I will give you a piece of candy." Then he will study hard, not for the sake of studying, since he does not know its value, but in order to . . . get something that he does desire—a nut or a piece of candy.[4]

Maimonides' son, Abraham Maimuni, also refers to this common technique: "We encourage the small children to study Torah in school during the weekdays so that they will have qaliyot and nuts on the Sabbath."[5]

This way of rewarding and encouraging small children is also noted in the Rhenish *Sefer Ḥasidim* (Book of the Pietists), where R. Judah b. Samuel, the Pietist (d. 1217), casually refers to the same idea in one of his exempla: "There once was an old Torah scholar . . . (who) used to stand around where small children went to school and give them fruit and nuts to make them want to study Torah. When they left school, too, he would give them more fruit and nuts and ask them what they were studying, thus making them review."[6] The Bulgarian-Jewish writer Elias Canetti, who began his schooling in Vienna before the First World War, recalled in his autobiography how his grandfather took him to the *Kaffeehaus* Sunday mornings, where the boy had *"café au lait* with whipped cream and, most important of all, a crisp *Kipfel* (a Viennese croissant). At eleven o'clock, the Talmud-Torah School at 27 *Novaragasse* began; it was there that you learned to read Hebrew . . . ; he wanted to be sure that I arrived at the school every Sunday morning, the *Kaffeehaus* and the *Kipfel* were supposed to make it more palatable for me."[7]

Although the Ashkenazic ceremony includes this widespread custom of giving sweets, it is much more complex. It features inscribed foods, the incantation against POTAH, the prince of forgetfulness, and a visit to the riverbank. But complexity alone does not distinguish it from other accounts. In an elaborate narrative claiming to be an ethnographic report of Jewish life in North Africa in the seventeenth century, we find a lengthy description of a Jewish child's first days of school. The customs it portrays differ from the Ashkenazic ritual, despite some resemblances. This narrative seems to be part of a Sephardic-Mediterranean variation that is built from some of the same ancient elements that were integrated into the Ashkenazic rite and yet is distinct from the northern European form of the ritual.

A Sephardic-Mediterranean Variation

In 1675 Lancelot Addison, an English civil servant stationed in Barbary (Morocco) published an account of Jewish life in North Africa which he called *The Present State of the Jews (More particularly relating to those in Barbary)*. The narrative includes this description of how Jewish boys began their formal schooling:

When the Jews have taught their children some decent modes of salutation, and imprinted them with an awful reverence of God's Name, and the essays of hating all religions but their own, their next endeavour is to instruct them in the elements of book learning. Where the first lessons are about the name and figure of the Hebrew letters: in which they use this method: First, upon a smooth stone or board they cast two or more letters of the alphabet, and acquaint the child with the name and figure thereof. And when the child is able to pronounce these letters, they proceed to more, according to the capacity and towardliness of the scholar. And so forward, till the whole alphabet be run over. When this task is finished, the children are taught to joyn the letters into short and easie sillibles; and having attained to read a little, they are put into the first Book of Moses, and so pass through the whole Pentateuch. In teaching their children to write they use as the Spaniards, a plana, which is a draught of very large letters upon a fair paper, which they imitate upon a thin paper laid thereon.

When the parents have at home pretty-well grounded their children in these prelusory rudiments, they send them to school; and every morning before they go thither, it is the mothers office to provide them something to eat, which is sweetened with sugar or honey; which serves them both for beakfast [sic] and an instruction. For at giving the child the sweet morsel she useth these words; As this is sweet to thy palate, so let learning be sweet to thy mind.[8]

Addison's description, like the examples from Maimonides, Abraham Maimuni, R. Judah the Pietist, and even Canetti, deals with a Jewish child who is fed something sweet when he is a beginning student. It is not explicitly associated, as it is in the Ashkenazic ritual, with the first day of school. In addition, Addison clearly states that it is the parents who send them to school after they have taught them the Hebrew alphabet at home. In the Ashkenazic rite, the father or a scholar brings the child to the teacher, who in a highly ritualized manner combines foods with the instruction of the alphabet. Moreover, in Addison's description, at the end of the ritual the mother states its purpose: to make learning sweet for the child. In the Ashkenazic initiation, the foods and other gestures are designed to "open the heart," that is, to increase the student's capacity to learn and to retain what he studies.

It is not clear what Jewish community Addison was describing. As Elliott Horowitz has cautioned,[9] much of Addison's ethnographic account purporting to be about North African Jewish life was lifted, sometimes verbatim, from a book about Jewish life in northern Europe by the Christian Hebraist Johannes Buxtorf the Elder (1564–1629). And when we compare Addison's description with Buxtorf's remarks about Jewish children's elementary schooling, we see that Addison's second paragraph is a slightly modified and unattributed quotation from Buxtorf. That passage, as translated in Alexander Ross's *A View of the Jewish Religion*, reads:

> At the fifth year they begin to learn letters and Paintings. . . . And when the boy is first able to read, he is taught to translate the Pentateuch into his country tongue.
>
> In the book intituled *Shevilei Emunah* Schevile Amunah,[10] that is, ways of Faith; it is thus written, "When the Childe is first brought to the Rabbins School, his Mother must give him pieces of Bread, spread with hony and Sugar, adding these words; As this bread is sweet and delightful, so will the law be to thy heart: Like Sugar to thy tongue, and like hony to thy lips, Etc."[11]

Addison's concluding passage is based on Buxtorf's and Ross's acknowledged source, *Shevilei Emunah* (Paths of Faith), a late fourteenth-century Spanish-Jewish collection of natural and moral philosophy.[12] But is Addison describing the early schooling customs which Spanish Jews brought to Morocco or the customs of former Iberian Jews who lived in northern Europe? His remark that "they use as the Spaniards, a plana" raises both possibilities.

We need to consider some additional evidence. A twentieth-century ethnographic account of a Jewish child's preschool initiation in the northwestern Saharan trading town of Ghardaia, in present-day Algeria, bears only a marginal resemblance to Addison's account and raises further doubts about his claims, but there are correlations between Ghardaia and ethnographic evidence from Morocco.[13]

At age five, which in Ghardaia meant during the year preceding the fifth birthday, a Jewish boy undergoes an initiation called *kittab* (literally, "one who writes with speed and ease"). It is spread out over thirty days of festive parties hosted by fathers of the kittab boys. Each boy's hair is cut at home, and he is bathed and dressed in a white shirt and other garments covered with amulets and symbolically marked. He is introduced in the synagogue to the rabbi or other elders, who place a turban on his head and stick flowers into it. His father parades him around the synagogue, and everyone gives him coins.[14]

The kittab ceremony is very different from Addison's account, but then

Ghardaia is not in Morocco. Yehoshua Sobol and Shlomo Bar, of the Israeli-Moroccan folk troupe Ha-Bereirah ha-Ṭivʿit (The Natural Gathering), perform a song called "Tudra Village," which seems to allude to the idea in Addison's borrowed quotation connecting sweet foods with making the Torah sweet for the small child:

> In our village of Tudra, in the heart of the Atlas Mountains, they used to take the child who had reached the age of five and make him a garland of flowers. In our village of Tudra they put the garland on his head when he reached the age of five.
>
> All the kids on the street gave him a party when he reached the age of five in our village of Tudra.
>
> And then the guest of honor,[15] who has reached the age of five, in our village of Tudra, was brought into the synagogue, and they wrote on wooden boards the letters of the alphabet in honey, and they said to him, "Darling, lick!"
>
> And the learning (ha-torah) in his mouth was sweet as the taste of honey, in our village of Tudra, in the heart of the Atlas Mountains.[16]

Although the age of five, the garland of flowers, and the parties all recall the kittab ceremony, which is from a different region of North Africa,[17] the conclusion of the song echoes the idea also found in Addison. "And the learning in his mouth was sweet as the taste of honey" is very close to Addison's pirated quotation from Buxtorf based on the Spanish-Jewish Shevilei Emunah: "As this is sweet to thy palate, so let learning be sweet to thy mind."

The data in the song are in fact consistent with a genuine ethnographic account reported by Ḥaim Zafrani about North African Jewry, from the "Valley of Todga (Tudra?)"[18] in the Atlas Mountains:

> Parents were concerned about two things when the boy reached the age of five: to teach him Torah and to choose a bride for him, following the words in the Talmud.[19] On the eve of the Shavuot festival, in remembrance of Sinai, they would arrange a "miniature wedding."[20] The boy and the girl his age appointed for him were brought together in a real marriage ceremony followed by a festive meal. After morning services, the men went to the groom's house. The rabbi wrote the Hebrew alpha-

bet in honey on a clean board, told the boy to lick the letters, and said: "So may the words of the Torah be sweet to your palate."[21]

Although Addison does not mention the rite of a child's marriage on Shavuot, licking the alphabet written with honey is familiar, as is the reiteration of the explanation for the ritual first attributed to the Spanish-Jewish collection *Shevilei Emunah*. It is possible that both the wedding motif of a first-day schoolchild and the custom of licking honey from a school tablet were related to contemporary Muslim practices.

In his book *The Search for God at Harvard*, Ari Goldman recounts a lecture in which the Islamicist Annemarie Schimmel "told us of a wonderful ceremony that takes place when a boy reaches the age of four years, four months and four days.[22] On this day, the boy is dressed up like a little bridegroom and sent to school to recite his first verse of the Koran. The verse is written in honey on a slate and, after the boy masters it, the honey is dissolved in water. The boy drinks the sweet holy words as a spiritual and physical nourishment."[23]

In contrast to the Ashkenazic ceremony, which stipulates that the alphabet first be written on a tablet, which is then covered with honey, the Tudra song, Zafrani's Moroccan informant, and Schimmel's recollection state that the alphabet itself is written on the slate in honey. The Muslim practice of dissolving the honey in water and drinking it differs from the ceremonies described in the Tudra song and Zafrani, both of which require that the Jewish boy lick the honey from the slate. The method of dissolving and drinking resembles well-known forms of ancient magical rituals in which inscriptions are written in bowls or other objects, filled with liquid, dissolved, and drunk.[24]

The ethnographic data, then, seem to support the conclusion that at least the end of Addison's account does reflect customs of former Spanish Jews living in North Africa. Although Schimmel's report is not specific to North Africa, its correlation with Zafrani's informant's report from Morocco and with part of Addison's account suggests Muslim, not European Christian, provenance.

Other features of Addison's report, such as his assumption that the boys began to study "the first book of Moses," are possible but unlikely.[25] The Tudra Village song, Zafrani's informant, parts of the Jewish kittab ceremony, and the passage from *Shevilei Emunah* quoted in Addison all suggest that a Spanish-

Mediterranean initiation tradition existed which both resembled and differed substantially from the Ashkenazic ritual. Thus both Ashkenazic and Spanish-Mediterranean variations incorporated the practice of rewarding small children at the beginning of their studies. The *Maḥzor Vitry*, one of the Ashkenazic texts, observes this nearly universal practice but puts it differently: "First we entice him and afterward we use the strap." Addison's and the North African Jewish accounts were based in part on this widespread practice.[26]

But the medieval Ashkenazic initiation ceremony differs from the Sephardic-Mediterranean one. Nor is it a simple folk custom, even if the practice today of giving a Jewish child honey cake or candy on the first day of Hebrew school is. It is something else and something more. Like the Spanish-Mediterranean variations, the Ashkenazic ceremony drew on ancient and early medieval elements from the East, but did so in a unique way. It is a highly articulated initiatory rite of passage, with a defined structure that may be read in many ways because of the many layers of symbolic associations embedded in it.

It also has a history. Whereas the Sephardic ceremony was closely related to Muslim practices, the Ashkenazic rite was configured in the cultural context of Latin Christendom. It appeared and disappeared at specific times and places. And because the Ashkenazic variation is unique to Christian Europe, studying it enables us to understand better the culture of Ashkenaz and the ways it interacted with the culture of Latin Christendom.

The German-Jewish Versions

Although all of the written versions of the Ashkenazic Jewish initiation ritual agree as to its basic structure, they divide into two types. The three written descriptions and the manuscript illumination, which all come from Germany, indicate that the child's initiation is to take place on the festival of Shavuot. Accordingly, each description is placed in the part of the book that discusses the laws and customs of Shavuot. In contrast, the three texts from northern France and Provence do not mention when during the year the ceremony should be held. They imply instead that only the child's age or maturity, not the calendar, is the determining factor. As a result, the descriptions of the ceremony from these Hebrew works appear in the sections of the book that deal with the individual's life cycle, right after the laws and customs about an adult's marriage and a male child's circumcision.

Despite this difference between the Hebrew sources from Germany and France, all seven compare the child's initiation into Hebrew literacy with the revelation of the Torah on Mount Sinai to biblical Israel, an event that early rabbinic tradition understood as having taken place on the Shavuot festival. Consequently, all seven versions associate the ceremony, if not its actual observance, with Shavuot. And yet, although the versions agree about many of the elements that make up the rite, each contains distinctive features.

To a greater or lesser extent, the texts that record the initiation rite all contain two types of material. They describe the ritual gestures that constitute a unique version of the ceremony, and each also contains commentary about what certain elements mean. The simplest and earliest account is in *Sefer ha-Roqeah* (Book of the Perfumer) by R. Eleazar b. Judah of Worms (ca. 1160–1230).[27] Among the remarkable features of this version is the very first statement: "It is the custom of our ancestors (*minhag avoteinu*) to sit the children down to study (the Torah for the first time) on Shavuot because that is when the Torah was given." Although Eleazar insists that the ceremony is old, he offers no explicit evidence to confirm this. To be sure, several key elements in the ceremony can be traced back to earlier Jewish and even Greco-Roman practices, while others derive from early medieval East Mediterranean Jewish settings, but that is true of individual elements, not of their combination in a Jewish boy's initiation ritual. The complete initiation itself is unattested before the late twelfth or early thirteenth century.

Following his claim that the ceremony is old, Eleazar describes it in detail and occasionally cites prooftexts from the Book of Exodus which are designed to prove that certain details in the ceremony correspond to details in the theophany at Sinai. They interrupt the description of the ritual itself but support the author's introductory statement that the rite takes place on Shavuot because "that is when the Torah was given":

> A (scriptural) indication that (the boy should be covered so that he will not see a Gentile or a dog on the day he is instructed in the holy letter) is ("No one else shall come up with you, and no one else shall be seen anywhere on the mountain;) neither shall the flocks and the herds graze at the foot of this mountain" (Exod. 34:3).

The boys are brought (on Shavuot morning) at sunrise, according to (the verse): ("On the third day,) as morning dawned, there was thunder, and lightning" (Exod. 19:16).

He is covered with a cloak on the way from their house to the synagogue or the teacher's house, according to (the verse): "and they took their places at the foot (or: nether part) of the mountain" (Exod. 19:17).

At this point, Eleazar compares the relationship between the small child and the teacher in school to that between the images of biblical Israel as a child and of Moses and God as its nurturing parent:

> The child is placed on the lap/bosom (ḥeiqo) of the teacher who sits them down to study, according to (the verse): "and Moses said to the Lord, . . . 'Did I conceive all this people, did I bear them, that You should say to me, "Carry them in your bosom as a nurse carries an infant" ' " (Num. 11:12); (and according to the verse): "I have pampered Ephraim, taking them in My arms" (Hos. 11:3).

The biblical words now shift from being rationales for parts of the ceremony to becoming rituals themselves. Apart from the two themes of Israel and God at Sinai and of Israel as Moses's and God's child, the rest of the ceremony is no longer linked to scriptural prooftexts. Instead, specific biblical verses are to be written on a school tablet, on a cake, and on an egg. Nowhere does Eleazar even hint about the antiquity of the central part of the ritual involving licking honey from the tablet or eating specially inscribed cakes and eggs:

> They bring over the tablet (luaḥ) on which is written (the alphabet forwards, beginning) alef, bet, gimel, dalet; (the alphabet written backwards, beginning) tav, shin, resh, qof; (and the verse) "When Moses charged us with the Torah as the heritage of the congregation of Jacob" (Deut. 33:4); (the phrase) "May the Torah be my occupation";[28] (and the first verse of Leviticus, beginning,) "The Lord called to Moses . . ." (Lev. 1:1).
>
> The teacher recites aloud each letter of the alphabet (forwards), and the child (recites them) after him; (then the teacher recites) each word of tav, shin, resh, qof and the child does so too; similarly, (they both recite the verse beginning) "When Moses charged us with the Torah . . ." (Deut. 33:4); (the phrase beginning) "May the Torah be . . ."; and likewise (the verse beginning) "The Lord called Moses . . ." (Lev. 1:1).

And (the teacher) puts a little honey on the tablet, and with his tongue, the child licks the honey which is on the letters.

After this, they bring over the cake kneaded with honey on which is written, "The Lord gave me a skilled tongue, to know how to speak timely words to the weary. Morning by morning, He rouses, He rouses my ear to give heed like disciples. The Lord God opened my ears, and I did not disobey, I did not run away" (Isa. 50:4-5). The teacher recites aloud each word of these verses, and the boy (does so) after him.

After this, they bring over a cooked egg which has been peeled and on which is written, "as He said to me, 'Mortal, feed your stomach and fill your belly with this scroll that I give you.' I ate it, and it tasted as sweet as honey to me" (Ezek. 3:3). The teacher recites aloud each word and the boy (does so) after him.

They feed the boy the cake and the egg because it is good for the opening of the heart (li-petiḥat ha-lev).

Eleazar concludes his description of the rite by reinforcing his opening claim about the custom's antiquity. But he does this by citing rabbinic texts that stress the importance of observing customs in general, not this one in particular:

"Let no one deviate" from (following) this custom, as we say in (Tractate) Pesaḥim, in the Ch(apter beginning) "Maqom she-Nahagu" ("Where they were accustomed"); and (we read) in Genesis Rabbah, section "Va-yeira eilav" ("And He appeared to him") (Gen. 18:1ff): "When you come to a (new) place, follow its custom"; and (we read) in Ch(apter) I of Palestinian (Talmud, Tractate) Taʿanit and in the Ch(apter beginning) "Maqom she-nahagu" [29] and in Haggadah Shir ha-Shirim (?):[30] that custom is valid.

Eleazar's style is laconic. Only occasionally does he add a helpful comment to explain the strange details. For example, he tells us that the child is covered when taken from his house to the teacher in order to protect him from seeing a "Gentile—read: Christian—or a dog." And near the end, he offers a practical reason for performing the rite, by saying that the specially inscribed cakes and eggs are eaten because "this is good for the opening of the heart." But for the

most part, he provides no explanations for the peculiarities of the ritual. There
is no comment about why the child reads the different permutations of the
Hebrew alphabet and then certain texts. We find no explanation about the
honey or the cake and eggs. We are not even told who brings the boy from his
house to the teacher. Nor do we know if anyone else is present when the ceremony takes place. Who brings over the various objects? Where are the child's
parents during this important event? We do not know.

Although Eleazar presents the ceremony within the context of the Sinai
theophany and the festival of Shavuot, most of the ritual's features remain
unexplained. And Eleazar offers no proof that this ceremony is in fact "the
custom of our ancestors." He cites no talmudic sources, which are common
in his pietistic tracts, nor does he appeal to geonic or earlier European Jewish
authorities to prove the rite's antiquity. He cites only Scripture. Finally, the
rabbinic sources that he does cite at the end of the passage are not related specifically to this ceremony but to the importance of following custom per se.
The omission of rabbinic sources about the ritual suggests that had Eleazar
been able to cite texts that supported his specific claim, he certainly would
have done so here. From the citations in the text, then, we have reason to won-
der exactly what Eleazar means by his opening remark that the ritual is "the
custom of our ancestors."

The first line of Eleazar's account is also found in a second Hebrew version from thirteenth-century Germany, the anonymously compiled book of
customs and laws called Sefer ha-Asufot (Book of Collections).[31] Despite its identical beginning, the passage in Sefer ha-Asufot contains significant variations and
additions. Unlike Sefer ha-Roqeah, Sefer ha-Asufot omits Numbers 11:12 and Hosea
11:3, which were quoted to explain the child's being placed on the teacher's
lap or bosom. The verses that Sefer ha-Asufot stipulates are to be inscribed on
the cake and egg also differ from those mentioned before. In Sefer ha-Roqeah,
the cake is to be inscribed with Isaiah 50:4–5 and the egg with Ezekiel 3:3.
In Sefer ha-Asufot, the cake is to be inscribed with the same verse from Ezekiel
and the same verses from Isaiah (50:3–4), but also, significantly, with verses
from Psalm 119 (9, 11, 12, 18, 34, 97, 130, 140); the egg is to be covered with
other verses from that Psalm (99, 100, 103, 105). Psalm 119 is an eight-fold
alphabetic acrostic and contains several allusions to "expanding the heart" and
not forgetting the Torah. Apart from its use in this ceremony, it played a significant role in other rituals associated with learning the Torah.[32]

In addition to Psalm 119, *Sefer ha-Asufot* also introduces as an entirely new element the incantation against POTAH, the prince of forgetfulness. That formula is also a tradition associated with the *havdalah*, the Separation Ceremony, which takes place at the end of each Sabbath or festival as the new week or postfestival day begins: "Ten times he should say these three words: NGF, SGF, AGF. I adjure you, POTAH, the prince of forgetfulness, that you extract and remove from me a fool's heart, I so-and-so, son of so-and-so, and throw it on a high mountain, in the name of (line blank)."[33] The ritual names are omitted at this point in *Sefer ha-Asufot*, but they can be recovered from the parallel texts that use this formula in the havdalah ceremony.[34]

Toward the end, *Sefer ha-Asufot* introduces a third significant new element: "After the study session, the boy is brought to the riverside, according to the Torah's being compared to water and (the verse), 'Your springs will gush forth (in streams in the public squares)' (Prov. 5:16), so that the boy should have an expanded heart." This version concludes with a recipe for baking the cakes and includes additional biblical associations for the various ingredients: "The cake is prepared from three measures of fine flour corresponding to the manna, the well and the quail (in the desert). And one mixes into it honey, oil and milk, as in (the verse) 'He fed him honey from the crag, (and oil from the flinty rock)' (Deut. 32:13), and it is written, 'honey and milk are under your tongue' (Song of Songs 4:11)."

Thus far, *Sefer ha-Asufot* has a version of the German ceremony which retains the structure of the rite as described in *Sefer ha-Roqeah* but also contains more ritual elements: the use of Psalm 119, the POTAH incantation, and the ceremony at the riverbank. It also connects the foods to biblical texts that refer to the divine gifts in the wilderness (manna, quail, and water), as well as verses from Deuteronomy and the Song of Songs about honey, milk, and oil.

The third Hebrew text from Germany is the longest and is found in a commentary on liturgical poems (piyyutim) in Hebrew MS Hamburg 17.[35] It consists of a description of the ritual and supplementary questions and answers about its details. In the description, the three key elements—the school tablet, cake, and egg—remain as before, but this text contains a few new twists. Now it is the father who brings the child to the synagogue by wrapping him in his talit. On the tablet is written not only the letters of the alphabet, Leviticus 1:1, and Deuteronomy 33:4, but also Psalm 119:9, 12, 17, 140, and 125. On the cake the alphabet is to be written again—another new detail—as well as Ezekiel 3:3

and Isaiah 50:4, 7, and 5, as in *Sefer ha-Asufot*. But on the egg, Psalm 19:8 and 11, again new, are inscribed.[36]

After the texts are read aloud and the child has eaten the cake and egg, as before, two other new features are mentioned. The child is to be given nuts and is to be covered up when he is brought home to his mother so that he will not be seen by a "dog, pig, ass, or Gentile." In *Sefer ha-Roqeah*, we recall, this explanation is offered for why the child is covered when taken to, not from, the synagogue. In addition, although the first part of the text refers to one cake and one egg, the second or exegetical part of the text specifies three cakes and three eggs.[37]

This presence of three eggs and cakes is also clearly portrayed in a visual representation of the rite found in a Hebrew manuscript illumination, which, like the three texts, is also from medieval Germany (see figure 5). The *Leipzig Mahzor*, an early fourteenth-century festival prayer book of German-Jewish provenance, contains a three-part depiction that portrays selected aspects of the ritual.[38] Like the German-Jewish texts, the illumination also explicitly associates the initiation ceremony with the festival of Shavuot and accompanies the Shavuot liturgical poem that begins *adon imnani* (the Lord Who taught me).[39] Moreover, on the facing page of the manuscript is an illumination depicting Moses as he receives the Ten Commandments. This programmatic juxtaposition clearly associates the medieval child's initiation ceremony with Israel's receiving the Torah on Shavuot.

In the illumination representing features of the ceremony we see a male adult carrying the child wrapped in a cloak. The child faces away from the man, but one of the child's hands caresses the man's cheek and the other holds a round cake. In the left scene, the child is sitting on the teacher's lap. The teacher holds a gilded tablet, and the child holds up an egg in one hand and a round yellow cake in the other. Two other children stand facing the seated teacher and child and each of them, too, holds up an egg and cake. Finally, the scene on the right shows the teacher pushing two children, still holding up eggs and cakes, toward the riverside.

Like the version in *Sefer ha-Asufot*, the illumination includes the riverside scene as an integral part of the ceremony that is not mentioned in the other German texts or in the French texts.[40] The featuring of three cakes and three eggs, rather than one of each, is also stipulated in the oldest of the French-Jewish texts, the *Mahzor Vitry*, to which we now turn.

The French-Jewish Versions

The Maḥzor Vitry is a collection of laws and customs focused especially on the liturgy. Its description of the ceremony is much less elaborate than the one in the German versions. For example, it says that only the alphabet is to be written on the tablet, not biblical or other passages, and nowhere does it prescribe that anything should be written on the cake or egg. Like the German illumination, but unlike the German written versions, the Maḥzor Vitry states that three cakes and three eggs are to be eaten, not just one of each.[41]

The Maḥzor Vitry ceremony also exhibits more of the universal elements we encountered in sources about elementary schooling that are not related to most of the other details of the initiation ceremony, such as its recommendation that someone bring the child apples and other fruits. A general pedagogic principle is articulated here for the first time: "first we entice him and afterward we use the strap." To be sure, elements can carry more than one meaning, but these features of Maḥzor Vitry, like the provision in MS Hamburg that the child be given nuts, seem to be examples of the general pedagogic practice of giving small children desirable foods before they go to school or do something else that is difficult, rather than belonging specifically to the initiation ceremony.

Despite the Maḥzor Vitry's tendency to include these elements, it also mentions additional features specific to the Jewish initiation ritual. Thus, the text stipulates that the child is to sway with his body when studying and is to use a melody when learning. Learning to chant, not just read, the biblical text receives special emphasis. After the boy has learned how to recite Leviticus 1:1, he is to continue studying that text through the words "it is a law for all time" (Lev. 3:17) and is expected to chant it as the Torah is chanted in the synagogue. When the boy has learned to do this, a festive meal is to be held in celebration of this accomplishment.[42] The requirement to chant the first portion of Leviticus and conclude with a party is not mentioned in the German-Jewish texts.

Although the Maḥzor Vitry never mentions that the ceremony takes place on Shavuot, it concludes with an elaborate comparison between the father's bringing his son to the teacher for the first time and Moses's receiving the Torah at Mount Sinai which, we recall, Jewish tradition fixed at the Shavuot festival. It also dwells on the metaphor that a child who studies Torah is like a Temple sacrifice and brings vicarious atonement to other Jews.[43]

The two nearly identical surviving versions of the ritual from southern France are modeled on the description in the *Mahzor Vitry*. In R. Aaron b. Jacob ha-Kohen of Lunel's *Orhot Hayyim* (Paths of Life) and the anonymous *Kol Bo* (Miscellany), both from the fourteenth century,[44] the description follows the sequence in *Mahzor Vitry* but omits certain items, such as the requirement of eating eggs. We also hear for the first time that the letters of the alphabet may be written "on parchment or on a tablet" covered with honey and licked off. The use of parchment may be implicit in the other sources as well, as it was the practice to place parchment on a wooden writing tablet. Still another significant additional element comes at the end of *Orhot Hayyim*, which states: "This custom was the custom of the ancestors (*qadmonim*). The people of Jerusalem did it and even today it is done in some places."

Following this comment, the editor of the book adds a description of a completely different custom. People in Jerusalem would begin training their small children "from the ages of three and four" to learn to fast. This concluding section again reinforces the emphasis in the French versions that the child's initiation ceremony takes place according to the child's readiness or age, not the time of the calendar year. Finally, the peculiarities found in *Orhot Hayyim* are also found in *Kol Bo*, and the two are closely related to one another.

Historical Questions

With the historical claims at the end of the versions in *Orhot Hayyim* and *Kol Bo*, we return to the opening statement in Eleazar's *Sefer ha-Roqeah*, which is repeated in the anonymous *Sefer ha-Asufot*, that the ceremony is *minhag avoteinu* — the custom of our ancestors. Although the ritual is unattested in classical rabbinic or early medieval Jewish sources, the authors of two of the German versions claim that it has a pedigree. But how old is the ceremony, and why do the most elaborately crafted variations of ancient and early medieval elements appear only in medieval Germany and northern France? Can we make sense of both the exotic features of the ceremony as well as its having been preserved in authoritative rabbinic legal and liturgical texts? And what implications does this have for our understanding of European Jewish culture in the Middle Ages and of how Jewish acculturation took place there?

In order to interpret this ceremony historically, I will first analyze its constituent elements. Many of them originated in ancient Palestine or in the Muslim East and were later transformed in Christian Europe—as well as in the Sephardic Mediterranean variations—into a complex ceremony redolent of new cultural and historical meanings. I propose first to take the ceremony apart and then to put it back together. Each element will be intentionally wrenched from the context of the medieval initiation ceremony so that it can be studied in its earlier contexts. I will then reexamine it as an integral part of the medieval ceremony as a whole. In so doing, I will try to recapture some of the earlier historical meanings of a particular element and discover how they were later modified. For customs, like stories, are made up of constituent parts that move from culture to culture and through time and place within a culture. They have their histories.

To trace back to their earlier history the various elements that were melded together in the medieval European initiation ceremony is not to explain the whole by reference to the parts. On the contrary, to appreciate the meanings of the ceremony we must also analyze the complete ceremony itself. Nevertheless, the cultural baggage each element brings with it from its earlier contexts adds to the final semantic and cultural load of the ceremony as a whole. The ritual is more than the sum of its historical parts, but it is made up of a refiguring of those parts. First, then, the history of the ceremony's various components: once we appreciate what was old, we will understand better what was new.

Chapter Three

Ancient Jewish Pedagogy

Considering the importance of Jewish literacy in premodern times, it is striking how little we know about Jewish schooling in late antiquity or even in medieval times. Despite the religious obligation that fathers teach their sons the Torah, we do not know much about how children actually began their studies, what they learned, and how or even if elementary or more advanced studies developed into a program of adult learning.[1]

To be sure, some rabbinic sources take for granted that children began their education at an early age, but no special ceremony marks the occasion. We find references to many of the elements that later appear in the medieval European initiation rite, but no ancient precedent for the ceremony itself. Despite the fact that few rabbinic sources refer explicitly to the ways small boys studied, we may infer how they learned from traditions that describe the initial learning experiences of two categories of Jewish adults who are similar to children: converts to Judaism and adult native Jews such as R. Akiva who began to study their letters late in life.

The Talmud tells us that "a proselyte who has converted to Judaism is like a newborn child,"[2] and in a tale about a would-be Jewish convert who approached the first-century sage Hillel, we see an indication that Jewish children learned the Hebrew alphabet in different combinations. Learning the Hebrew alphabet backwards and forwards, as required in the medieval Jewish initiation, was a common practice among Jews in late antiquity; in the Hellenistic schools some pagan children learned the Greek alphabet from *alpha* to *omega* and in reverse, from *omega* to *alpha*. The talmudic account runs this way: "On the first day, (Hillel) taught (the convert) *aleph, bet, gimmel, dalet*. On the following day he reversed the letters for him."[3]

Jewish children continued to learn the Hebrew alphabet from *aleph* to *tav* and from *tav* to *aleph* in medieval Ashkenaz, as required by the initiation rite, as well as in ancient Palestine. English still retains a trace of this ancient regimen when we say that we know something "backwards and forwards." In the ancient world, Greco-Roman and Jewish children literally did.[4]

Ancient pagans and Jews also taught their children the alphabet a third way, by making them memorize it in symmetrical pairs of letters, a technique borrowed from the Ancient Near East.[5] The Greek child learned the letter combinations *alpha/omega* (first with last), *beta/psi*, (second with next-to-last), *gamma/khi* (third with third-from-last), and so on. Echoes of a Jewish child's way of learning the Hebrew alphabet are heard in a story about R. Akiva:

> What were the beginnings of R. Akiva? It is said: When he was forty years of age he had not yet studied a thing. . . . He went together with his son and they appeared before an elementary school teacher. Said R. Akiva to him: "Master, teach me Torah." R. Akiva took hold of one end of the (writing) tablet and his son (took hold of) the other end of the tablet. The teacher wrote down *aleph bet* for him and he learned it; *aleph tav*, and he learned it; the book of Leviticus, and he learned it. He went on studying until he learned the whole Torah.[6]

The tradition about Akiva suggests that Jewish children, like the ancient Greeks, learned their alphabet not only forwards and backwards but also by pairing first and last letter combinations (*aleph-tav, bet-shin,* etc.). The rabbis called this method *at-b(a)sh,* after the pairs *a[leph]-t[av]* and *b[et]-sh[in],* and the entire set of letter pairings became part of an exegetical technique in rabbinic and medieval textual interpretation. Reading a text by transposing symmetrical pairs of letters in the Hebrew alphabet might reveal unexpected meanings in the text. An early example of this practice occurs in the Hebrew Bible, where the meaningless name "Sheshak" (Jer. 25:26; 51:1, 41), transposed by *at-b(a)sh,*[7] is interpreted as a code word for "Bavel," that is, Babylon.[8]

Eaten Texts

In addition to requiring that a boy learn the Hebrew alphabet in three different ways, the medieval initiation ceremony prescribed that the child must read and symbolically eat three sacred texts that were written on the writing tablet and smeared with honey. These texts, too, have ancient roots. The first is Deuteronomy 33:4: "When Moses charged us with the Torah as the heritage of the congregation of Jacob." From at least the days of Ben Sira (Ecclesiasticus, ca. 200–180 B.C.E.) this verse was viewed as a summary of the entire Torah.[9] Rabbinic sources feature it prominently in elementary education, beginning with the child's earliest years, and the third-century Babylonian master R. Hamnuna names it as the first Torah lesson a father taught his son—perhaps even the basis of an oral primer.[10] Another Babylonian tradition further elaborates the pedagogic function of this verse: "The Rabbis said to R. Hamnuna: R. Ami wrote four hundred Torah scrolls. He said to them: Perhaps he wrote (four hundred times), 'When Moses charged us with the Torah (as the heritage of the congregation of Jacob).' "[11]

Here the single verse from Deuteronomy stands for the entire Torah, and this made it an appropriate first text for a father to teach his son even before going to school. R. Jacob b. Meir, the twelfth-century northern French talmudic jurist known as Rabbeinu Tam (d. 1171), noted about this passage: "That verse is called 'Torah,' as we learn in Chapter Three of (Tractate) Sukkah: 'When a minor knows how to speak, his father must teach him Torah.' "[12] These talmudic and medieval traditions regarded the verse as an epitome of the entire Torah which was to be taught to young children as a catechism.

Yet another talmudic teaching supports this equivalence:

> R. Simlai expounded: Six hundred thirteen commandments were told to Moses, three hundred sixty-five negative precepts, corresponding to the number of the solar days (in the year), and two hundred forty-eight positive precepts, corresponding to the number of limbs in a person's body.
>
> R. Hamnuna said: What biblical verse (proves this)? "When Moses charged us with the Torah as the heritage of the congregation of Jacob" (Deut. 33:4). Torah in gematria[13] is 611 (to which you should add) "I am the Lord your God" (Exod. 20:2) and "You shall have no other gods besides Me" (Exod. 20:3), which we heard (directly) from the mouth of God.[14]

Here, too, R. Hamnuna claims that Deuteronomy 33:4 stands for the entire Torah. Although many verses include the word torah in them, he chose to equate it in this verse with all of the commandments that Moses received from

God. For R. Hamnuna and for the medieval Ashkenazic initiation ceremony as well, Deuteronomy 33:4 was a condensed expression of the entire Torah. It is certainly an appropriate one, in that it states a central claim of rabbinic Judaism: Moses received the Torah and transmitted it to Israel. The rabbinic chain of tradition which authenticates the validity of the Oral Torah, parallel to the Written Torah mentioned in Deuteronomy 33:4, begins as a paraphrase of that verse: "Moses received Torah from Sinai and transmitted it to Joshua." [15] In addition, the rabbis interpreted the verse as a requirement that every Jew should study the Torah.[16]

Apart from the traditions attributed to R. Hamnuna, another source refers to Deuteronomy 33:4 as a text that young schoolchildren learned. It is found in the midrash on Leviticus, *Midrash Vayyiqra Rabbah* (*Leviticus Rabbah*): [17] "He replied to him: It is as the children say: 'When Moses charged us with the Torah as the heritage of the congregation of Jacob' (Deut. 33:4). It does not say 'the congregation of Yannai' but 'the congregation of Jacob.'" That is, the Torah belongs to all Jews, not just to R. Yannai.

The statement clearly associates this verse with schoolchildren in light of the immediate context, not quoted here, which stipulates that small schoolchildren begin to study Leviticus and not Genesis. Another version of the passage explicitly connects reciting this verse with children in school. "Once when I was walking past an elementary school (*beit safra*), I heard children saying, 'When Moses charged us with the Torah as the heritage of the congregation of Jacob.'" [18] This verse has retained a special significance for young children in school, and I remember learning it myself to a melody when I began to study the Hebrew alphabet.

In addition to learning to recite the various permutations of the Hebrew alphabet and Deuteronomy 33:4, the child symbolically begins his study of Scripture by learning the beginning of the Book of Leviticus, the first verse of which is also inscribed on the writing tablet. This ancient custom is mentioned in the late rabbinic period in *Avot de-Rabbi Natan* in connection not only with R. Akiva's elementary education but also with Hillel's initiation of a pagan into Judaism: "First Hillel wrote out the alphabet for him and taught it to him. Then (Hillel) taught him Leviticus." [19] *Midrash Vayyiqra Rabbah* offers a rationale for this custom: "R. Isi said, Why do children begin their study of Torah with Leviticus? They should start with Genesis! The Holy One, blessed be He, said: Since sacrifices (in Leviticus) are pure and children are pure, let the pure (children) begin by studying (the laws about) purities." [20]

This custom is probably very ancient and related to the fact that the Temple was the place where the Priests and Levites transmitted sacred knowledge in biblical times. A number of scholars have suggested that well into the Hellenistic era, only Levites taught their children to read the Torah.[21]

Although the priestly origins of literacy may lie at the heart of this tradition, it may have been reinforced in part by the mystical interpretations drawn from the first chapter of Genesis. As Philip Alexander points out, Origen noted in the prologue to his commentary on the Song of Songs that "Jews did not study the beginning of Genesis, the beginning and the end of Ezekiel, and the Song of Songs, until they had mastered the rest of Scripture and the oral law." This indicates that there was an ancient Jewish inhibition to begin studies with Genesis, clearly indicated in M. Ḥagiga 2:1. The association between pure children and sacrifices in R. Isi's tradition is a secondary rationale, but it achieved a life of its own in post-Temple Judaism and in the medieval school rite.[22]

The Hebrew alphabet permutations and the study of the first verse from Leviticus are both documented in the earliest preserved Hebrew alphabet primers from the Cairo Geniza. Several pages include outlines of the alphabet written forwards, backwards, in first-last combinations, and with the opening verses from Leviticus (figure 2). Similarly, at the end of the version of the ceremony found in the JTS (Reggio) Manuscript of *Maḥzor Vitry*, a torn alphabet primer appears that also ends with the first verses of Leviticus and also contains the forward alphabet, the alphabet in *atbash*, the backward alphabet, numerological combinations of letters equivalent to ones, tens, and hundreds, known as AYQ BKHR, and a mnemonic sentence containing all of the letters of the alphabet (figure 3).[23]

The alphabet combinations, Deuteronomy 33:4, and the first part of Leviticus are all elements of the medieval ceremony that derive from children's elementary education in the ancient world. Others are preserved in ancient adult contexts and were later transferred to the child's initiation ceremony. An example of this is the fourth text which is written on the child's writing tablet, the post-biblical phrase "May the Torah be my occupation." In the Talmud this expression applies to adults, not small children. It appears in a passage that lists the personal prayers that several rabbis said after completing the required

2. Primer Leaf, Cairo Geniza, Cambridge, Cambridge University Library, Taylor-Schechter K.5.13 f. 1a and 2b. Reproduced by permission of the Syndics of Cambridge University Library.

daily Prayer (ʿamidah) [24]: "On concluding his (recitation of) the Prayer, R. Ḥiyya added the following: May it be Your will, O Lord our God, *that Your Torah be our occupation.* . . ." [25] Another version is found in a different adult context: "It was taught: If scholars are busy studying, they must interrupt their study to recite the Shema, but not to recite the Prayer. R. Johanan (third-century Palestine) said: This was taught only of someone like R. Shimon bar Yoḥai and his colleagues, *whose study was their occupation,* but we must interrupt our study for both the Shema and the Prayer." [26]

Here, too, a phrase associating study of the Torah with an occupation is found in connection with adult behavior. The medieval Ashkenazic ceremony is the first time this phrase appears in connection with a child's beginning to learn the Torah. The formula now changes to the first-person singular: "May the Torah be my occupation." It is possible that an early rabbinic tradition listing a father's obligations to his son helped change an adult idiom into one applied to small children. The following lists several rites of passage and juxtaposes teaching a son Torah and teaching him an occupation: "What is a father's religious duty toward his son? To circumcise him, redeem him (if a first born), teach him Torah, teach him an occupation, marry him off." [27]

This text means that a father must teach his son a practical occupation or livelihood, and it does not mean, as the adult passages do, that some individuals devoted their time exclusively to the study of the Torah as an occupation. Nevertheless, by the time of the medieval ceremony, the adult phrase defining the pursuit of the Torah as one's occupation now refers not to an adult's dedication but to a child's aspiration.

Some time in the modern period, the phrase was incorporated into an abbreviated "Morning Prayer for Children" and modified still further. [28] The rabbinic phrase appears alongside the ancient catechism of Deuteronomy 33:4, but the last word has been changed from *omanuti*, "my occupation," to *emunati*, "my faith." The ancient adult association of the Torah with one's occupation is now transformed into a child's statement of faith. This shift took place under the influence of the medieval initiation ceremony, in which the original adult phrase was adapted for children.

3. *Maḥzor Vitry* (formerly Reggio, Italy). Forward alphabet (lines 1–2), first-last letter paired alphabet (lines 2–3), backward alphabet (lines 3–4), *ayq bkhr* or multiples of ten (lines 5–6), alphabet letter mnemonic (lines 6–7), Lev. 1:1–2 (lines 7–10). France, 1204. New York, Library of the Jewish Theological Seminary of America, MS Microfilm no. 8092, f. 165a. Reprinted courtesy of the Library of the Jewish Theological Seminary of America.

Two Schooling Traditions: *Age Alone or Age and the Festival of Shavuot*

The elements in the medieval ceremony discussed so far derived from ancient practices associated with small children — the alphabet, Deuteronomy 33:4, and the first verses of Leviticus — even though some of the earliest direct evidence is preserved in sources about proselytes and adults who began their studies late. The phrase "May the Torah be my occupation," on the other hand, was based on an expression applied in the ancient period to adult Torah scholars and was later transferred to the children's initiation ceremony.

Regardless of the original ancient settings of the texts inscribed in medieval times on the child's writing tablet, it is the child's age alone that marks the time when he is to begin studying the Torah. Beginning school on Shavuot was not a practice preserved in early rabbinic sources. Nor do we have evidence that the rabbis prescribed most of the other elements in the ritual, such as eating specially inscribed foods or the incantation to POTAH. Rather, rabbinic texts point only to the child's age or readiness as the criterion for when he should enter Torah study. The focus on age is preserved, we recall, in the French-Hebrew witnesses to the medieval ritual, such as the *Mahzor Vitry*, but the German-Hebrew sources all state or imply that the child of school age is initiated on Shavuot. What is the basis of this assertion in the German-Jewish texts?

A second, nontalmudic tradition underlies the choice of Shavuot as the time to initiate the child, and it leads us to the basis of those other elements of the ritual that are derived from the type of ancient or early medieval Eastern magic that was designed for memory training. These gestures lie at the heart of the rite: they include eating certain foods on which words have been inscribed and pronouncing an incantation. These mnemonic devices and the Shavuot tradition derive from adult practices, although there are hints that children may have been involved in them as well.

At first it may seem perfectly obvious that the initiation ritual should take place on Shavuot because that biblical festival was interpreted in rabbinic sources as the occasion when ancient Israel received the Torah on Mount Sinai. What could be a more appropriate time for a Jewish child to begin his study of the Torah? Such a celebration would give to Shavuot, a two-day festival otherwise lacking in unique rituals, a rite parallel to the Seder meal and special foods eaten during the eight-day Passover festival and to the ritual use of temporary huts and of the citron, palm branch, myrtle, and willow on the eight-day festival of Sukkot.[29]

Remarkably, despite the importance of religious study in ancient Jewish rabbinic culture, nowhere is a date in the calendar year specified as the time when Jewish children should begin their studies. Beginning school on Shavuot is a historical phenomenon that seems to appear for the first time in the medieval European ceremony. We need but review the standard ancient rabbinic passages that allude to when children begin school to see that the child's age or readiness, not a particular time of the year, determined when he began his formal studies.[30]

The postbiblical sources offer various starting points for the child to begin learning informally at home. For example, a father should begin to teach his son "once an infant begins to talk"[31] or "at age three,"[32] and the child is certainly no longer under his mother's authority from age six.[33] Formal schooling is discussed with reference to a child's age as well. The only Jewish text that discusses elementary education from Second Temple times is in the Rule of the Congregation, from Qumran, which prescribes study of Scripture ("Book of Hago") until age ten, and then, "according to his age they shall instruct him in the laws of the covenant . . . for ten years," until age twenty.[34]

The factor of the child's age is also stressed in B. Bava Batra 21a, which describes the institutionalization of elementary schooling in Palestine, which supposedly took place either in the first century B.C.E. or in the first century C.E. but in fact can be dated no earlier than the third century C.E.[35] This passage states that children should begin their studies at age "six or seven"[36] but makes no mention of Shavuot or any other fixed time of the year.

Age is also at the center of the best-known rabbinic text about schooling, the pseudo-mishnaic passage appended sometime in the Middle Ages to Mishnah Avot. This ages-of-man text[37] begins with the time when a small child should study Scripture and proceeds through life-cycle events decade by decade:

> At age five (one begins studying) Scripture; at ten, Mishnah;[38] at thirteen, (fulfilling) the commandments; at fifteen, (studying) the Talmud; at eighteen, (entering) the bride-chamber; at twenty, pursuing (a calling); at thirty, authority; at forty, discernment; at fifty, counsel; at sixty,

being an elder; at seventy, grey hair; at eighty, special strength; at ninety, a bowed back; and at a hundred, a man is as one that has (already) died, passed away, and departed this world.[39]

This passage was not yet part of the Mishnah when the Babylonian Talmud was redacted, ca. 500 C.E., because the editor of the talmudic passage in B. Bava Batra 21a does not mention it in the discussion about the age when a child should begin his studies. After the opinion is expressed that the boy should begin at "age six or seven," the anonymous editor does not immediately object by citing the contradictory view in the more authoritative Mishnah, "at age five (one begins studying) Scripture." He does not do this because that passage was not yet part of the Mishnah. Indeed, *Avot de-Rabbi Natan*, the first commentary on Mishnah Avot and of uncertain date, does not comment on that ages-of-man passage at all, from which we may also infer that it was not yet considered part of the Mishnah.

But by the twelfth century, it was.[40] The Tosafists, or northern French Talmud glossators, point out the contradiction, for them, between the Mishnah—"At age five (one begins studying) Scripture"—and the conclusion in the Talmud—"age six or seven." They resolve the contradiction by assuming that the different ages mentioned in the two texts refer to different situations and are not contradictory. Since the Talmud mentions the ages of six and seven explicitly in a discussion about the onset of formal schooling, those ages must refer to that situation.[41] The Tosafist understands age six to be the age when a healthy child should begin schooling; only when a boy is too weak or ill at age six to begin his studies must they be delayed until he reaches age seven. The distinction of healthy or ill is analogous to the case of circumcision, which is supposed to take place on the eighth day after the child's birth but may be delayed if the eight-day-old is too ill to undergo the procedure.

The Tosafists interpret the Mishnaic text, "at age five (one begins studying) Scripture," which does not mention schooling explicitly, to mean that the father should begin to teach his son Scripture at home when the child is only five. When he turns six, he should begin formal schooling with a teacher, the father's surrogate. Regardless of the differences that these texts display and their casuistic, rather than descriptive texture, they agree about one point: it is the child's age, not a festival or some other time of the year, that determines when the child is to begin his first Torah studies.

Nevertheless, at least the German-Jewish versions of the medieval European rite stipulate that it should begin on Shavuot.[42] If we look into this further, it turns out that there is evidence from pre-European Judaism that some Jews considered the Shavuot festival to be especially appropriate for religious study, not so much for children as for adults. This was the case for Jews associated with the special study of the vision of the prophet Ezekiel, recorded in Ezekiel 1 and 10 and in other biblical and postbiblical traditions that are usually referred to as *heikhalot* (palace) texts, or *merkavah* (chariot) mysticism and magic.

Ultimately derived, as David Halperin has argued,[43] from sermons given on Shavuot, when Ezekiel 1 was read in the synagogue to complement the reading about the Decalogue on Mount Sinai, some heikhalot texts are accompanied by other texts that are clearly designed to conjure divine powers from heaven in order to achieve earthly goals. Among the most important of these magical acts is the recitation of secret names for the purpose of acquiring knowledge of the Torah and not forgetting it. These theurgic texts are commonly called *sar ha-torah* texts, after the name of the power being conjured (prince of the Torah), but are sometimes known as *sod/ot ha-torah* (secret/s of the Torah). These late ancient or early medieval texts — it is impossible to determine which at present — deal with magical techniques by which one can master the Torah and retain it. They are part of an early Jewish tradition of magical mnemonics and are a major source for elements in the medieval Jewish initiation ceremony.[44]

According to sar ha-torah texts and heikhalot magic, on the festival of Shavuot Jews who knew how could draw down the power revealed on Mount Sinai, which is described in Exodus 19:20 as the one time when "the Lord came down upon Mount Sinai."[45] These mystical circles applied to Shavuot what rabbinic tradition had affirmed about the Passover Seder's reiteration of the biblical Exodus from Egypt. The Haggadah, or rabbinic Passover liturgy, states that when the Jews recite the Haggadah they should think of the Exodus not as a past, one-time event, but as though they were reenacting the Exodus in the present: "It is as though *you* went out of Egypt." Similarly, the merkavah mystics thought of the study of the Torah on Shavuot as reexperiencing Moses' ascent of Mount Sinai and the descent of God's power from the mountain in the form of sar ha-torah, whom adepts could even conjure forth with the correct gestures and words.[46]

That Jews could have entertained the idea that Shavuot was the annual time of special revelation or divine proximity may be inferred from the Christian tradition of Pentecost as recorded in the Acts of the Apostles. There we see that the early Jerusalem church remembered that it was on Pentecost that the twelve apostles "were all together in one place. And suddenly a sound came from heaven like the rush of a mighty wind and it filled all the house where they were sitting. And there appeared to them tongues as of fire, distributed and resting on each one of them. And they were all filled with the Holy Spirit and began to speak in other tongues, as the Spirit gave them utterance" (Acts 2:1–4).

The early Jerusalem church understood that its formation took place on Pentecost, Shavuot, and it is likely that this early Christian tradition relies on a prerabbinic Jewish source, the import of which was not only that God gave Israel the Torah on Pentecost (Shavuot) but also that every year "the Lord came down" on that day and, consequently, that students of the Torah may achieve special divine aid in their study if they observe certain rituals on that festival. The Jewish merkavah study circles, whose activities are preserved in the so-called heikhalot texts, like the author of Acts 2, seem to have taken the rhetoric of Exodus 19 that "the Lord came down" and institutionalized it in a unique way. The early Jerusalem church understood Pentecost as a one-time event, but the special association between it and the presence of the Holy Spirit led to the celebration of baptism on Pentecost in addition to Easter.[47] Rabbinic tradition understood Shavuot as a commemoration of the original one-time event on Mount Sinai, but Jewish mystical students of Torah understood the divine descent as a potential annual event, for "the Lord came down" on every Shavuot if they performed certain acts.

The medieval initiation ceremony grew from a confluence of these two traditions: the rabbinic idea that a father is religiously obligated to teach his son Torah when he is ready or at a certain age, and the second tradition, derived from the ancient Jewish mystics, that Shavuot is an especially propitious time for a special, ritualized study of Torah because that is when "the Lord came down." We do not know exactly when elements from these two traditions were combined in the ceremony for a Jewish child, and not just for adults, to begin the study of Torah on Shavuot and thereby reenact symbolically the moment when biblical Israel originally received the Torah on Mount Sinai. But by the late twelfth century the ceremony was established enough to be noted as "the custom of our ancestors."[48]

Chapter Four

Food Magic and Mnemonic Gestures

Ancient Mnemonics and Magic

The school initiation ceremony consists of a complex set of mnemonic magical elements. To appreciate them, we need to consider the alternative methods of memory training practiced in Judaism and in the pagan cultures of the Greco-Roman world. Two types of mnemonic techniques can be distinguished. Although the Greeks and Romans advocated repetition and rote learning to memorize traditions,[1] they also developed a technique that involved the visualization of a building, or palace, into which topics or words were mentally placed. The visual method of mnemonics ascribed to the early fifth-century B.C.E. poet Simonides of Ceos was preserved in the writings of Quintilian and Cicero and in an anonymous text called *Rhetorica ad Herennium*. The rabbis developed their own version of repetition assisted by mnemonic acronyms and other abbreviations (Hebrew *simanim*), and this was a verbal method.[2]

The Greco-Roman technique of visual memorization has been discussed by several scholars.[3] It is summarized by Frances A. Yates in the opening chapter of *The Art of Memory*:

> At a banquet given by a nobleman of Thessaly named Scopas, the poet Simonides of Ceos chanted a lyric poem, in honour of his host but including a passage in praise of Castor and Pollux. Scopas meanly told the poet that he would only pay him half the sum agreed upon for the panegyric and that he must obtain the balance from the twin gods to whom he had devoted half the poem. A little later, a message was brought in to Simonides that two young men were waiting outside who wished to see him. He rose from the banquet and went out but could find no

one. During his absence the roof of the banqueting hall fell in, crushing Scopas and all the guests to death beneath the ruins; the corpses were so mangled that the relatives who came to take them away for burial were unable to identify them. But Simonides remembered the places at which they had been sitting at the table and was therefore able to indicate to the relatives which were their dead. The invisible callers, Castor and Pollux, had handsomely paid for their share in the panegyric by drawing Simonides away from the banquet just before the crash. And this experience suggested to the poet the principles of the art of memory of which he is said to have been the inventor. Noting that it was through his memory of the places at which the guests had been sitting that he had been able to identify the bodies, he realised that orderly arrangement is essential for good memory.[4]

Yates continues, quoting Cicero's account: "He inferred that persons desiring to train this faculty [of memory] must select places and form mental images of the things they wish to remember and store those images in the places, so that the order of the places will preserve the order of the things, and the images of the things will denote the things themselves, and we shall employ the places and images respectively as a wax writing-tablet and the letters written on it."[5]

As Yates points out, the technique or art of memory is part of the art of rhetoric. It is a method by which the orator can improve his memory and deliver long speeches accurately. As Quintilian describes it, one must think of a building with many rooms. In each room one pictures specific objects and associates each with a different subject in the speech. The orator mentally walks through the building, adding the topics of the speech as he encounters the images in his imaginary building. This art of memory had a lasting influence on Western culture.

Despite the fact that Judaism emphasized a sacred oral tradition and placed — still places — great religious value on the memorization of rabbinic tradition,[6] the visual art of memory is unattested in the documents that form the rabbinic canon: Mishnah, Tosefta, early Midrash, or the Talmuds. Apparently the rabbis did not know of the rhetorical art of memory. There are no clear signs that they polemicized against it, though well they might have, since it smacks of idolatry. The visual art of memory enters Jewish intellectual history only in the Renaissance, when some Italian Jewish authors became aware of classical Greco-Roman rhetoric and began writing about it, as we find in Judah Messer Leon's *Sefer Nofet Zufim* and, later, Leon Modena's *Lev ha-Aryeh*.[7]

What, then, did ancient Jewish authorities recommend as a means for remembering the oral tradition? The predominant technique was sheer repetition, facilitated by stylistic patterns of composition that aided memorization.[8] This technique is implicit in the tradition about R. Akiva and his willingness to begin the study of Torah at an advanced age:

> One time he stood by the mouth of a well. "Who hollowed out this stone?" he wondered.
>
> He was told, "It is the water which falls upon it every day, continually." It was said to him: "Akiva, have you not heard, 'The waters wear away the stones'?" (Job 14:19).
>
> Thereupon R. Akiva drew the inference with regard to himself: If what is soft wears down the hard, all the more shall the words of the Torah, which are as hard as iron, hollow out my heart, which is flesh and blood! Forthwith he turned to the study of the Torah.[9]

The first part of the tale is a straightforward *a fortiori* argument to support the efficacy of persistent Torah study, but the imagery is striking when compared to the phrase "broadening the heart" in Psalm 119 and in the texts about the medieval initiation ceremony.[10] The heart is compared to a stone to be hollowed out, and the Torah is compared to water, which is yet another association in the initiation ceremony and an ancient Jewish commonplace.[11] Here, however, the image is not the standard association of Torah/water/life but a specific reference to Torah study as the agency of mental enlargement. Just as water hollows out a stone, so the study of Torah will enlarge the heart, that is, expand the mind's capacity to contain Torah. This metaphor is very similar to the mishnaic image of the mind as a cistern to be filled up with Torah traditions before it can ever become a self-sustaining "fountain" of independent understanding.[12]

But unlike the initiation ceremony, the rabbinic use here of the image of widening the heart lacks any hint of a magical technique for carrying it out.[13] In fact, the Akivan tradition graphically expresses the common rabbinic technique of memorization by repetition. For the religious commandment of

Torah learning (Hebrew *talmud torah*) refers not simply to learning a tradition once and for all, but to studying the same traditions over and over again. Steven Fraade has noted the polemical overtones of the doctrine of rabbinic scholastic piety in contrast to other models that rely on mystical ascents.[14] I would add that there is a relationship between the rabbis' doctrine of continuous study of the Torah and their advocacy of the technique of repetition, on the one hand, and an alternative mnemonics using magic, which the rabbis considered impious, on the other. Another heikhalot tradition portrays angels as urging God not to let mortals know the secret names and crowns which they could then use to learn Torah magically and never have to labor again to acquire it.[15]

The primary source about the rabbinic repetitive mnemonic techniques is B. 'Eruvin 53a, and it assumes that verbatim memorization preceded verbal abbreviations, which were a secondary technique: ["First in Hebrew] R. Judah stated in the name of Rav: The Judeans who learned verbatim retained their learning, but not the Galileans who did not. [Now in Aramaic] But does (learning) depend on whether one pays attention to the language (of the traditions)? Rather say: The Judeans, who learned verbatim and who prescribed mnemonics (*simanim*) as an aid, retained their learning; but the Galileans, who did neither, did not."[16]

Adding to the pressure to study by repetition, some rabbinic authors found biblical mandate not only to study Torah but also not to forget what one had learned. The need to ward off forgetting was often linked to repeated study. The primary biblical text was Deuteronomy 4:9. Thus:

> R. Dosethai b. Yannai said in the name of R. Meir: He that forgets one word of his study, the Scripture reckons it to him as though he endangers his own soul, for it is written, "But take utmost care and watch yourselves scrupulously, so that you do not forget the things that you saw with your own eyes" (Deut. 4:9).[17]
>
> (Elisha ben Abuyah) used to say: Like gold vessels, the words of the Torah are hard to acquire, and like glass vessels they are easy to wreck.[18]
>
> (Hillel) answered (Ben He He): He that repeated his lesson one hundred times is not as good as someone who repeated it a hundred and one times.[19]
>
> R. Joshua b. Karḥa said: Whoever studies the Torah and does not review it is like one who sows without reaping. R. Joshua said: He who

studies the Torah and then forgets it is like a woman who bears (a child) and buries (it).[20]

What is striking about the two standard rabbinic techniques of repetition and verbal mnemonic is the difficulty of applying them to large bodies of text. Unlike the Homeric poets, the Druids, the Brahmins, or the Scandinavian bards, who learned lengthy bodies of lore in semantic equivalent phrases, not verbatim,[21] the oral Torah is to be mastered word by word—not just by virtuosos, but potentially by all adult Jewish males. Even if we consider the probability that in actuality it was the rabbis, not most Jews, who did this in antiquity, it is a daunting challenge. No visual aids were available other than the words themselves. Before printing was invented, not even a standard page existed with which one could visually enhance the memory. Once the first printed edition of the Babylonian Talmud appeared, a Talmud prodigy could dare someone to stick a pin through the pages of an open folio volume and offer to announce the letters through which the pin had penetrated.[22]

But no such visual aid was available in the ancient Jewish schools.[23] And so, it is not surprising that some tried to get around the laborious and risky business of trying to memorize by repetition. This need was especially acute in light of the rabbis' view that forgetting Torah was a sin. Perhaps the emphasis on the religious reward for constantly repeating what one had already studied reflects a polemic not against the pagan visual art of memory but against an alternative Jewish method, a method so reliable that it claimed that it permitted one to study a tradition once and never forget it. Given the frailties of the human mind confronting the universal obligation for Jewish males to study Torah and not forget it, such a technique must have been very alluring.

One rabbinic text, which may be postclassical, hints at just such a technique. It is a commentary in *Midrash Qohelet Rabbah*, 1:13, on the phrase "I set my mind to study . . . ; wisdom . . . is a bad thing" (Eccles. 1:13):

> R. Abbahu said: This refers to the futility of study—a man learns Torah and then forgets it. . . . (Others said:) (No,) it is for man's benefit that he studies Torah and (then) forgets (it). For if he studied Torah and did not forget it, he would study it intensively for two or three years and then spend the rest of his life working at his trade (bi-melakhto) and never study it any more. But since a man studies Torah and forgets it, he will never stop laboring over it.

To be sure, this passage may simply express the commonplace rabbinic notion that the more one studies Torah, the more one receives a reward. But it is strange to find the rabbis defending the virtue of forgetting Torah, an action that elsewhere they refer to as sinful. The author of this text seems to argue against a different possibility when he stresses that forgetting what one has studied is beneficial in that it makes Jews continue to study the Torah throughout their lives, a religious activity that the rabbis called *talmud torah*, the continuous study of the Torah traditions. And yet, it is not clear that everyone had the time to study "the rest of his life" and not spend most of his time making a living. From classical and clearly from postclassical times, there is evidence of an alternative Jewish mnemonic technique, which sought the same goal as the standard rabbinic method of constant repetition and also served the ends of Jewish piety; but unlike the method of laborious repetition, this technique offered a shortcut. It also guaranteed success, because it did not rely on human capacities alone.[24]

This other technique was magical. Unlike the rabbinically documented methods of repetition and mnemonic signs, the magical method involved studying the Torah by ritual procedures that appealed to a supernatural power, sar ha-torah. The technique might also involve an incantation to ward off POTAH, the prince of forgetfulness.

Although David Halperin has proposed that the origins of sar ha-torah and heikhalot traditions lie in antirabbinic circles of ʿamei ha-arez of the lower classes,[25] I consider it more plausible that the proponents of these magical practices were relatively learned nonrabbinic circles, at least some of whom lacked the wealth and leisure to follow the early rabbinic ideology of continuous Torah study, a Jewish way of leisure living analogous to pagan aristocrats who studied classical authors in the same period, the first two Christian centuries.[26] The reference from *Midrash Qohelet Rabbah* to "working at his trade" may reinforce this interpretation, although we lack any concrete data about the socioeconomic backgrounds of the authors of the texts in question. Perhaps it was just such nonrabbinic Jews who persisted in institutionalizing the practice of reading Ezekiel 1 in the synagogue on Shavuot when the Mishnah, M. Ḥagiga 2:1, explicitly opposed reading that text in public.[27] As the rabbis yielded to this practice, so they eventually accepted many of the magical techniques of adult Torah study, which accounts for their being preserved in medieval rabbinic works, as well as in anonymous magical manuscripts.[28]

Food Metaphors and Ritualized Mnemonics

As we have seen, some parts of the initiation ceremony included elements, such as learning the letters of the alphabet in various combinations,
that were primarily designed to teach children how to read. Other elements of
the rite were primarily adult magical techniques for enhancing the memory
that might also be pedagogically effective with children. The distinction between "pedagogic" and "magical" is somewhat artificial and risks anachronistic
distortion. Whereas magical techniques might seem to us to be of no practical educational use, to the ancients and medievals they might have appeared
to be the most effective teaching methods available. In using these terms, my
intention is to distinguish between those features of the ceremony that were
primarily associated with children's schooling and those others that arose from
the types of magic used for adult memory training or Torah study, usually on
Shavuot.[29]

A magical and mnemonic function can especially be attributed to elements such as licking honey off the alphabet written on the tablet, eating
letters and words written on cooked eggs and on a baked honey cake, as well
as reciting an incantation to ward off POTAH, the prince of forgetfulness. Such
a function is also suggested in the gestures of bringing the child down to a
riverbank and covering him en route to school to protect him from sources of
impurity, and in the singing and body motions. In ancient or early medieval
sources, each of these practices is found in isolation from the others but often
connected with the enhancement of an adult's memory. In medieval times
these practices were adapted and transformed into an initiation ceremony for
young boys learning their letters.[30]

In contrast to rabbinic mnemonics, which is based on an ideology of
constant repetition aided by simanim, or Greco-Roman mnemonics, which
resorts to visualizing a multi-chambered memory palace, the Jewish initiation ceremony draws on several ancient magical techniques that involve food,
verbal formulas, and sympathetic river magic. Although some of these are
mentioned briefly in the sources of ancient Judaism, they are not nearly as
central as the mnemonics of constant repetition.

I begin with the prominence in the medieval ceremony of the association
of eating certain foods with learning and remembering the Torah. Many cultures make the association of food and study. We need only think of such com-

monplace English expressions as "to digest" what one learns, "to ruminate" when one deliberates, and "food for thought."[31]

In ancient Judaism, each side of the study-as-eating equation was given several specific meanings. The object of one's study was to be the Torah as the word of God, and the foods that were compared to the Torah tended to be specific as well: honey, milk, oil, and flour (bread, cake). Already in the Hebrew Bible, foods are sometimes associated with the oral transmission of God's words to a prophet. When rabbinic Judaism adopted the Hellenistic ideal of studying sacred knowledge as a means to achieve personal salvation, the scriptural images that compared acquiring God's words to ingesting them were applied to the study of the written text. This association, which was eventually interpreted ritually as the actual eating of foods to enable one magically to study Torah and not forget it, was based on the biblical theme that God puts His words into the mouth of His prophets. We should realize that this image can be used to support the standard rabbinic mnemonics of constant repetition of divine words, as well as the magical mnemonics of ingesting inscribed foods.[32]

The theme occurs in the Hebrew Bible whenever a classical prophet is described. For Moses, the paragon of biblical prophets, the image is introduced in statements declaring that God will be with Moses and give him the words that should be said (Exod. 3:12; 4:10–16). In Deuteronomy we find the notion that later legitimate prophets will be like Moses: "I will raise up a prophet for them from among their people, like yourself: I will put My words in his mouth and he will speak to them all that I command him" (Deut. 18:18).

The image continues in the call to prophecy of two of the great literary prophets. In his initiation into prophecy, Jeremiah draws directly on the Deuteronomic language, as is his wont: "The Lord put out His hand and touched my mouth, and the Lord said to me: Herewith I put My words into your mouth" (Jer. 1:9).[33] But it is Ezekiel who takes the image to a new literal dimension by envisioning himself actually eating God's words and then adding that God's words taste sweet: "He said to me, 'Mortal, eat what is offered you; eat this scroll, and go speak to the House of Israel.' So I opened my mouth, and He gave me this scroll to eat, as He said to me, 'Mortal, feed your stomach and fill your belly with this scroll that I give you.' I ate it, and it tasted as sweet as honey to me" (Ezek. 3:1–3; figure 4).[34] This new metaphor of eating God's sweet words as the interpretation and extension of the image of God's words

4. Ezekiel eating the Book. Paris, Bibliothèque Nationale, lat. 16744, Bible, f. 81a. Reprinted with permission. Photo: © cliché Bibliothèque Nationale de France, Paris.

being in the prophet's mouth is echoed again in Psalms: "How pleasing is Your word to my palate, sweeter than honey" (Ps. 119:103). And again in Proverbs: "My son, eat honey, for it is good; let its sweet drops be on your palate. Know: such is wisdom for your soul" (Prov. 24:13–14a; cf. Ps. 19:11).

Ezekiel gave concrete meaning to Jeremiah's image of God's putting words into the prophet's mouth, but he also drew on another biblical image to reach the conclusion that the content of God's words is sweet: the manna in the desert. In the biblical account of the gift of manna, the divinely sent food is described as being "like coriander seed, white, and it tasted like wafers in honey" (Exod. 16:31). Moreover, the manna is sent to test whether Israel is observing all of the commandments, and in Deuteronomy it is presented as being equivalent to God's words: "He subjected you to the hardship of hunger and then gave you manna to eat, which neither you nor your fathers had ever known, in order to teach you that man does not live on bread alone, but that man may live on anything that comes out of the Lord's mouth" (Deut. 8:3).

Ezekiel, then, combined the metaphor of the word of God as manna with the motif of the prophet's receiving in his mouth the words of God. The dramatic result is a vision in which the prophet eats a scroll on which God's words are written and which he says are sweet. We recall that Ezekiel 3 and Psalm 119 are both cited in the initiation ceremony as scriptural prooftexts, but the text from Ezekiel is central. The ceremony, in effect, compares the child's beginning to study the written words of God with the prophet Ezekiel's initiation into receiving the words of God. This comparison is appropriate when one considers that the sages viewed themselves as the successors to the biblical prophets,[35] and that literacy is the first step toward becoming a Torah scholar. The ceremony, then, is a ritual gloss on the passage in Ezekiel: the generic "words" are given concrete forms in the alphabets, verses, and phrases, and they are sweet because honey has been smeared over the tablet or baked into the cakes.

Expanding the metaphor of eating God's words from prophets to all Jews is already anticipated in the Hebrew Bible. Second Isaiah develops the idea of Israel as a prophetic people and transfers the image, formerly reserved for prophets, to all Israel: "And this shall be My covenant with them, said the Lord: My spirit which is upon you, and the words which I have placed in your mouth, shall not be absent from your mouth, nor from the mouth of your children, nor from the mouth of your children's children—said the Lord— from now on, for all time" (Isa. 59:21). Second Isaiah's view that Israel is to be a prophetic nation (Isa. 51:16; 49:1–3) is translated in rabbinic parlance as the idea that the Jews are to be a Torah-studying people, and the image of divinely uttered oracles being placed in ancient Israel's mouth becomes the image of God's Torah words being placed in every Jew's mouth.

Ezekiel's vision of a ritualized eating of God's sweet words resonates with associations between God's words and other references to honey and mouth. For example, in Deuteronomy: "He fed him honey from the crag, and oil from the flinty rock" (32:13). Or in Song of Songs, the lover (God) says to his beloved (Israel): "Honey and milk are under your tongue" (4:11). In this fashion, foods such as oil and milk were added to the menu of Torah symbols to be ingested and found sweet.[36] Both of these verses are cited in the initiation ceremony and are there based on standard rabbinic exegesis that equated each of these food references to the Torah, God's words.

But the medieval initiation ceremony does not merely stipulate that certain foods are like the Torah. Nor does it envision eating foods as the ingestion of God's words, as did Ezekiel. Rather, it ritualizes these metaphors and actually directs that words be written on these foods and that the boy eat them for the purpose of "opening his heart." Although the ultimate inspiration for such a possibility is the biblical association of God's words and the prophet/scholar/young student's mouth, the use of ancient magic as mnemonics led to the concretization of specific acts, foods, and words for this purpose.

Eating God's words written on different types of food is one of the main features of the ceremony, which was drawn from the tradition of magical mnemonics. Although a talmudic tradition stating that eating certain foods is either good or bad for one's memory anticipates this part of the ritual, the specific types of eating in the ceremony derive from other contexts as well. In B. Horayot 13b we find the following statement about remembering and forgetting one's Torah:

> Our rabbis taught: Five things make one forget one's studies: Eating something from which a mouse or a cat has eaten; eating the heart of a beast; frequent consumption of olives; drinking the remains of water that was used for washing; and washing one's feet one above the other. Others say: He who puts his clothes under his head.
>
> Five things restore one's learning. Wheat bread and much more so wheat itself; eating a roasted egg without salt; frequent consumption of olive oil; frequent indulgence in wine and spices; and the drinking of water that has remained from kneading. Others say: Dipping one's finger in salt and eating it is also included.[37]

Talmudic commentaries on this passage gloss parts of the statement as follows: On "frequent consumption of olive oil": "This corroborates the view of R. Johanan who said: 'Just as the olive causes one to forget seventy years of study, so does olive oil restore seventy years of study'"; on "frequent indulgence in wine and spices": "This corroborates the view of Rava who said: 'Wine and spices have made me wise.'"

These traditions express the idea that eating certain foods causes retention or loss of memory, and they are part of the magical tradition of Torah mnemonics that was further developed in the medieval initiation ceremony and in another ritual in Judaism. In particular, the notion that wine and spices enhance the memory has an echo elsewhere. The special time in Jewish celebration when one drinks wine and smells spices together is at the end of the Sabbath at the havdalah ceremony.[38] And it is not surprising that the incantation against POTAH, the prince of forgetfulness, a salient feature of the child's initiation ceremony, is also found in the weekly havdalah ceremony. This particular incantation is not found in the Talmud, but its use at the havdalah ceremony builds on the talmudic tradition that connects wine and spices with memory enhancement. In effect, the inclusion of wine, spices, and the incantation against POTAḤ means that celebrating havdalah helps one not forget one's Torah learning as one moves from the Sabbath to the secular week.

Other parts of the ceremony were inspired not by the talmudic passage but by other considerations. In contrast to eating a baked loaf and a hard egg, which can be related to the talmudic tradition of food mnemonics, the practice of the child's licking honey off a school tablet does not seem to depend directly on any specific ancient or early medieval models. There is no ancient Jewish tradition that claims that licking honey off a tablet or piece of parchment enhances one's memory, although honey has broad associations with ancient initiations.[39] Rather, this part of the ritual seems to be an adaptation of two ancient elements. It draws on the fact that in antiquity, pagan, Jewish, and Christian children all used wooden writing tablets covered with wax from which to learn their letters.[40] Such a tablet is mentioned, we recall, in connection with the middle-aged Akiva, when he went to learn his letters with his young son. In addition, the honey smeared on the tablet is a concrete way of giving meaning to Ezekiel's image of eating God's sweet words. In the ceremony the tablet now functions as a primer, as in antiquity, but also symbolizes the scroll in Ezekiel 3 on which God's words have been written and which the prophet (now, child) eats. The honey makes the words inscribed on the tablet sweet, both literally and metaphorically.

The use of the tablet, rather than something edible, to concretize Ezekiel's vision meant that the child must lick the honey off the slate, since he cannot eat an inedible object. This limits the extent to which the child is similar to Ezekiel, who envisions himself actually eating God's words. In some other cultures, in fact, children did eat cakes baked either in the shapes of individual letters of the alphabet, or they ate a whole alphabet primer, or abecediary, made from a flat cake onto which the alphabet was imprinted with a mold. The more obvious solution, of eating a sweetened cake on which God's words were written, did become part of the medieval Jewish ceremony, but the tablet remained as well. Perhaps one reason that the school tablet was retained, despite the addition of the honey cake, was that it was meant to represent the tablets (luḥot) of the Ten Commandments given on Mount Sinai, the occasion to which the entire ceremony was linked.[41] In addition, there was historical continuity from antiquity for using such tablets in elementary education in medieval Europe.[42]

Honey Cakes and Torah

In the ceremony, besides licking honey off the alphabet tablet, the child is to read and eat inscribed honey cakes and hardboiled eggs as two additional ways of ritualizing Ezekiel's vision. Just as the school tablet gave a new specific form to Ezekiel's vision of eating a scroll, so other contexts led to the use of honey cakes and eggs. The honey cake on which words have been written combines several associations: the sweet manna that God gave the Israelites in the desert on the way to Sinai; the loaves of the first wheat harvest (lehem bikkurim) associated in the Hebrew Bible with the Shavuot festival; the talmudic tradition that bread baked of wheat flour enhances one's memory; and, of course, Ezekiel's vision that he ate God's words, which were sweet.

But unlike the practice of licking honey from an alphabet tablet, about which we find no allusion prior to the medieval European initiation ceremony, there is an early tradition of eating an inscribed cake as a means of "becoming wise." One passage occurs in the eleventh-century Italian rabbinic dictionary 'Arukh (Arrangement), compiled by R. Nathan b. Yehiel of Rome. And since early Italian Jewish culture was a bridge between ancient Palestinian traditions, on the one hand, and Ashkenazic Jewish culture, on the other, we must pay special attention to an Italian Jewish source that might possibly provide an important clue as to earlier meanings of this part of the ceremony.

Under the entry QLR, the same consonants that make up the name of the early medieval Byzantine-Jewish liturgical poet Eleazar birabbi Qalir,[43] we find the following: "We have heard that there is a place where a cake is called qalir. That is how R. Eliezer ha-Qalir (got his name). He ate a cake ('ugah) on which was written an amulet (qamei'a) and he became wise (ve-nitpaqah)."[44] The connection between the name Qalir and eating memory cakes was taken up by others in the nineteenth century; some even speculated that there was a historical connection between that name and the medieval initiation ceremony. In 1845 Leopold Zunz commented on this passage in the 'Arukh: "The Jacobites had something similar, see Michaelis, Syr. Lex., p. 801."[45] In his Syriac dictionary, Johannes Michaelis notes under the entry "kalyris": "A crust of bread, on which Jacobites write a certain prayer which is found in their Psalter, and which is to be eaten when they bring boys (to school)." [46]

The introductory Syriac rubric of the text is quoted and translated into Latin in the catalogue of Syriac manuscripts in the Bodleian Library in Oxford: "A prayer for a boy whose parents wish to introduce him to book learning: they should bring him to the priest who gives him to eat this prayer written out on the loaf of bread." [47] The prayer or magical text to be inscribed on the bread is the following:

> Come, Holy Spirit, from the supernal heights; come, come, O Spirit of Wisdom and Understanding to N son of N and fill his mind with wisdom, knowledge and understanding, so that he may speak and learn all that he wishes from the knowledge of truth. And may he receive the (?) of the economy of all true doctrine, memre, madrashe, qale, meters (or tones) and chants, (containing) all true doctrine. And if Satan stands up in opposition to him, may (Satan) flee from him. Yes, O revered God, Lord of lords, who was named in the Scriptures Ehyeh Asher Ehyeh and El Shadday Saba'ot, at (whose) word the sun runs (its course), may your word run upon your servant's lips, and may they (sic) raise up to you praise and thanks, Father, Son, and Holy Spirit, now and always, for ever. [48]

Although it is difficult to date this text, Sebastian Brock indicated to me that it has linguistic features that are peculiar to texts that are as old as the sixth century. [49] Moshe Idel pointed out to me in conversation that the several Jewish formulations that it contains likely reflect an earlier Jewish source. [50] Even if there existed a Jewish model on which the text itself rests, this need not mean that a Jewish children's initiation ceremony was the original setting for the incantation. It is possible, but it is even more likely that the Jacobite Christian tradition derives from adult Jewish circles who indulged in magical techniques designed to improve their memories. This Syriac passage is the only direct reference, outside of the medieval Hebrew sources, to children eating inscribed food in order to learn and remember better.

Another Syriac text, although metaphoric and midrashic in character, suggests that there was an eastern Christian, and probably a Jewish, tradition behind many of the magical practices and associations that worked their way westward into Europe. The text is by the early seventh-century Nestorian bishop Barhadbsabba (literally, "Sunday's child"), who wrote a narrative called *The Cause of the Founding of the Schools.* The text presents the stages of sacred history in the form of the foundation of schools:

> As soon as He created Adam and Eve, he passed before them, in the order of the letters (of the alphabet), all of the animals and beasts. (God) inspired (Adam) invisibly so that he would read out to Him (what God had told him). Adam read out these first (unwritten) tablets (consisting of) the names of all the animals, the beasts of the desert, and the birds of the heavens. The name that Adam gave to each living animal became its name.
>
> After Adam had correctly repeated these unwritten letters, forming from them the individual names, God transported his school to the Garden of Eden. There He taught him the commandments of the law. First, He composed for him a short psalm on a beautiful tree so that he could read it and learn from it the difference between good and evil. And because God knew his weakness, He warned him as follows: "The day that you will erase one of the letters of this tablet, or when you will eat of the fruit of this tree, your teacher, you will die."
>
> But He didn't leave him only with a warning, but He promised him, as a teacher to his pupil, and as a father to his children, that if he read and meditated on this commandment and if, during the desired time, he would repeat the names which He had read before him, and preserve all the letters so that they were not erased, He would give him the tree of life from which to eat and thereby live forever.[51]

This text combines learning the alphabet and the importance of remembering and not forgetting the letters with eating special foods that confer salvific knowledge. Despite the significant differences between it and the medieval versions of the Jewish children's ritual in Europe or the Mediterranean, the Nestorian text is further support that ancient Christian and possibly even earlier Jewish antecedents are behind the medieval ceremony. Still, in the specific case of the eating of inscribed cakes, associated with Qalir and the first-mentioned Syriac text, it is not possible to determine why there are no allusions to a Jewish practice of children eating inscribed bread or cake in antiquity, if in fact it antedated the Christian Jacobite example.

This paucity of hard fact has tempted others to speculate on how the initiation ceremony originated in the East. In 1883 Shmuel David Luzzatto (Shadal) published in one of his scholarly letters a theory about the ceremony's origins based on the statement in the 'Arukh, on the etymology of "Qalir" as "cake," and on the Syriac Christian text. Luzzatto argued that the entry in the 'Arukh that explains how the great liturgical poet Eleazar Qalir got his name need not be accepted as fact today but could instead represent what contemporaries thought to be the case.

After quoting at length the passages about the medieval initiation ceremony from the Maḥzor Vitry and Sefer ha-Asufot, Luzzatto cites the comment in Michaelis's Syriac dictionary about the word qalyra and indicates that this passage supports the 'Arukh's comment about the meaning of Eleazar Qalir's name. He then offers the following explanation of the connections among all of the facts he has assembled:

> This (Syriac text) also supports my view that R. Eliezer birabbi Qalir was Babylonian. The likelihood that he and his father were born near Syrians (Christians) is supported by the likelihood that his father took from them the custom of the cake which they called "Qalira" and fed it to his son Eliezer. It subsequently happened that he became a precocious student, and everyone began to call the father "Qalir," that is, Cake-Wise. Rabbi Eliezer himself also believed that the cake he had eaten made him smart and enabled him to be a good student. He was thankful to his father for feeding him the cake and showed his respect by signing his name, "son of Qalir," because he ate the cake and became wise. The Babylonian (Jews) learned about this from R. Qalir, and they too fed cakes to their children when they first took them to study Torah. The custom spread from Babylonia to France and Germany, for they all desired that their sons become as wise and successful in Torah study as R. Eliezer, the great liturgical poet, whose poems were widely used in Italy, Germany, and France.[52]

This fanciful reconstruction is valuable for what it tries to do, and also for what it cannot do. Luzzatto senses correctly that there is a link between the Franco-German children's initiation ceremony and Eastern sources, and we have seen that several elements are derived from ancient Palestinian and early medieval settings. He also tells us that the only element in the medieval children's ceremony with an earlier analogue specifically related to the beginning of a child's schooling is the eating of inscribed cakes. We cannot, however, fill in the gap between the Syriac ceremony and the medieval Jewish initiation by invoking Luzzatto's "Qalir connection." It is clever, but it is only speculation. There is no basis for thinking that Eleazar Qalir was born and lived in Babylonia. His poems reflect a liturgy that is fundamentally Palestinian, with some Babylonian influence. It is more likely that Qalir was not his father's name but was an epithet of uncertain meaning. Later generations tried to explain its meaning, and one of these interpretations connected the homonym *kalyra* (cake) with the name Qalir. This resulted in the pseudo-etymology found in the *'Arukh*.[53]

It is not clear where this pseudo-etymology and its awareness of the magical-cake custom arose. What is significant here is that some Jews in eleventh-century Italy were aware of the custom of eating magical cakes with inscribed words on them to make one wise. We should also note that the tradition in the *'Arukh* does not stipulate that Eleazar Qalir ate the cake when he began school or when he was a small child. Luzzatto assumes this in order to make a connection between the Syriac text, which is about a Christian child entering school, and the medieval Jewish child's initiation ceremony. The setting of the Jewish practice might have been an adult setting, and a magical ritualization of the talmudic tradition, quoted earlier, which stated that eating a baked loaf of wheat will help one to remember one's studies.

Further references to Qalir are found in the *Maḥzor Vitry*, one of the liturgical compilations in which the medieval ceremony was preserved. Unlike the geonic tradition that seems to make Qalir into a Babylonian, the text in the *Maḥzor Vitry* claims that Qalir was a Palestinian and also a *tanna*, that is, one of the earliest rabbinic authorities. This report further strengthens the impression that Qalir was a legendary figure in Italo-Ashkenazic Jewish memory.[54]

In addition to these connections, there was an important Ashkenazic esoteric tradition that claimed to derive secret lore from ancient Babylonia via Italy, although it actually masked a fundamental historical path from ancient Palestine via southern Italy to the Rhineland.[55] In a collection of early medieval traditions, we find the magical ingestion of inscribed cakes as a means to strengthen an adult's memory. A tradition is ascribed to the great tenth-century head of the rabbinic academy of Sura in Baghdad, Saadia ben Joseph al-Fayumi (882–942), whose philosophical writings were known in north-

ern Europe from a Hebrew paraphrase that linked him with early medieval
Byzantine Palestinian lore. In this text a specific calendar date can be inferred:

> For forgetfulness, tested and reliable, and R. Saadia b. R. Joseph, may his
> memory be blessed, would use it. He found it in the cave of R. Eleazar
> Qalir, where all the sages of Israel and their students were using it suc-
> cessfully.
>
> On the New Moon of Sivan, take wheat flour and knead it when
> you are standing. Make it into loaves and bake it. Write on it "He made
> a remembrance (zekher) of His wonders. The Lord is gracious and com-
> passionate" (Ps. 111:4). Take an egg and cook it well. Peel it and write
> on it: ASPIYAM KISTAM TRMT ANUN DKHZUH. Eat the loaf every day with
> an egg for thirty days. And you will learn whatever you see and not
> forget it.[56]

Although it is not possible to date this tradition, the association of Saadia with the Palestinian poet Qalir is suggestive. Evidently, the tradition in the
'Arukh that connected the poet Qalir with eating an inscribed cake was based
on a Palestinian recollection that also involved Saadia Gaon. Although we cannot trace how such a tradition developed, it seems clear that Qalir became
associated in later memory with learned and magical lore.[57]

We find other examples of magical recipes for the improvement of memory and Torah study connected with inscribed cakes. One is recorded at the end
of Sefer Razi'el, a compilation of mystical lore that concludes with a selection of
magical formulas. Although published only in 1701, it clearly contains very old
material that can be found in geonic and other early medieval texts. Sefer Razi'el
further confirms that we are dealing with techniques designed not specifically
for children but for adult Jews. Among the formulas for not forgetting what
one learns is one that involves an inscribed loaf that is to be eaten on Shavuot.
The text reads:

> It is mainly to be done on the New Moon of Sivan and the eve of
> Shavuot even though it is not eaten until the next day. . . . He should
> take barley flour and if he cannot find barley, wheat flour, but barley
> is preferable. He should knead it in a state of ritual cleanness and say:
> I am doing this for N. May it be [Your] will, our God in heaven, that
> I succeed in (making) this "opening the heart" which I am preparing

for N son of N (mother). May he be open to the study of the Torah and
everything else and not forget anything he studied and knows. "This
sentence is decreed by the Watchers; this verdict is commanded by the
Holy Ones" (Dan. 4:14). In the name of Yah Adonai Zeva'ot.

He should knead the flour thoroughly and make clean fine flour.
From the fine flour he should make a round cake, a handbreadth in
diameter. He should take ink and make on the cake four lines (one on
top of the other) in the middle of the cake. He should write in the spaces
the following three Names in large, perfect lettering, one above the
other, not all in the same line, nor on two lines but on three separate
lines: ARIMAS, AVRIMAS, ARMIMAS. On the other side of the cake, opposite the squares (just mentioned), he should write out in ink another
(set of) boxes made of six lines. In them he should write the following
five Names, one above the other, each Name separately, in large letters:
ASI'EL, ANSI'EL, ANSIFI'EL, U-FETAH'EL, U-FATHA.

After writing all the Names on both sides of the cake, he should
bake the cake on the oven and heat the oven with wood from grape-
vines. After baking it he should take a cup of red wine and eight myrtle
leaves and write on them the eight Names written above in the boxes.
He should write each Name on a separate myrtle leaf and dissolve the
Name in the red wine and place the leaves in the wine cup and drink
after saying seven times: ADA BAR PAPPA, RAFRAM BAR PAPPA, RAMI
BAR PAPPA, YAKHISH BAR PAPPA, SURHAV BAR PAPPA, DARU BAR PAPPA,
HAMA BAR PAPPA, AHI BAR PAPPA, NAHMAN BAR PAPPA, MARI BAR PAPPA.
"Blessed are You, Lord, train me in Your laws" (Ps. 119:12). May my soul
live and praise You. May Your laws aid me. You are good and beneficent.
Blessed are You, Lord, Who is good and beneficent (cf. Ps. 119:68).

I adjure you, POTAH, the prince of forgetfulness, that you remove
from me a foolish heart and throw it on a high mountain in the name of
the holy Names: ARIMAS, AVRIMAS, ARMIMAS, ASI'EL, ANSI'EL, ANSIFI'EL,
U-FETAH'EL, U-FATHA. "But Noah found favor with the Lord" (Gen. 6:8).

He should say this six more times and afterward he should eat
the cake.[58]

This elaborate text combines several elements associated with the magical
use of a cake as a mnemonic technique. Based on the talmudic association of

wheat and cakes with remembering the Torah, the magical names are inscribed and the cakes ingested as a sure means of retaining what one studies. *Sefer Razi'el* adds the formula of the ten sons of Rav Pappa, based on the geonic version of the magical havdalah ceremony.

Aside from eating inscribed cakes, two major components of the medieval initiation ceremony are also found in these two texts. In the Saadia-Qalir tradition there is reference to cooking an egg, and in the lengthy procedure from *Sefer Razi'el* we find use of the incantation against POTAḤ. Each of these elements of mnemonic magic requires careful examination.

Magical Eggs

The practice in the medieval initiation ceremony of eating an inscribed hardboiled egg is derived only in part from the talmudic statement that eating a roasted egg enhances one's memory. It can also be traced to traditions of Jewish magical mnemonics such as the Saadia-Qalir tradition quoted above. In addition, another source can be found in the collection of Hebrew heikhalot writings.

Among the Torah formulas associated with the magical acquisition of Torah knowledge is one attached to specific ritual actions. It is found in a composition that Gershom Scholem called *Ma'aseh Merkavah* (Chariot Magic). In JTS MS 8128 we find various acts that an adult should do to "become wise." Some of these acts are preserved in the magical text quoted from *Sefer Razi'el*, and the time of the year is specified as Shavuot: "R. Yishmael said: A student who wishes to make use of this great secret should sit fasting from the New Moon of Sivan until Shavuot." [59]

Like the magical formula attributed to Saadia Gaon, this text also specifies a number of magical techniques. They involve incantations to guarantee the memory of one's study of Torah and gestures such as writing the incantation on a fig leaf and then eating it with wine; writing another on an olive leaf, dissolving it in wine, and drinking the wine and reciting a prayer twenty-four times; and reciting another prayer over a cup of wine forty-one times and drinking it on Friday when lying down, and fasting the following day.

The last element involves an egg ritual:

Egg. L'YGNSS BPSA PR. [You][60] are the great Prince of the Torah, who was with Moses on Mount Sinai and crowned him.[61] Feed me and put into me everything that he learned and that his ears heard. Remove the stone from my heart, speedily and without delay. Amen. Amen. Selah.

Write (the above) on a fresh egg from a black hen. Roast the egg, and after it has been roasted, peel it. Write this incantation on the egg, and then eat it. Do not drink (anything) afterward. Let him fast that day and go to bed (hungry).[62]

We know from other Jewish sources, such as the early medieval Ḥarba de-Moshe (Sword of Moses) that the egg was used as a symbol of hidden knowledge.[63] R. Eleazar of Worms and the author of the Zohar used the nut for a similar image.[64] Here, then, we have another early case of eating an inscribed egg on Shavuot in order to gain permanent knowledge of the Torah. This magical practice, related to but different from the talmudic tradition that eating a roasted egg enhances one's memory, was incorporated into the child's initiation ceremony in medieval Europe.[65]

POTAḤ, the Prince of Forgetfulness

In addition to the ancient magical food techniques for remembering Torah, the medieval children's ceremony also draws on other forms of ritualized or magical mnemonics, specifically, the incantation against POTAḤ, the prince of forgetfulness. This incantation is derived from the heikhalot texts that describe the use of theurgy in studying Torah on Shavuot,[66] a time that is parallel in its potency to Pentecost in the Christian tradition. We saw in chapter 2 that the incantation against POTAḤ is found in a magical version of the havdalah ceremony recited at the end of the Jewish Sabbath each week.[67] A third occasion when a related text is prescribed is in a formula to be recited after a student has completed a tractate (masekhet) of Talmud. In that case, a memory formula developed beginning with the word hadran (beauty).[68] The hadran formula is printed in the Vilna edition of the Babylonian Talmud, after each tractate, and is still recited liturgically at a siyyum, or ceremony of completing the study of a Talmud tractate.[69]

The children's ceremony, the weekly Sabbath havdalah, and the hadran rite all involve a moment of boundary or transition. They are liminal occasions and were considered dangerous without supernatural protection.[70] Another set of liminal moments that posed a danger was the seasonal transitions of solstices and equinoxes (*tequfot*). In medieval Europe, Jews considered it dangerous to drink water "between seasons" (*bein ha-tequfot*), because demons might have poisoned the water at those moments.[71] As a precaution against the danger of the liminal, the practice of enhancing one's memory of Torah learning by use of a magical formula developed. In each boundary situation, supernatural aid was needed to prevent one from forgetting what one had learned, or to enhance one's memory in the future.

As is the case with most of the elements that became part of the initiation ceremony, the adjuration against the prince of forgetfulness is primarily an adult mystical gesture found as often as not in rabbinic, not folk, contexts. An example is the havdalah text with the incantation against POTAH in the first known Jewish prayer book, *Siddur Rav 'Amram Gaon*, from ninth-century Baghdad.[72] The incantation is also found in a nearly contemporaneous early medieval magical text that Gershom Scholem published, *Havdalah de-Rabbi 'Aqiva* (R. Akiva's havdalah).[73]

The regular havdalah ceremony is earlier than the time of the Mishnah (ca. 200), the first document of rabbinic Judaism, in which the weekly recitation of the havdalah ritual was already associated with wisdom. M. Berakhot 5:2 states: "Havdalah (is recited) as part of (the blessing of the required Prayer read on the Sabbath night) that refers to God who 'graciously grants knowledge.'" By association, then, granting knowledge is linked to the havdalah passage that is inserted in the Saturday night liturgy.

No later than the early medieval period—and possibly much earlier— the havdalah ceremony was expanded from this rational association to a more theurgic function, even in rabbinic circles. In the responsum that the mid-ninth-century gaon R. 'Amram b. Sheshna wrote, part of the same text appears that later found its way into the European medieval initiation. But in 'Amram Gaon's version of the incantation, the names of the supernatural beings are not omitted as they are in *Sefer ha-Asufot*: I adjure you, POTAH, the prince of forgetfulness, that you remove from me a fool's heart and throw it upon a high mountain in the name of the holy names, ARIMAS, ARIMIMAS, ANSISI'EL, and PETAH'EL.[74]

This text contains four of the eight magical names that are present in the magical memory formula from *Sefer Razi'el*. This special elaboration of the havdalah traveled from Babylonia to Spain, the destination of R. 'Amram's responsum, and then to Provence. The incantation against POTAH is also found in early editions of R. Jacob b. Asher's standard code of Jewish law, *Arba'ah Turim* (The Four Pillars),[75] which in turn became the basis of R. Joseph Karo's authoritative law code, *Shulhan 'Arukh* (Prepared Table). This continuity indicates that the magical technique of learning the Torah, attested in early medieval Babylonian geonic sources, came from and remained in the very heart of rabbinic Judaism as part of the weekly havdalah rite. The text was meant for adults, and only later was it incorporated into the medieval European Jewish children's Torah initiation ceremony.

Purity and Memory

The mnemonic technique of eating inscribed eggs, which derived from ancient Jewish magic and was associated with the magical learning of the Torah on Shavuot, was also related to a special concern in the ceremony for ritual purity. In the heikhalot texts, including those that specifically deal with the magical acquisition of Torah by conjuring sar ha-torah, ritual purity is stipulated as a prerequisite for the magical acts to be effective. One who uses the magical Names of God must first become ritually pure.[76] Although there is a Jewish tradition which holds that an act of purity ablution in a ritual bath should take place on the eve of the Day of Atonement[77] — in imitation of the Jerusalem Temple high priest, who must stay awake all night and guard himself against ritual pollution — the adult Torah acquisition ceremony takes place on Shavuot. Here the appropriate archetype is not the Temple but the sexual purity demanded of the Israelites three days before the theophany on Mount Sinai (Exod. 19:10, 14).

In any case, ritual purity is required for the techniques to be effective, and achieving and maintaining purity is an integral part of the children's initiation ceremony. The form that the guarantee of purity takes is specific as well. The child is wrapped in a garment so that he cannot see certain objects — a dog, an ass, a gentile, and a pig — which confer impurity on sight.

The idea that visual contact confers ritual impurity upon an otherwise pure individual recalls a similar attitude that is taken in regard to a menstruant adult woman and her efforts to become ritually pure by immersion in a miqveh or ritual bath.[78] The main source is a text called Baraita de-Niddah,[79] which apparently derives from Palestine in the fifth to eighth centuries. The text prescribes that a woman who purifies herself in a ritual bath and who subsequently sees "a dog, an ass," and so on, must return to the bath and immerse herself again. Otherwise the offspring of sexual relations with her husband will be adversely affected. The purification of the bath is nullified by her seeing a source of pollution.

Another stipulation of the Baraita de-Niddah involves knowledge and forgetfulness: "A sage who partakes of food prepared by a menstruant will forget his learning."[80] From this statement one might suppose that, in general, sources of ritual impurity cause forgetfulness. The converse is supported by the precaution to wrap the child in the initiation ceremony: avoidance of sources of impurity prevents forgetfulness or protects memory.

A second concern about purity, associated with performance of the ritual, might have been to prevent the male adult carrying the child from experiencing any sexual arousal and thereby polluting the child, as was the concern with the ancient high priest on the Day of Atonement. This source of apprehension is in fact affirmed in a comment of Gregory of Tours about one Nicetus of Lyon, who "refused to take a child into his arms unless the child were wrapped in clothes."[81] By definition a child is pure, and the fear of impurity is reinforced in the emphasis on the study of Leviticus because of the association of the pure child with the laws of sacrifices, or purities. This was incorporated into Latin in monastic culture by playing on the words puer (young boy) and puritas (purity).[82] A similar wordplay—pure (child), purities (sacrifices)—underlies the explanation in Midrash Vayyiqra Rabbah for the substitution of Leviticus for Genesis as the child's first biblical text, although that is only part of a moralistic explanation for a custom the origins of which remain obscure.

The tradition of wrapping the child in a talit, as the French-Jewish versions stipulated, may also be a symbolic adaptation of an ancient adult Jewish practice to the children's initiation rite. In ancient times, wrapping oneself in a talit was a gesture that signified the transition from adult to sage or elder. Thus, "A parable about an elder who possessed one prayer shawl and would shake it out regularly and fold it. He said: I am very careful with it, because I put it on when I was appointed an elder."[83]

The gesture of wrapping the child when carrying him through the streets may have been inspired by these two ancient or early medieval motifs: the fear of impurity and the symbolic initiation into wisdom. In combination they serve the new purpose of protecting the child as he begins the process of learning the Torah.[84]

Water and Torah

Apart from the important symbolic meanings attached to water[85] and rivers in Jewish and Christian cultures, which will be discussed in chapter 5, the Talmud records a custom of studying Torah near a river. This seems to be a pedagogic technique designed to enhance one's mastery, or power of retention, as is hinted in the following: "R. Mesharshya said to his son: . . . when you study any tradition, do so near a (river), for as the (river) is drawn out, so your learning may be prolonged."[86]

Rashi interprets the phrase "your learning may be prolonged" to mean: "so that it not cease (coming out of) your mouth, as this spring that (continuously) flows on." It is still not clear, however, whether studying by a river is meant to be a helpful didactic hint to the student to imitate the river by studying continuously or if it is an act of sympathetic and contagious magic.

Study and river are associated with small children in another rabbinic text. A commentary on the verse "like gardens beside a river" (Num. 24:6) states: "Gardens are teachers of little Jewish children who bring forth from their hearts wisdom, understanding, and discernment, and teach them to do the will of their Father who is in Heaven."[87] The association of study and river is incorporated into the initiation ceremony as described in Sefer ha-Asufot and as illustrated in the Leipzig Maḥzor, where the teacher takes the child to the riverside. A general piece of advice for all students has been transformed into a part of the special, onetime experience of small children when they first begin to learn their letters.

Singing and Swaying

Two other mnemonic gestures that the initiation rite requires of the child are singing or chanting when studying and movement of the body, or swaying. These, too, are based on ancient rabbinic traditions that the *Mahzor Vitry* and the Hamburg MS included in the ceremony.

Singing derives ultimately from the biblical association of the Torah with the Temple Priests and Levites. The prescription to begin studies with Leviticus instead of Genesis is probably one such trace of the biblical idea that "the lips of a priest guard knowledge (of the Torah)" (Mal. 2:7). In addition, there are ancient traditions connecting the Levites, who sang Psalms in the Temple, with the concept of a student who studies the Torah. Thus, the first mention of the later rabbinic Hebrew word *talmid* (student) is preserved in 1 Chronicles 25:8 in the context of the Levites: "They cast lots for shifts on the principle of 'small and great alike, like master like apprentice (*talmid*).'"[88]

In light of the biblical legacy connecting the Temple to the Levites' singing and the Torah, it is not surprising to find post-Temple rabbinic traditions about singing the Torah as one studies.[89] In one, the Torah speaks to R. Akiva, asking him to "sing me again and again."[90] Elsewhere, the verse "Moreover, I gave them laws that were not good and rules by which they could not live" (Ezek. 20:25) is applied to a person "who reads Bible without melody or who studies the Mishnah without song."[91] The practice of chanting or singing what one studies, as opposed to the common modern habit of reading silently, to oneself, is well known from ancient Greco-Roman and medieval European schools. It persisted in the Jewish academic world as well. Thus, a Tosafist, commenting on the last passage, observes: "The scholars used to recite the Mishnah with a melody because they studied it by heart and because of this they remembered the text more easily." Or again, the word "song" in the phrase "and in the night his song is with me" (Ps. 42:9) was interpreted to mean study of the Torah at night.[92]

Reciting the text out loud with a melody involved motions of the mouth, and some traditions stress the mnemonic value of this physical aspect of studying the Torah with song. One talmudic tradition depicts R. Meir's learned wife Bruriah scolding a student for studying silently: "She said to him, 'Is it not written (in the Bible), "(an eternal pact)[93] arranged and prepared every one and preserved" (*'arukhah ba-kol u-shemurah*) (2 Sam. 23:5)? This means if (your learning) is arranged in every one of the two hundred and forty-eight parts (of your body), (what you study) will be preserved; and if it is not, it will not be preserved.'" Forgetting what one had studied is attributed to studying silently (*shoneh be-lahash*); moving the entire body will enhance one's memory.[94]

This passage brings us from singing to swaying, another important mnemonic gesture in the initiation rite. Called *shukkeling* in Yiddish, pious swaying is mentioned in early Arabic sources that warn Muslims not to imitate the Jews, who sway when they read the Torah in public. As Walter Ong has observed, it illustrates that oral memory has "a high somatic component": "The Talmud, though a text, is still vocalized by highly oral Orthodox Jews in Israel with a forward-and-backward rocking of the torso, as I myself have witnessed."[95] One can still see traditional yeshivah students—or Muslims chanting the Qur'an— follow the gesture of rhythmic swaying when seated at study or when standing at prayer.

The earliest Jewish source in Europe that refers to swaying during Torah reading or study comes from the Muslim-Spanish tradition of the *Kuzari* (II:79– 80) by R. Judah Halevi (ca. 1075–1141).[96] The first Ashkenazic reference occurs in the mnemonic technique that the *Mahzor Vitry* prescribes for the young boy during the school initiation rite.[97]

The various elements of the initiation rite that I have discussed combine several traditions from ancient Palestinian sources and practices, many of which went underground, so to speak, and reemerged in the combination before us as an elaborate rite of passage for a child first entering school. Within this overall historical development, three basic patterns emerge from our investigation of the various elements that comprise the medieval Ashkenazic initiation ritual. These are: (1) pedagogic and mnemonic themes and practices; (2) rabbinic literary commentary and magical gestures; and especially (3) children's schooling practices and adult Shavuot Torah rituals. In the following two chapters I will first consider different readings of the ceremony taken as a complete symbolic system, and then look at the historical processes that the emergence and disappearance of the ritual suggest about Jewish and Christian attitudes toward childhood and toward the symbols of the other culture.

Chapter Five

Symbolic Readings

I turn now to a "thick description" of the initiation ceremony, which is an elaborate ritualization of key metaphors that can be read in different ways. To tease out these meanings, I will consider not only the various written accounts and visual representations of the ceremony's gestures, but also the internal exegesis found in the texts and manuscript illuminations.[1] The child's Torah initiation ritual is a complex rite of passage, which is at the same time a communal affirmation of Judaism celebrated on Shavuot. After considering readings of the ceremony as a whole, I will examine ways in which this affirmation is expressed as a social polemic against Christianity, and will show that the specific magical techniques chosen to constitute the ritual — especially the inscribed honey cakes — suggest correspondences with a contemporary Christian symbolic vocabulary and polemical argumentation.

Some of the metaphors that Jews applied to the Torah or Torah child Christians applied to Christian figures. Thus, the image of the Torah as wheat, bread, or manna is akin to Christ's being compared to these foods. Moses is pictured as a Madonna figure; and for Jews the schoolchild, like the Christ Child for Christians, can be seen as a pure sacrifice who brings vicarious atonement for the community. Pre-Christian Jewish traditions persisted in both medieval Judaism and in Christianity. New reworkings of some of these symbols in medieval European Christian culture — especially the Child Jesus and the eucharist — precipitated a Jewish polemical response that drew on the repertoire of ancient Jewish symbols and reconfigured them.

Rites of Passage

The ceremony is not merely a chapter in the history of Jewish elementary education or mnemonics. As the texts make explicit, entering school is considered a Jewish boy's next stage of life after circumcision and prior to the later stages of social maturation at age thirteen, at marriage, and in full adulthood. It is an example of van Gennep's *rites de passage*, those rituals of transition by means of which cultures mark the various social stages of life. Such rites may, but need not, correspond to biological changes such as sexual maturation (puberty, menses). Cultures invest certain moments in a person's social and cultural maturation with special meanings. They mark the individual's adjustment to a new stage of life and also express the community's collective self-affirmation.[2]

Van Gennep posited three characteristic structural elements in rites of passage: separation from a previous situation, a transition or liminal passage between stages, and incorporation into a new phase of life.[3] The child's initiation in Ashkenaz illustrates van Gennep's general schema of a three-part ceremony. The child leaves home (separation), goes through the streets of the town, and when seated on the teacher's lap undergoes the complex ceremony of initiation (transition), after which the teacher leads the boy to the river (incorporation). At the same time, the initiation rite takes place in three types of social space: the home, a private Jewish space; the streets and the school or synagogue, public Christian and Jewish spaces; and the riverbank, a different public Christian space.

Separation

At first, the child is taken from his mother at home. She is present only in the background, but he leaves his house and natural mother to become part of the male study circle of his Torah teacher and fellow students. As he grows, he will continue to leave home daily to go to school with other boys. Even if well-off parents might hire tutors to teach a boy in his own house, the act of becoming a Torah student among other males under the tutelage of a male teacher is basically the same regardless of the actual location of the lessons. Later, when he marries, the young man will leave his house permanently to make a home of his own or move in with his wife's family. But for now, the child's leaving home for school is a symbolic act of initial separation—he stops being a "momma's boy" in order to become a novice Torah student.[4]

Transition

A boy's transition from being seen as a baby and toddler at home with mother, father, and younger siblings to having the status of a Torah student in the company of males his age and older is carefully orchestrated. His father or a local learned man carries the boy from his house. In religious terms, the father brings the son to the teacher, who is the father's agent in fulfilling his religious obligation to teach his own sons Torah. This is parallel to circumcision, the boy's first initiation. A Jewish father is obligated to circumcise his own sons but may appoint a mohel as his agent. Similarly, in the initiation ritual, the father brings his son to a teacher as his religious surrogate.[5]

But first the boy must go through the streets of the town, a public Christian space, which is presented in the texts as polluting and hence requiring the father to take preventive measures to protect the pure Jewish child from being contaminated. The texts stress that the child is carried, even though at age five or six he could clearly walk the short distance in the Jewish quarter from a private house to the synagogue or to the teacher's house. He is to be wrapped in a garment, either a coat or a talit. In some of the German-Jewish versions, this gesture is explained as a means of protecting the child from seeing any sources of impurity, such as "a Christian or a dog"[6] or "a dog, pig, ass, or a Christian." The French-Jewish version in the Maḥzor Vitry declares that the purpose of wrapping the boy in a talit is "to teach him modesty and humility," but MS Hamburg adds, as a second reason, "so the evil eye does not harm him."[7]

The journey from the private Jewish space of the home to the public Jewish space of the school or synagogue is a liminal or boundary zone, an in-between time in which harm may befall the child as well as the community. In Victor Turner's phrase, the person is "betwixt and between," no longer part of his prior status of being at home nor yet part of the social structure of life as a schoolboy. As a result of his indeterminate status he is in a state of danger,[8] and the danger is expressed as a state of potential pollution from Christians, purity and pollution being the typical Ashkenazic rhetorical categories for defining Jewish-Christian contact.[9]

In his discussion of initiations, Mircea Eliade sheds additional light on the symbolism of the rite: the acts of separation and incorporation can express symbolic death and rebirth.[10] In the ritual, the child's being wrapped in a coat or talit not only serves the function of protecting him from liminal danger but also symbolizes the tomb of his "dead" first stage of childhood[11] and the womb of his "rebirth" as a schoolboy.[12] Being wrapped is also a sign of his return to symbolic infancy, as may be seen in numerous manuscript illuminations depicting medieval infants wrapped as if in cocoons, a practice found in other cultural initiations as well.[13]

In addition to being portrayed as ritually pure, the child is likened to a Torah scroll. This is connoted not only by the requirement that the child be wrapped in a talit but also by the stipulation that he be escorted from home to school by a Torah scholar or another respected adult who is knowledgeable in Torah. The combination of sacred wrapping and escort is associated with carrying a Torah scroll from one place to another, often from synagogue to home and back, as at the beginning and end of the week of mourning (shiv'a), when daily religious services might take place at home. Abraham Joshua Heschel intuitively pointed this out,[14] and Harvey Goldberg has explored it in more detail.[15] The similarity between the child's being wrapped and carried from home to synagogue in the initiation ceremony and customs about carrying a Torah scroll from ark to ark is but one of several similarities in Jewish culture between the treatment of small children and of Torah scrolls.[16]

In Ashkenaz a tradition developed further linking circumcision, a small boy's first rite of passage, and the Torah. Attested only beginning in the fourteenth century but reflecting the earlier association of Torah and children, the wimpel, or cloth in which the baby was held during circumcision, was set aside and later embroidered with the baby's name and possibly this statement from the circumcision ceremony: "as he has entered the covenant (brit) so may he enter the Torah, the marriage chamber, and (a life of) good deeds."[17] This wimpel would later be used as a Torah binder during the child's public bar mitzvah ceremony, a rite of passage that developed only in late medieval Ashkenaz.[18]

Although the transition, or liminal stage, begins in the public Christian space of the streets, it continues after the child reaches the teacher in public Jewish space. Initiation ceremonies often have very elaborate transitions, and this one is no exception. After the child is seated on the teacher's lap, the teacher shows him the writing tablet, honey cake, and egg on which the

Hebrew alphabet or biblical verses have been written. The two of them recite the texts, and the child licks honey off the tablet and eats the inscribed cakes and eggs.

These gestures are a bold illustration of symbolic inversion. The child enters the Torah (*nikhnas la-torah*) by means of the Torah's entering the child in the form of special foods on which verses from the Torah have been written.[19] Ingesting Torah foods is the central act of the rite, and it is emphasized by its three-fold repetition: licking the alphabet tablet, eating the inscribed cake, and eating the inscribed egg. The pattern of three is further reinforced in the texts that stipulate that three eggs and three cakes are required.[20]

Incorporation

Following the gestures of carrying, reading, feeding, and invoking the incantation to protect the child's memory, the teacher leads the boy to the riverside. This is the third and final stage of the rite — incorporation. As he goes to the river, the child no longer is held in an adult's arms, as he was when he arrived at school. Nor is he sitting on an adult's lap, as he is during the transitional initiation. Instead, he now walks on his own, signifying that he has been initiated and is now a schoolboy who can stand on his own two feet, even in Christian public space.

Like the incantation to POTAH, going down to the riverside is a mnemonic gesture designed to guarantee that the boy remembers and persists in his future Torah study. It also denotes Torah ("water means Torah")[21] and may connote ritual immersion, a rabbinic motif associated with the purification rites preceding God's revelation at Sinai,[22] the concluding rite in adult Jewish conversion, as well as a requirement of Jewish magical purity rituals. By requiring that the child go near but not into the river, the gesture may also allude to Christian baptism, which was carried out in rivers.[23]

Social Drama and Communitas

Between the child's departure from home and the closing scene by the river is the central scene of transition in the schoolroom, where the child ingests the symbolic sweetened foods as Torah, a ritualization of Ezekiel's metaphoric vision of eating the sweet scroll of God's words. Victor Turner noted that the first and third stages of rites of passage presuppose structured living, whereas the liminal transition lacks structure. This in-between character of the liminal is dangerous, but it also offers an opportunity for closeness otherwise less likely to occur in more structured living. Turner overemphasized the spontaneous and unstructured character of transitions,[24] for the bonding of the initiate with the rest of the community is a significant aspect of the ceremony. The child who undergoes the ceremony enables other members of the adult community to visualize, act out, and rehearse the deepest values and worldview held by all the members of the community.

The school initiation takes place on Shavuot,[25] when the local Jewish community celebrates the festival that marks Israel's receiving the Torah for the first time. In this way the rite of passage involves not only the child and his immediate family but also the community. Symbolically, the three parts of the rite recapitulate the Jewish spring festival trilogy of Passover, the semi-mourning period of the Counting of the Omer (sefirah),[26] and Shavuot. In the Hebrew Bible the Passover celebration represents the primal exodus of Israelite slaves from bondage in Egypt (separation). It is followed by the dangerous trek through the desert and the arrival at Mount Sinai, where the epiphany takes place (transition). Ultimately, the Children of Israel as a new covenantal people reach the river Jordan, the border of the Promised Land (incorporation).

Like the transition stage in the rite, the celebration of sefirah and Shavuot is complex and symbolically powerful. Shavuot marked the termination of sefirah, a protracted period of semi-mourning during which Ashkenazic Jews did not marry. This denial recalled the memory of the sages martyred during the Hadrianic persecution in second-century Roman Palestine. But in medieval Germany, sefirah also marked the deaths of Rhenish Torah scholars and communities in anti-Jewish riots in the late spring of 1096, following the call for the First Crusade.[27] Poems and historical narratives read or recited during sefirah commemorated these acts of terror and sacrifice and reaffirmed the truth of the Torah and Judaism.[28] This period ends at Shavuot, an elaborate drama between God and Moses played before the assembled community of Israel.

In addition to expressing symbolically the lived holiday cycle of Passover-sefirah-Shavuot, the rite also consciously represents events in the biblical narrative that portray the original formation of the covenanted community of

Israel.[29] During the ritual, then, the child not only bonds with other Jews in the local community but also participates symbolically in the collective memory of the Jewish people as preserved in the Hebrew Bible. The child's personal journey to school is a symbolic reenactment of the biblical narrative of ancient Israel's exodus (Passover), the desert trek (sefirah), and the approach to Mount Sinai to receive the Torah (Shavuot) and alludes to the river Jordan and beyond.

Parts of this symbolic reenactment are explicit and parts are implicit in the ritual. Thus, the child's separation when leaving home recapitulates biblical Israel's exodus from Egypt, which had been their home for four hundred years. The sojourn in Egypt is recalled in the Bible both as a time of good living in the land of Goshen and as harsh slavery.[30] It is the former meaning that resonates in the analogy: the child leaves home, which is likened to Egypt when it had been Israel's home, the Egypt which they later remembered as a place where they had been well off.[31]

Carried through the streets of the potentially harmful Christian town, the child symbolically acts out Israel's dangerous journey through the wilderness to Sinai. The journey provoked so many complaints that God gave the Israelites special gifts, among them the manna or sweetened cakes, as a sign of his divine caring, just as the child receives the sweetened foods. When the child is carried and wrapped in a coat or talit to protect his ritual purity before he gets to school, he is like the adult Israelites whom Moses told to remain sexually pure three days prior to receiving the Torah at Sinai. The child seated on the teacher's lap is like biblical Israel receiving the Torah from Moses on the mountain. Finally, the approach to the river has overtones of the end of Moses' career and anticipates the Israelites' reaching the Jordan. The Pentateuch ends at the riverbank, not across the river in the Land of Israel.[32]

In this way, the child's personal rite of passage as he enters the Torah is a symbolic representation of Israel's formative national experience recorded in the collective memory of leaving, journeying, and receiving. As a result of this correspondence between the ritual and the biblical narrative, the child who experiences the ritual becomes a symbol of the biblical people of Israel. In some ways, he is a Jewish equivalent of the Christian iconographical representation of the Jew in the images of the synagoga. But instead of being represented by a woman who portrays the Jew from a Christian perspective as powerless and blind, the child embodies biblical Israel and contemporary medieval Jewry from a Jewish point of view.[33]

A graphic confirmation of this interpretation is provided in a manuscript illumination that depicts the ritual in the *Leipzig Mahzor*. Two facing pages in the Shavuot liturgy feature the liturgical poem that begins *adon imnani*, and each is illustrated by an illumination at the bottom of the page (figure 5). On the right, where the poem begins, is one of several preserved scenes depicting the giving of the Torah to Israel at Mount Sinai. Opposite it, on the left side, is the unique three-part representation of the children's Torah initiation ceremony. This pairing dramatically interprets the child's personal initiation as a recapitulation of the collective memory of the people's original initiation at Sinai.

The *Leipzig Mahzor* illumination represents the school initiation ceremony selectively in three scenes. The central scene shows the father or scholar carrying the child wrapped in a garment.[34] The home is not represented, but the adult's carrying the child indicates that the separation stage has already occurred. The child looks away from the adult carrying him, but his hand gently caresses the adult's cheek, and he gazes toward the teacher at the left. The boy is next pictured sitting on the teacher's lap in the left scene of the illumination. The child holds an egg and a round, yellow cake. Two other children stand facing the pair, also holding an egg and cake. The teacher holds a gilded tablet. The third scene, to the right, portrays two children led by the teacher toward the river, in which fish are visible.

Divided into three scenes, the ceremony is read from the center to left and finally to right. This sequence is strange: Hebrew illuminations usually read from right to left, like the Hebrew language. As portrayed, the ceremony is divided visually as two representations of the teacher and child surrounding the parent, or other adult, who is carrying the child in the center. On the left, we see the stage set for the child symbolically to ingest the Torah; on the right, the riverside that may magically help perpetuate his Torah learning and prevent forgetting. The child and natural parent in the center, then, are surrounded by the Torah teacher with foods as Torah, on the left, and water as Torah, on the right.

Although when taken by itself the narrative of the three parts of the school illumination is out of sequence, it makes visual sense, especially when viewed in comparison with the facing illumination, which depicts Mount Sinai.[35] For

5. The school initiation scene (left) and the giving of the Torah (right). *Leipzig Maḥzor*, Leipzig, Universitätsbibliothek, Hebrew Manuscript Vollers 1102, vol. 1, f. 131a and 130b. Reprinted with permission. Photo: Suzanne Kaufman.

there are clear correspondences between the two. Most dramatic is the visual symmetry between Moses on the mountain, in the Sinai illumination, and the teacher on the raised chair or *cathedra*, in the school scenes. Structurally, the two illuminations constitute a program that must be seen and read as a complementary metaphoric interpretation: the child's Torah initiation is like Israel at Sinai.

In addition to the equation of the school with Sinai and the Torah teacher with Moses, other correlations follow from the *Leipzig Maḥzor* pair of illuminations. The child or children in the school can be compared to biblical Israel, the "Children of Israel" (*benei yisrael*). There is also a striking correspondence between the tablets of the Torah that Moses holds in the Sinai illumination, on the righthand page, and the writing tablet that is in the teacher's hands in the school illumination, on the left. Apart from the semantic identity of the two images — both are called luḥot — they are visually linked by being the only gilded surfaces in each illumination. This cannot be seen in the facsimile, but upon direct inspection of the manuscript the gilding is obvious. Moreover, the clothing, facial features, and hats of the Moses figure and the Torah teacher are similar. The beardless figure in the center may signify a young father of a five-year-old child, and his bare chin sets him apart from the bearded figure of the teacher in the lefthand and righthand parts of the school illumination.

Bread, Manna, Torah, Christ

Within the dynamic process of the transition stage, the foods the teacher gives the child to eat are powerful symbols charged with historical and religious meanings. Above all, they have strong ancient metaphoric associations with the Torah. Although the ceremony features many foods, including cake, honey, milk, oil, and eggs, metaphors about bread and its components play a central role. Bread symbolism was important in early Judaism and Christianity, and it continued to be part of a polemic between the two religions in medieval Europe. This cultural interaction is reflected in the initiation ceremony.

Bread as a metaphor for the Torah or the word of God is a biblical image that became part of Judaism even earlier than rabbinic sources (second century). We know this because the bread metaphor is employed in early Christian sources as a polemical response to Jews and Judaism. Thus, in the Gospel of John, Jesus says, "I am the bread of life. Your fathers ate the manna in the wilderness, and they died. . . . I am the living bread which came down from heaven, if any one eats of this bread, he will live for ever; and the bread which I shall give for the life of the world is my flesh" (John 6:48–49, 51). In addition, at the center of the Christian liturgy is the statement attributed to Jesus at the Last Supper: "Take, eat; this is my body" (Matt. 26:26). This equation of bread and Jesus in the New Testament led to the development of the ritual of the eucharist, the central rite of Christianity.[36]

The persistence of these elements and associations in the Jewish school initiation ritual suggests that the Jewish rite is articulated in the symbolic language of the eucharist partly as a social polemic against it. Thus, the polemic came full circle: early Christian writers affirmed that Jesus, not the Torah, was the bread; the medieval European Jewish proponents of the schooling rite reaffirmed the priority of the Torah, not Jesus, by ritualizing it as a form of the Christian eucharistic loaf.

In Judaism, no symbol is more central than the Torah, and things equated metaphorically with the Torah take on primary cultural significance. The earliest basis for equating wheat with the Torah is the biblical and rabbinic interpretation of the Shavuot festival. Biblical tradition understood Shavuot, the Feast of Weeks, as the time of the wheat harvest: "You shall observe the Feast of Weeks, of the first fruits of the wheat harvest" (Exod. 34:22). It is marked by a wheat sacrifice: "You must count until the day after the seventh week—fifty days; then you shall bring an offering of new grain (lehem bikkurim) to the Lord. You shall bring from your settlements two loaves of bread as an elevation offering . . . as first fruits to the Lord" (Lev. 23:16–17).[37] Since rabbinic tradition understood Shavuot to be the time when the Torah was revealed to Israel at Mount Sinai, wheat and Torah became linked with the festival of Shavuot and with each other in antiquity, and this link generated still other associations.

A rivalry between Judaism and early Christianity over what or who is the true bread can be educed from comments in early Judaism such as the following:

(1) Scripture says, "That man does not live on bread alone"—referring to Midrash—"but by everything that proceeds out of the mouth of the Lord" (Deut. 8:3), referring to halakhah and aggadah.[38]

(2) Thus the Holy One, blessed be He, said to Israel, My children, I created an inclination to evil in you than which there is none more evil. . . . Busy yourselves with words of Torah, and the inclination to evil will not rule over you; . . . as it is said, "If your enemy is hungry, give him bread to eat; if he is thirsty, give him water to drink. You will be heaping live coals on his head, and the Lord will reward you" (Prov. 25:21–22).[39]

(3) "With no bread or clothing in my house" (Isa. 3:7) (means): I possess no Bible, Mishnah, or Talmud.[40]

(4) "For lo! The Sovereign Lord of Hosts will remove from Jerusa-

lem and from Judah prop and stay; every prop of bread and every prop
of water" (Isa. 3:1): "prop" means masters of Bible; "stay" means masters
of Mishnah like R. Judah b. Tema and his colleagues . . . ; "every prop of
bread" means masters of Talmud, for it is said (Wisdom = Torah says),
"Come, eat my bread and drink the wine that I have mixed" (Prov. 9:5);
"and every prop of water" means the masters of aggadah who draw the
heart of man like water by means of the aggadah.[41]

In the dispute between two Babylonian scholars as to who should become the head of the talmudic academy of Pumpeditha, the candidates were
Rabba, a master of dialectic, and R. Joseph, learned in accurately memorized
Torah traditions. The Talmud concludes that R. Joseph is to be preferred because "everyone needs the master of the wheat,"[42] that is, someone proficient
in mastery of the oral traditions of Torah.

In the introduction to *Song of Songs Rabbah*, which Rashi quotes in the
eleventh century, Scripture is compared to different grades of flour: "R. Eleazar
ben Azariah said: This is like a king who took a *se'ah* (measure) of wheat and
gave it to a baker. He said to him: Take out so much fine flour, so much
medium-grade flour and so much coarse flour. Make from the finest flour a
perfect, refined loaf. Similarly, all of Scripture is holy and the Song of Songs
is the Holy of Holies." Compare: "The full soul loathes the honeycomb" (*nofet*;
Prov. 27:7)—just as a sieve (*nafah*) sets apart flour, bran, and coarse meal, so
does a student sit and sift words of Torah and weigh them."[43]

The Torah is compared not only to bread, but also to manna, the sweet
food that was a divine gift to biblical Israel and which Christian tradition
identified with Jesus. For example: "R. Shimon bar Yoḥai says: 'The Torah was
given to be studied only by those who eat manna.'"[44] And the early church
writers picked up on this theme in the New Testament, as we have already seen
in John 6. The association of the word of God with manna is a theme that
permeated discussions of the eucharist throughout the Middle Ages.[45]

In the schooling ritual, the honey cakes combine both flour and honey,
and represent the manna or Torah for the child. By eating an inscribed cake,
the child eats manna and ritualizes Ezekiel's metaphoric vision of eating God's
sweet words of Torah. This symbolic refiguring is selective: the divine desert
gifts of the water well and the quail are ignored;[46] only the manna is represented because it is a sweet cake.

The association of the Torah with manna persisted into medieval Judaism and is illustrated in the *Bird's Head Haggadah*, an early fourteenth-century German manuscript of the Passover Seder ritual. On the page that contains the prayer of praise "Dayyeinu" ("It would have been enough"), in which reference is made to several divine gifts to Israel, among them the Land of Israel and the Torah, there is a pair of illuminations (figure 6). The prayer is constructed around a formula: "Had God only given us the (Sabbath, manna, land, Torah, etc.), it would have been enough." At the bottom of the righthand page there is an illumination that depicts Israel receiving the manna and the quail in the desert. On the left side is a representation of Israel receiving the Torah. Although the quail, not mentioned in the prayer, is depicted along with the manna, it is striking that the only gifts that are both mentioned in the text of the Haggadah and illuminated on the page are the manna and the Torah, thus indicating a visual tradition connecting them.

In the scene on the right, the upper part of the illumination represents the manna as two large, round, yellow or gilded disks that bear a striking similarity to the way in which the inscribed cakes are depicted in the *Leipzig Mahzor*. A comparison between the manna–Mount Sinai pair in the *Bird's Head Haggadah* and the child's initiation–Mount Sinai pair in the *Leipzig Mahzor* suggests that a symbolic vocabulary is being used in both which merges the manna-as-Torah with the child's cakes-as-manna-as-Torah. However, unlike the biblical manna, which is described as being white cakes (Exod. 16:31), the color of the manna in the *Bird's Head Haggadah* is yellow, just like the cakes in the initiation illumination in the *Leipzig Mahzor*. Yellow round circles as representations of bread or cake are also found in the *Worms Mahzor*,[47] where the two first loaves offered on Shavuot are represented as two loaves of bread coming out of the oven. The color yellow, then, need not mean honey but simply bread, yet it is common to the representations of manna and the child's honey cakes.

The *Bird's Head Haggadah* illuminations make clear an additional association that bears on the *Leipzig Mahzor* illuminations. Each of the two illuminations in the *Bird's Head Haggadah* has two levels. The lower one on the left pictures an Israelite roasting a lamb on a spit; the lower scene on the right shows Israelites gathering small disks of manna and a quail falling from the sky. Although the lamb seems to be at the foot of Mount Sinai, it apparently connotes the eating of the Paschal lamb on the Passover holiday, and the gathering of the manna and quail portrays the Israelites preparing to eat those divine gifts.

6. The giving of the Torah (left) and of manna in the desert (right). *Bird's Head Haggadah*, Germany, fourteenth century, Jerusalem, Jewish Museum, MS 180/57, f. 23a-22b. Collection Israel Museum, Jerusalem. Photo: Israel Museum. Reprinted with permission.

Whereas the lower scenes portray Israel receiving and preparing to eat different foods, the upper scenes depict God giving the Torah, on the left, and giving two loaves of manna, on the right. These gifts are shown to be related in that each is pictured as being offered by a divine hand with the two pointed fingers of the "Latin blessing," a special gesture of divine beneficence also associated with the priest's offering of the eucharistic wafer.[48] By portraying the Torah and the manna in this way, the *Bird's Head Haggadah* reflects earlier rabbinic verbal traditions that equate the Torah with the manna. These visual associations further reinforce the interpretation of the illumination in the *Leipzig Maḥzor*: when the child eats the specially inscribed honey cakes, he is also eating the Torah-as-manna.

Several associations, then, run into and reinforce one another: Torah, manna, child's cake. A Jewish tradition held that manna was associated not only with the giving of the Torah but also with the child's receiving the Torah for the first time on Shavuot by eating honey cakes (and eggs). Symbolically, when he tastes the wheat and honey in the cake on which the Torah words are written, the child is taken back to the time when the Jewish people first received the Torah at Mount Sinai and is reborn as a Torah child.

Feeding the child the baby foods milk and honey, which are baked into the Torah cakes, is yet another symbol of rebirth. In antiquity and in medieval Europe, milk and honey were the first foods that a baby ate,[49] and as a pair they have additional symbolic meanings. Like honey, milk is an ancient Near Eastern symbol of divine beneficence. In Greek and Roman religion, the combination called *melikraton* had the power to revive the dead.[50] In biblical idiom, the Holy Land and the Torah—God's gifts to Israel—are associated with milk and honey, two foods that embody divine caring for Israel.[51] Human or animal milk is a natural food that is produced during and after pregnancy and is divinely sent to promote young life. Honey, understood in the ancient world as date honey or bee honey,[52] is, like milk, a staple Middle Eastern food. Because both can be produced without human cultivation, in ancient Judaism they came to signify God's caring enough about the people of Israel to give gifts with which He nurtures them.

Moses as Madonna

The association of the Torah with the baby foods milk and honey leads us to another key symbol in the ritual, clearly depicted in the *Leipzig Mahzor*, which also resonates with a contemporary Christian symbolic vocabulary. From classical rabbinic comments about these foods as symbols of Torah, a maternal vocabulary emerges that presents Moses, the rabbis, and Torah teachers as nursing mothers who feed their students with Torah. " 'More than the calf wants to suck, the cow wants to suckle' refers to teachers of Torah and their students," according to the Talmud.[53] This motif of the nursing Moses is expressed as a Jewish analogue to a certain type of the Madonna and Child.[54] Although the small child is in fact moving from his natural mother, and female space at home, to the male space of his Torah teacher and fellow students, Jewish and Christian symbolic images give new cultural specificity to this functional shift in the life of the small boy.

In rabbinic exegesis, the Torah is associated with milk and honey, as in Song of Songs 4:11: "Sweetness drops from your lips, O bride; honey and milk are under your tongue."[55] According to the allegorical interpretation of that book in the midrash, the male lover, or bridegroom, is understood as God, and the female lover, or bride, as Israel. Furthermore, the rabbis took praise of parts of the maiden's body to refer to attributes of Israel, such as the Torah, which was given to Israel, or the great masters of Torah, even Moses himself, who taught Israel. Thus, "sweetness drops from your lips, O bride; honey and milk are under your tongue" means "words of Torah must be acceptable (= sweet) to the audience; or the laws or the commandments of the Torah."[56] Another comment from that midrash on the phrase "sweetness (nofet) drops from your lips" reads:

> R. Yose b. Hanina and the rabbis (differed about the meaning of the word nofet): R. Eliezer said: If one preaches on the Torah and his words are not so palatable to his listeners, as the fine flour which sticks to a sieve (nafah), it is better not to have spoken. R. Yose said: If one preaches on the Torah and his words are not as palatable . . . as honey from the comb (nofet). The rabbis said: if one preaches on the Torah . . . as honey with milk. . . .

A midrash explains that the verse "I have come to my garden, my own my bride; . . . eaten my honey and honeycomb" (Song of Songs 5:1) refers to Israel studying Torah.[57]

Nurturing images are also derived from the opening verses of the Song of Songs. The second verse begins, "Oh, give me of the kisses of your mouth, for your love (dodekha) is more delightful than wine." The Septuagint, the Vulgate, and subsequent Christian tradition in the West read the unvocalized Hebrew consonants d-d-kh as dadekha ("your breasts"). What are the Bridegroom's/God's breasts? They are Christ. In Christian exegesis, especially in the twelfth century, nursing and nurturing images were applied to abbots and other clerics who taught other males.[58]

In classical Judaism, the "love" that the word dodekha conveys refers to the Torah, especially the rabbis' Oral Torah ("kisses of your mouth"). Thus, "R. Yuda b. Pazi said: 'The words of the sages (= Oral Torah) are sweeter to me than the Written Torah (= wine). . . . That is (the meaning of) what is written: "for your love (dodekha) is better than wine." ' "[59] Or, the association is sometimes stated elliptically: "When R. Dimi came (from Palestine to Babylonia) he said: 'Israel is saying to God, "Master of the World, the words of your love are sweeter to me than the wine of the (written) Torah." ' " [60]

Classical and medieval Jewish exegetes glossed images of the bride's (not the bridegroom's) breasts [61] to support the associations of Torah teachers with nursing, and of Torah with milk. [62] For example, on the phrase "Your breasts are like two fawns" (4:5), the midrash *Song of Songs Rabbah* comments: "These (breasts refer to) Moses and Aaron. . . . Just as whatever a (nursing) mother eats, the child eats when he sucks from these breasts, so too, all the Torah that Moses learned he taught Aaron." Rashi adds: " 'Your breasts' *that nurse you* refers to Moses and Aaron." The phrase is repeated in Song of Songs 7:4, and there Rashi glosses the phrase as meaning "the two tablets (of the Torah)." [63]

On Song of Songs 7:8, "your breasts are like clusters (of grapes)," Rashi echoes midrash *Song of Songs Rabbah*'s use of the metaphor but adds specific individuals: "These are Daniel, Hanania, Mishael and Azaria, who were for you like breasts to suck; they were compared to clusters which give forth drink. In the same way they give forth to suck and teach everyone that there is no fear like their fear (of God)." *Song of Songs Rabbah* and Rashi equate "breasts" with sages in several verse phrases, such as "Let your breasts be like clusters of grapes" (7:9). On the verse "We have a sister, whose breasts are not yet formed" (8:8) R. Yohanan said: "This (verse) refers to Elam, which merited being a place of the study (of Torah) but (unlike Babylonia) not being a place for the teaching of Torah." On the verse "I am a wall, my breasts are like towers" (8:10) we read: "R. Yohanan said: 'I am a wall' means Torah; 'my breasts are like towers' are Torah scholars; but Rava said, 'I am a wall' means the people of Israel; 'my breasts are like towers' are synagogues and houses of Torah study." [64] Rashi adopts the latter interpretation, to which he adds, "which nurse (Israel) like those breasts." [65] The images of the nursing sages mentioned throughout these comments on the Song of Songs implicitly build on Moses' powerful rhetorical statement in Numbers 11:12, one of the biblical verses inscribed on the food used in the ceremony: "Did I conceive all this people, did I bear them that You should say to me, 'Carry them in your bosom as a nurse carries an infant'?" Beyond Moses, the association between breasts, milk, honey, and Torah extended to all teachers of Torah.

The motif of the teacher as nursing mother is also expressed in the ritual in the way the child sits on the teacher's "lap" (ḥeq), an ambiguous term which also means "bosom." In the Book of Ruth, which Jews read in the synagogue on Shavuot, we find a striking usage of this term that resonates with the ceremony: "Naomi took the child and held it to her bosom (ve-ḥeiqah). She became its nurse (omenet)" (Ruth 4:16). Naomi was no more the natural mother of Ruth's child than Moses was the mother of the Children of Israel. Yet both carry a child to their bosom (ḥeq) and are compared to nurses. Although the precise meaning of the term omenet in the Book of Ruth is "foster mother," the classical and medieval Jewish interpreters understood the term to mean "nurse," even though only a natural mother or a wetnurse could actually nurse a child, and Naomi and Moses were neither. Like Naomi, Moses is metaphorically compared to a nursing mother in Numbers 11:12, but he is not portrayed as giving suck from the breast.

In medieval Christian art and writings about the meaning of nursing, a type of Madonna developed who is portrayed as breast-feeding the Christ Child or others seated or standing around him.[66] In Christian culture, then, the Mary as nursing mother was explicitly represented, but in medieval Jewish culture, where males, not females, were almost always the only teachers of Torah to boys and men, symbolism was limited to implication and to the identification of the Torah with different food substitutes for breast milk: milk and honey, eggs, cakes, and oil. In the medieval ritual, the male teacher acts out the response to Moses's rhetorical question in Numbers 11:12: he does carry the child as a nurse carries a babe to the bosom/lap. Moreover, the teacher proceeds to feed the child, not from the physical breast, as in Christian iconography, but with the symbolically equivalent baby foods, especially milk and honey.

The effect of the ceremony is to transform the young child who plays or helps his mother at home into a young student. As the Maḥzor Vitry explains the ceremony, "First we entice him and afterward we use the strap." The ceremony itself effects a smooth transition by making the child's very entrance into schooling a transformation of the old status: first he is nursed for Torah, then he is nurtured by the Torah teacher. Before, his mother fed him sweet foods, milk and honey; now, the Torah teacher feeds him Torah as a substitute.

The rich symbolic association of the Torah with certain foods and the representation of Torah teachers as surrogate mothers are part of the symbolic language in the school scene of the Leipzig Maḥzor. As Evelyn Cohen has noted, Christian iconography lies behind two parts of the Leipzig Maḥzor scene. The Jewish illumination seems curious in that it is unattested in earlier Jewish art and is

7. Madonna and Child as *mater amabilis*. The
Virgin of Jeanne d'Evreux, 1339. Silver gilt
with basse-taille enamel. Louvre, Paris.
Reprinted with permission. Photo: Agence
photographique réunion des musées
nationaux.

unique. Moreover, there are discrepancies between the pictorial representation
of the initiation and certain elements in the written accounts. Especially striking is the central section. Although the artist represents the child being carried
from home before the initiation, he already holds the round cake. This is puz-
zling until one recognizes the Christian model that the Jewish artist used. As
Cohen has convincingly argued, the image of the male adult carrying the child
who is caressing his cheek is a Jewish adaptation of the Madonna and Child
type known as *mater amabilis* (Mother deserving of love), in which the Child
Jesus touches either Mary's veil or her cheek (figure 7). The round cake is a

8. Enthroned Virgin and Child. North
French, Meuse region, from priory of
Oignies, about 1220. New York, Metropolitan
Museum of Art. Gift of George Blumenthal,
1941. 41.190.283. Reprinted with permission.
Photo: Photograph Services, Metropolitan
Museum of Art.

residual element, poorly integrated, from the Christian *mater amabilis*, where the
Christ Child holds a round object, an orb.

It should be noted, however, that the image of the young boy caressing
the father's or scholar's face, derived from the strong affective style of the *mater
amabilis*, has an emotional force which replaced the more formal and stilted
mother-child relationships of earlier depictions. The result is a powerful statement of parental affection which makes the image of separation affectively
compelling regardless of the awkwardness of the anomalous cake in the central scene.

In the image on the left, the artist portrays the teacher seated on a large
chair, with the child seated on his lap. This scene is also derived from a well-
known Christian model: the Madonna and Child seated on the Throne of Wis-

dom, or of Solomon, with either her or the child holding a book. This figure is sometimes understood as the Madonna herself symbolizing the throne upon which sits wisdom in the form of the Christ Child (figure 8). In the Jewish adaptation, the male teacher holds the child and the tablet, and both represent Jewish symbolic replacements for the Christ Child as logos and wisdom. Images of the cakes and eggs that the child is to eat are specific new elements. The acts of feeding and eating are not shown.[67]

Although two of the three sections derive from Christian models, the three parts have been made into a fresh, integrated whole. Formally, the two scenes with the teacher frame the one with the father and child to form a compositional unity. The sequence also depicts a progression through the developmental stages of the child's initiation into Torah study. The child first is carried like a swaddled baby,[68] then is seated on the teacher's lap/bosom, and finally stands in front of the teacher, who prods him toward the river's edge. The child moves from being his father's (and mother's) baby to being a nursling of his surrogate parent, the Torah teacher, who feeds him baby foods and Torah foods, and then stands nearly on his own, with his teacher, confronting the river and the Torah.

The Child Torah Student as Eucharistic Sacrifice [69]

The metaphor with which I conclude this series of readings is found not only in descriptions of the ceremony itself but also in the exegesis or interpretive layers of the ceremony in some of the texts. Based on ancient ideas and reiterated in the ceremony is the theme that the child who studies the Torah diligently, especially at a young age, is like a pure sacrifice with redemptive power as a form of vicarious atonement for the rest of the Jewish community. This child-sacrifice motif had special meaning in Ashkenazic Judaism, and it resonated with the new high-medieval European Christian image of the Child Jesus as the eucharist.[70] The initiation ceremony served as a social polemic and was understood as a Jewish equivalent of, and answer to, the eucharistic sacrifice: Torah children, not the Child Jesus, are an effective redemptive sacrifice.

Toward the end of the description of the various elements that constitute the rite, the *Maḥzor Vitry* states: "Know that this whole matter is as though (the father) brought (his son) near (hiqrivo) to Mount Sinai."[71] The form hiqrivo can also mean "he sacrificed him," but as the context immediately following suggests, the analogy between the boy's initiation ceremony and Israel nearing Mount Sinai is being invoked, and it is not a reference to sacrifice. The analogy with Sinai is found in all of the texts that describe the ritual.

In the Maḥzor Vitry additional explanations are offered about other elements in the ritual, and the author develops further the comparison with Mount Sinai: "Israel approached (nitqarvu) Mount Sinai when the Torah was (first) given (to Israel)."[72] Here, the verb form nitqarvu cannot be taken to mean "sacrificed," as the form hiqrivo can.

However, when the commentary reaches the issue of why the child begins to study Leviticus first, and not Genesis, the argument takes a new turn: "Why is Torat Kohanim (the Book of Leviticus) read first? As is taught, R. Yose said: The children begin with the Book of Leviticus. The Holy One, blessed be He, said: Let the pure ones occupy themselves with purities."[73] This quotation of R. Isi or Yose from Midrash Vayyiqra Rabbah is found in other descriptions of the rite, but the Maḥzor Vitry adds the gloss "and I count it as though he sacrificed him as a sacrifice before me (ke-'ilu hiqrivo qorban lefanai)." It is true that the biblical account of Sinai refers to a sacrifice offered up by young men (na'arei benei yisrael) at Sinai (Exod. 24:5), but that is different from the idea expressed here that the father sacrifices his son by bringing him to school.

The earliest extant manuscript of the Maḥzor Vitry concludes the description of the initiation ceremony at this point.[74] But the British Library manuscript, which dates from the late thirteenth century and is the basis of the critical edition, includes an elaborate additional comment on the motif of the child as sacrifice:

> Why does (the boy) conclude (his first text from the Book of Leviticus) with the verse, "you must not eat any fat or blood" (Lev. 3:17)? The Holy One, blessed be He, said, . . . It is on account of the the children (ha-tonoqot) whose fat and blood is reduced over words of Torah. I consider it as though they sacrificed them to me. . . . That is why (the boy) reads that verse as a chant: he gives forth song and praise before God because they have accomplished this commandment, and I consider it as though they sacrificed his blood and fat on the altar.
>
> For this reason one has to prepare a feast for him like the one made

on the day (the boy) was circumcised and his blood was also reduced. One who enjoys the feast (of the schoolboy) must bless him and say: "May God enlighten your eyes with his Torah." This is similar to blessing him at the circumcision with: "As he has entered the covenant, so may he enter the Torah, etc."[75]

Underlying these statements are several rabbinic traditions that may have suggested such unusual interpretations. The first is the idea that studying the laws about sacrifices in the Pentateuch and in rabbinic texts in the present age is equivalent to and an adequate replacement for the offering of sacrifices in the days of the Temple. This view is stated in *Midrash Vayyiqra Rabbah* immediately preceding the text that the ceremony cites to explain why the children (pure ones) should study Leviticus (pure sacrifices) before they study Genesis: "The Holy One, blessed be He, said: Since you study (lit. occupy yourselves) with the sacrifices, I count it as though you offer a sacrifice (*maqrivin qorban*)."[76] The rabbinic texts that mention that studying about sacrifices is equivalent to the priests' performance of the earlier Temple cult sacrifices refer to adult study, not children's, but the juxtaposition of the two passages in *Midrash Vayyiqra Rabbah* suggests that they may be applied to children as well.

A second rabbinic tradition connects the fasting and weeping of adult pietists (*ḥasidim*) with the sacrificial cult and in one case specifically refers to fasting as analogous to the fat offering and loss of blood on the Temple altar: "R. Sheshet used to pray on the evening after a feast day, 'Lord of the world, when the Temple was standing, one who sinned offered a sacrifice of which only the fat and the blood were taken on the altar, and thereby his sins were forgiven. I have fasted today, and through this fasting my blood and my fat have been decreased. Deign to look upon the part of my blood and my fat which I have lost through my fasting as if I had offered it to Thee on the altar, and forgive my sins in return.'"[77] Here, too, it is the fasting of adult Jews that is compared to the Temple cult sacrifices.

A third rabbinic tradition links childhood study with sacrifice: "The world exists by virtue of the breath of small schoolchildren who study the Torah in elementary schools."[78] Just as sacrifice sustained the world in the days of the Temple, so the breath of small children does now.[79]

These three motifs have been combined in the concluding passage in the British Library manuscript of the *Maḥzor Vitry*. The result is the idea that a small child's study of the Torah, which begins with the description of the sacrifices in Leviticus, is equated with the religious benefit once gained from the Temple sacrificial cult. That is what is denoted when the author of the Maḥzor Vitry says that when the father brings his son to the school room to study Torah it is as though he has sacrificed his son at Sinai. The passages, we recall, are part of an extended explanation about why the boy begins his study of the Bible with Leviticus and not Genesis.

The idea that small children's study is equivalent to the sacrificial cult is made explicitly in a commentary on the Song of Songs. It begins with the familiar question "Why do we start the children with Leviticus (Torat Kohanim)?" But it answers it in a different way: "Because the breath of schoolchildren makes the world exist. Another interpretation: Just as the sacrifices atone, so do the children atone, as it is written, 'From the mouths of infants and sucklings you have founded strength'" (Ps. 8:3).[80] This text suggests that there was an early Jewish tradition that understood the small child's study of Leviticus as the equivalent of the sacrificial cult and as religiously effective.

Since several related rabbinic texts are implied by the passage that connects the child in the ceremony with sacrifice, one might expect some reference to Abraham and Isaac, the archetype of this theme in the Hebrew Bible (Genesis 22). Not only are there congruences between a father bringing his son to school, in recapitulation of Israel at Mount Sinai, and the biblical Abraham bringing his son Isaac to Mount Moriah in Jerusalem as a sacrifice, but also a rabbinic tradition specifically links the two: "Whence did Sinai come? R. Yose taught: Sinai was made from material taken from Mount Moriah, the place where our father Isaac had been bound as a sacrifice, as a priest's portion of dough is pinched from the bread dough. For the Holy One, blessed be He, said: Since their father Isaac was bound upon this place, it is fitting that his children received the Torah upon it."[81]

This text has several important overtones. The comparison between Mount Sinai and the priest's portion of dough reiterates the metaphor of the Torah as bread while stressing at the same time the smallness of Sinai (a pinch of dough) as compared to other mountains. More significantly, the missing link between the motifs of the father sacrificing his son and the approach to Sinai is here supplied. Sinai is explicitly associated with both the priestly bread sacrifice and the sacrifice of Isaac. Together, these rabbinic associations suggest the possibility that bringing the child to school is like sacrificing him at Sinai. The pure child (wrapped, studying Leviticus) is brought to school (Sinai), where he will study so hard that he will himself become a sacrifice. And by taking him there, the father does something which, like the ancient Temple cult, enables the world to continue to exist.

Although the father's role in the ritual can be performed by any Jewish man, the small child who studies is like the ancient priests whose sacrificial cult brought atonement for other Jews.[82] The ancient rabbinic statements comparing prayer or Torah study to the defunct Temple rites were more democratic than the Temple cult, but some traditions of Jewish piety persisted in medieval Europe that gave a special religious role to some Jews—pietists,[83] kohanim (priests), or leviim (Levites)—as representatives of other Jews.

Although the idea of vicarious atonement is only implicit in the commentary in the Mahzor Vitry, it is stated explicitly in connection with a plan for a Torah school described in Huqqei ha-Torah ha-Qadmonim.[84] In this text, children who study Torah provide surrogate acts of piety for the redemption of others. As the rabbinic text puts it, "The world exists by virtue of the breath of small schoolchildren who study the Torah in elementary schools." This description of a school for young Jewish adults that resembles a monastery is very likely related to northern French, possibly Norman, Jewish culture.[85]

The text begins enigmatically with the introductory phrase, "This is the book of the ancient rules of the Torah (zeh sefer huqqei ha-torah ha-qadmonim). It stipulates that descendants of the branches of Jews claiming ancestry from Aaron (kohanim) and from the tribe of Levi (leviim) are "to separate one of their sons and devote him to the study of the Torah." The elders of the other Jews (ziqnei yisrael) are to do likewise. These young men are to live for seven years in a special school, and their active study of the Torah will vicariously fulfill the religious obligation all Jews have to study the Torah. Implied is the proposition that their study will also earn a religious reward for the rest of the local Jewish community.

Although the acts of vicarious Torah study in Huqqei ha-Torah ha-Qadmonim resemble the theme of the child as sacrifice, there is an important difference. In this text, older children are compared to liturgical chanters in the synagogue, the hazzanim, in that both the children and the hazzanim vicariously fulfill the religious obligations of other Jews. In the initiation ceremony, it is the younger and not the older children whose study is compared to a sacrifice. Still, both

9. Miracle of the Child in the Host. Cambridge, Cambridge University Library, Ms Ee.3.59, *La Estoire de sent Aedward le rei*, f. 21a. Reproduced with the permission of the Syndics of Cambridge University Library.

are examples of a strain of Ashkenazic piety which recognizes that Torah study by some Jews can influence the religious welfare of others.

An important context in which to understand the concept of the Jewish schoolchild as sacrifice is in opposition to the contemporary Christian motif of the Christ Child in the eucharistic sacrifice, which developed in the late twelfth and thirteenth centuries (figure 9). For example, it is recorded of Father Peter of Tewkesbury:

> He was very intimate with the family of Galfrid Le Despensyr. On one
> occasion when he visited the house, the lord's son John, a little boy, ran

as usual to him with greatest familiarity. But when the boy had been to the chapel with his mother, where Father Peter had celebrated Mass, on returning home the child ran from the aforesaid Father and could not be compelled by his mother to approach him. When she asked why he had fled, he replied that he had seen Father Peter devour a little child on the chapel altar and feared a like fate for himself.[86]

In medieval Europe the sacrifice of small children was associated not only with the Jewish child's initiation ceremony and with the motif of the Christ Child in the Mass but also with earlier Jewish practices in the Rhineland of the ritual killing of Jewish children by Jews in extreme circumstances and the related Christian accusation that Jews must also kill Christian children — the ritual-murder accusation. At the same time, an accusation developed that Jews desecrated the Host, often associated with the Christ Child, as a form of deicide, since the consecrated Host was considered to be Christ. A variation of the ritual-murder theme argued that Jews not only ritually killed Christian children but also drank their blood as part of the Passover rite, that is, that Jews ingested Christian children.[87]

It has been conjectured that the Jewish ritual killing of Jewish children in 1096 to avoid subjecting them to forced baptism may have led some Christians in Germany to conclude a fortiori that if Jews kill their own children they certainly are capable of killing Christian children.[88] But there was also a powerful Christian tradition at work that helped Christians to imagine such Jewish behavior, namely, the tradition of seeing the Christ Child in the Host. This tradition represents the combined effect of the increased importance of the eucharist and transubstantiation and of the emphasis on viewing Jesus as a child.

The iconography of the twelfth century emphasized Christ as a child, and the cult of the Virgin Mary was accompanied by images of the Madonna and Child in various forms. As an awareness of the importance of the eucharistic sacrifice grew in Latin Christendom,[89] it increasingly took the form of combining the Incarnation — the Christ Child — with the Passion — Jesus' sacrifice on the cross. The result was to understand the ritual of the eucharist as a child sacrifice in which one eats Christ as a small boy. Thus, in iconography and in ritual, Christians understood that the Host was the Christ Child and could imagine that the Jews as killers and eaters desecrated what Christians held sacred.[90]

The blood libel can be understood better in light of both Jewish and Christian cultural shifts. Jews sacrificed their children 1096, and Christians, aware of those acts, imagined that Jews certainly killed Christian children out of hatred. But the Christian tradition developed that idea only when Christians who took the eucharist imagined that they ate Christ as a small child and that Jews certainly would desecrate what Christians held sacred by killing or eating the blood of small Christian victims.[91]

The vocabulary of the Jewish initiation of a child into the Torah emerged in the twelfth and thirteenth centuries, exactly when Christian culture was aware of this meaning of the Christ Child in the eucharist. The idea that a Jewish child who studies the Torah is like a sacrifice consisting of blood and fat offered on the Temple altar is understandable within this cultural context. In the symbolic ritualization of the child's initiation in medieval Ashkenaz, a Jewish child is offered to God as a vicarious atonement. The commentary at the end of the *Maḥzor Vitry* reflects an awareness of the Christian notion of the child sacrifice in the eucharist and is yet another part of a Jewish social polemic in the initiation ceremony. In addition to the honey cake's representing a Jewish equivalent to the eucharist, the emphasis on the child's fat and blood reinforces the argument that it is the study of the Torah, not belief in Jesus, that brings salvation, and that Judaism, not Christianity, is true.

Although the eucharist remains at the center of Catholic devotion to this day, the Jewish school initiation soon disappeared, to be succeeded by a new initiation, at the age of thirteen: bar mitzvah. Just as a comparative context is helpful for reading the Jewish ceremony as a social polemic in a Christian society, so a comparison of the development of Jewish and Christian children's initiation ceremonies in the central and late Middle Ages is a useful aid toward understanding the historical changes that occurred within Ashkenaz and Latin Christendom.

Chapter Six

Childhood Initiations into Religious Cultures

The male child is at the center of my symbolic interpretations of the Ashkenazic school initiation rite. His personal drama recalls and evokes the biblical narrative of Israel's sacred journey from Egypt to Sinai. In Germany, the ceremony was performed at the very time that the local Jewish community commemorated and celebrated that ancient event, during the spring festival season of Passover to Shavuot. The gestures that express the relationship between the boy and the Torah teacher are a Jewish affirmation that arose in response to a pervasive Christian iconography that emphasized the centrality and truth of Mary and Jesus as Madonna and Christ Child. The rite of ingesting symbolic foods in the ritual arose from a similar tradition in Christianity, in which Christ in the image of the sacrificed child came to be identified with certain symbolic foods.

These themes suggest that the symbolic vocabulary of the Jewish school initiation reflects an awareness of the powerful Christian cultural symbols that surrounded the Jews of Ashkenaz. Even if the Jewish gestures were based, in fact or in imagination, on ancient Jewish customs and metaphors—some possibly antedating Christianity itself—their reemergence in the Middle Ages in patterns similar to contemporary Christian religious images and idioms is a form of inward acculturation. To deny something is still to be influenced by it; a negative imprint still leaves a mark.

An analogous process of acculturation can be detected in a comparative historical analysis of the school initiation ceremony. In a Christian child's rites of passage, such as baptism and confirmation with first communion, and in the history of parents devoting children to a monastic life—oblation—we see an increased concern with the child as a consenting subject and not as the passive object of someone else's decisions. In Ashkenaz as well, the emergence and disappearance of the school initiation ceremony, followed by the development of the bar mitzvah rite, reflects a concern with the child's age and consent prior to entering a life of full religious responsibility. Both cultures were reexamining older practices and assumptions about children, the stages of childhood, and the age of religious majority. A study of the historical developments in Jewish and Christian children's rites of passage offers another index of acculturation, one that complements my comparative reading of the symbolic language of the two cultures.

The new emphasis on consent and choice reflected in children's rites of passage is part of a European cultural transformation that began in the late eleventh century and reached its climax in the early thirteenth century.[1] Monastic culture was significantly modified and challenged by a more urbanized, more institutionally diversified, and more settled town culture which accompanied the reform papacy and the slow growth of feudal monarchies. An increase in population, the expansion of town walls, the beginnings of university life, increased trade, and technological improvements in agriculture influenced one another and helped to bring about a new sensibility based on human reason and consent rather than miraculous act, on individual choice instead of custom. The belief in miracles and authority continued, but it was now modulated by the increasing self-awareness that human reasoning and decision-making could make a difference.[2]

One sign of a new climate was the vociferous defense of the old one. Spokesmen for the older monastic culture objected to the changes going on all around them. The times belonged not only to the Paris Schoolman Peter Abelard but also to Bernard of Clairvaux.[3] A similar process of cultural innovation and conservative protest occurred in Ashkenazic culture,[4] and the ebb and flow of these historical processes are reflected in changes that took place in children's rites of passage in the Christian and Jewish subcultures within Latin Christendom.

The Dynamics of Ashkenazic Acculturation

To understand the emergence and gradual disappearance of the Ashkenazic school initiation ceremony and its eventual replacement by bar mitzvah in the late Middle Ages, we need to look more closely at developments that were taking place both in the history of Christian initiations and in medieval Jewish culture in the twelfth and thirteenth centuries. Ashkenazic inward acculturation involves the complementary processes of preservation and transformation: Ashkenazic Jews continued to observe ancient Jewish traditions yet reshaped them in light of a contemporary Christian context in a polemical fashion. The medieval Christian environment contributed to the process of Jewish self-definition. Jews drew on an earlier Jewish legacy, but at the same time they selectively absorbed parts of the Christian culture in order to negate them symbolically. This interactive dynamic was possible in medieval Europe because of the public character of Jewish rites of passage then, as compared with those of late antiquity. Their public nature made it possible for Jewish rites of passage to be formulated as social polemics.

The introduction of Jewish children to Torah schooling on Shavuot by the use of symbols that resemble Christian ritual symbols illustrates this twofold process of inward acculturation. In Ashkenaz, important cultural changes were under way. The earliest Ashkenazic culture of the Rhenish towns of Mainz and Worms resembled the monastic culture of the early Middle Ages in that it was grounded in local custom and did not yet know dialectic.[5] It was shocked by the scholastic culture of the Tosafists, who presented a challenge similar to the one which the Paris Schoolmen posed to contemporary monastic leaders. In response to this challenge, very early traditions that had been brought to the Rhineland from Byzantium, southern Italy, and even ancient Palestine were written down and discussed.[6] Provoked by the new dialecticians, German Jews reaffirmed their old customs and practices as minhag avoteinu (the custom of our ancestors) going back generations and generations, even to prerabbinic Judea. Among the practices that contemporaries considered to be ancestral was the German-Jewish schoolchild's initiation rite on Shavuot.

A comparative analysis of Jewish and Christian children's rites of passage suggests that the Ashkenazic ritual may have been influenced by changes that took place in Christian children's rites of passage. By the thirteenth century, confirmation and first communion in the West were delayed from infancy to age seven, the age of schooling, and the eucharist was taken then for the first time. This created a rite with which the Jewish school initiation resonated. To be sure, the new Jewish school initiation drew on ancient and early medieval adult magical practices of Shavuot, but it emerged when it did in part as a Jewish adaptation of the Christian children's confirmation rite.

The dynamic and interactive combination of these two trends—a Jewish scholastic challenge to early Ashkenazic culture and a new Christian emphasis on children taking first communion at school age—contributed to the appearance of the child's initiation rite in the late twelfth and early thirteenth centuries. But unlike its Christian counterpart, which was motivated by a requirement that the child be of the age of consent and of minimal maturity, the Jewish initiation reflects the persistence of older cultural attitudes that still regarded a child as someone on whom magical rites were performed. And yet, even though the initiation rite expressed aspects of an older Ashkenazic culture, its ritual vocabulary was shaped as a polemical response to the Christian rite of confirmation and first eucharist at age seven, which was a contemporary phenomenon.

This is not to say that medieval Jewish writers did not notice that children had inner lives. There is evidence that they did in *Sefer Ḥasidim*, a major source about religious mentality in medieval Ashkenaz. The cultural process is complex. On the one hand, the appearance in the late twelfth century of the German Pietists' writings was a conservative response to Tosafist innovation. On the other hand, the reshaping of the ancient adult Torah rituals of Shavuot into a children's Shavuot initiation reflects an innovative emphasis on childhood in late twelfth-century Ashkenaz.[7]

First Initiations: Circumcision and Baptism with Confirmation

Between late antiquity and the Middle Ages, important changes took place in Jewish and Christian childhood rites of passage.[8] Although several Jewish life rituals began as domestic or private events in the life of a particular family, they became ritualized as shared moments in the life of a community. Circumcision is described in rabbinic sources as taking place in the home, but in medieval times it was done in the synagogue. In ancient times, a child who could speak was taught something by his father and went to a teacher, but no ritual marked the occasion until the Ashkenazic initiation, which took place in the synagogue. The age of thirteen and a day, for boys, or twelve and a day, for girls, was a legal sign of becoming responsible to observe certain religious duties like fasting, but no public act set off the transition for boys until the fifteenth century in Ashkenaz, when the bar mitzvah rite apparently first developed. Similarly, marriages were celebrated in the home in talmudic times and moved into a public space only in the medieval period. Mourning followed a similar pattern as well.

Personal moments of transition were increasingly shared with a community, and as Jewish rites of passage became more public, collective symbols were added to the personal ones. In circumcision, for example, the Chair of Elijah, a symbol of messianic days to be enjoyed by the entire Jewish people, was added, thereby placing a onetime event in the life of a particular child into a cosmic framework. The addition of such collective symbols meant that the rites operated on two social and cultural levels. They continued to be opportunities for the individual to enter a new phase of community membership. A newborn became a Jew; a minor came of age; a single person left one family and joined another and added a new family unit to the community at large. And the community also celebrated and affirmed its collective identity even as it welcomed the individual into its ranks.

Although the timing of Jewish infant circumcision on the eighth day after birth has persisted from ancient times to the present, subject only to the modification of a temporary delay in the case of the child's illness, it was first associated with an adult rite undertaken by Abraham (Genesis 17). The "first Jew" was an adult, not an infant. Circumcision was the only Jewish initiation rite of childhood in late antiquity. In rabbinic Judaism there was no ceremony for entering school, which is first documented only in Europe in the late twelfth century, nor was there a public bar mitzvah rite, which emerged in central Europe even later.

Christian baptism, too, started as an adult ceremony of initiation, because the first converts to Christianity were adults, not Christian infants born to baptized Christian parents.[9] By requiring immersion in water, baptism was analogous in some respects to ancient Jewish adult conversion ceremonies,[10] although it was also modeled on Jesus' baptism in the New Testament. The baptism of adults into Christianity was accompanied by the additional rite of confirmation, which included taking the eucharist for the first time, administered by a bishop.[11]

But adult baptism began to change in the first four centuries as the Christian population began to grow more from natural increase than from adult conversion. Augustine's theological arguments about original sin made clear that measures had to be taken to protect the newborn, who might die before maturing.[12] Infant baptism became nearly universal in the West until the Anabaptists opposed it, in the sixteenth century, as an innovation not mentioned in Scripture.[13]

When the age of baptism was changed from adulthood to infancy, a new form of adult sponsorship developed.[14] Since an infant could not perform the rite alone or present himself or herself to an adult, the institution of godparents at infant baptism was introduced in the early Middle Ages to perform that function. The presence of Christian godparents at baptism eventually influenced the Jewish circumcision ceremony, which introduced the concept of a godparent called *syndekos*, a Byzantine Greek term that marks the approximate time of the innovation in the early Middle Ages.[15] In later Ashkenazic Europe, two additional godparents were added, whose names were taken from the parallel German Christian terms for co-parents, *Gevatter, Gevatterin*.[16] All three terms eventually entered Yiddish as *Sandek, Kefatter,* and *Kefatterin*; along with Elijah's Chair, they remain integral parts of the Jewish circumcision ritual to this day.[17]

Second Initiations: Delayed Confirmation-Eucharist and Jewish School Initiation

In the Christian tradition, the new emphasis on infant baptism presented a further problem. In the East, a bishop performed the rite of confirmation together with first communion, immediately after adult baptism. But as adult baptism was replaced by infant baptism, confirmation often had to be delayed. In the less densely populated areas of Europe, it was also more difficult to find a bishop than it had been in the East. As the culminating ceremony of confirmation became more problematic, it was deferred, and by the thirteenth century it was administered close to the age of seven, at least in parts of the West. This delay was advocated by theologians and canonists who were part of the cultural transformation that emphasized the interior life of the mind and spirit and who taught that the child should not be given communion before the age of awareness and consent.[18]

Although we will see that other factors were at work as well, the Christian association of school-age children with first communion played a role in shaping the Jewish child's school initiation. There are striking formal similarities between communion and the Jewish school initiation rite introduced in

the late twelfth century. Both took place when the child was of school age—
at seven for Christians, at five, six, or seven for Jews. Both were administered
by a figure embodying religious authority, either a bishop or a Torah teacher.
Both were administered in the spring: the Christian ceremony at Easter or Pentecost [19] and the German-Jewish one at Shavuot (Pentecost). And both required
that the child ingest symbolic foods among which a special kind of ritually
sanctified cake or bread had a prominent place.

To be sure, they were not the same ceremony. In the late twelfth-century
Jewish initiation, the child who studies Torah is understood as a sacrifice; the
eucharist is a sacrifice of Jesus understood as a child. The eucharist is a re-
membrance of Jesus' words at the Last Supper and is a Passover meal, but it
also presents Jesus as the paschal sacrifice which the faithful must eat. Christians commune with God by eating his body in the form of a leavened cake,
as is still done in the Eastern churches, or an unleavened wafer, as has been
the practice in the West since the ninth century. Did the Jewish custom, based
on eating a cake, like the Christian Syriac school initiation rite, preserve the
Eastern Christian eucharistic rite long after it had disappeared in the West?

The faithful who consume the bread that has become the body of Christ
must be in a state of religious purity. The child as sacrifice in the Jewish initiation also is first to be ritually pure. Although the theological meanings of
the eucharist developed in stages, its public observance reached new heights
in the late twelfth and early thirteenth centuries, just when the Jewish initiation rite appeared. In 1215 the Fourth Lateran Council included a canon which
stated that every Christian adult must take communion annually, usually at
Easter.[20] Communion also became the subject of public ritualization in the new
festival of Corpus Christi, established in 1264 but practiced earlier in northern Europe.[21] With the increased sacralization of this symbol, new regulations
were promulgated to prevent the desecration of the consecrated Host by Christians, especially children who might play with consecrated wafers. It is also at
this time that Jews were accused of desecrating the Host.[22] Christians expressed
esteem for their newly important *sancta* by viewing the Jewish Other as having
desecrated it. These events are indices of a changing Christian culture.

The similarity between the Jewish school initiation and the first eucharist taken at confirmation by a young Christian schoolboy can also be viewed
historically as a Jewish social polemic. Ancient Jewish writings such as *Toledot
Yeshu* (Life of Jesus) parodied the Gospels and Christian rituals and doctrines.[23]

In these texts, Jewish authors relished imputing sexual perversities, ritual impurity, and other heinous sins to Mary and Joseph. The holy family became a bordello; the savior was made a magician whom Jews justly put to death; Mary became a menstruant prostitute; and the miracle of the virgin birth was parodied as having occurred when Mary was menstruating, a biological near-impossibility.[24]

Many of these rhetorical attacks on Christianity appear in Hebrew narratives that interpreted for a twelfth-century Jewish audience the meaning of the acts of Jewish ritual slaughter and suicide that accompanied the anti-Jewish riots in the German towns of Mainz and Worms in the spring of 1096.[25] These same texts portray Christian attackers as having desecrated Jewish *sancta* by tearing Torah scrolls and burning them.[26]

It is likely that the different elements that constitute the Jewish child's initiation rite were chosen from many alternatives, in part to use Christian symbols as vehicles for denying the truth of the eucharistic devotion and to affirm that the Torah, not Jesus, is the true bread, the true manna, the true gift of milk and honey from a loving God. There are certain obvious points of similarity between the Jewish child's initiation ceremony and the eucharist. Both reenact ancient historical events, the giving of the Torah at Mount Sinai and the Passion of Christ. One immediately senses the power of the referents, Torah and Christ, the two central symbols of each religious culture.

Recall that on the writing tablet the alphabet was written forward and backward and in symmetrically paired letters (*atbash*). Aside from its function as a mnemonic device, *atbash* represents the divine name. In Revelation 22:13 Jesus says, "I am the alpha and the omega," and in France today the wafer is stamped with those two Greek letters. In Jewish mystical tradition the Hebrew alphabet is a formulation of the divine name.[27] In licking honey off the Hebrew alphabet, then, the child is eating God's name. Moreover, according to another Jewish mystical tradition, the Torah itself is God's name. Thus, by eating cakes and eggs on which verses of the Torah have been written, the child is again consuming the holy name.[28]

Two additional sources—one, in *Sefer ha-Asufot*, directly related to its description of the initiation ceremony, the other a commentary from medieval Germany on the Hebrew Bible—mention a custom that is supposed to be part of the child's initiation and is also a Jewish polemic against Christianity. "Why is it that we are accustomed to teach the children the alphabet and to read QRST (the Hebrew letters *quf, resh, shin,* and *tav*) in the alphabet twice? How are these four letters different from the rest of the alphabet so that we do not make a word out of them but only from these?"[29] Although this text does not state explicitly that it is referring to the child's initiation rite, it is most probable, given the requirement in the ritual of reciting alphabets and the existence of alphabet charts that show two- and four-letter combinations used at the ceremony, including QRST, at the end of the forward alphabet. The text poses the question to a R. Leontin/Judah, who explains:[30] "It is because these (four) letters appear two times in the verse 'When Moses charged us with the Torah (as a heritage for the congregation of Jacob)'" (Deut. 33:4).

We recall that the verse "When Moses charged us . . ." is one of the sacred texts that is inscribed on the writing tablet in *Sefer ha-Roqeah* and has ancient associations as a Jewish Torah primer. But is R. Leontin's explanation an explanation at all? For if we look at the Hebrew text of that verse, it is obvious that other letters of the Hebrew alphabet also appear twice. Another sign of the artificiality of the explanation is the existence of a second justification for the same custom. It is found just before the description of the initiation ceremony in *Sefer ha-Asufot.* The very uncertainty in the explanations for this strange custom suggests that we are dealing with an early rite whose presence was being rationalized by reference to Deuteronomy 33:4.

When we pronounce the Hebrew letters QRST as one word and say it twice, we get something that sounds very much like *Christe, Christe.*[31] Now, it is highly unlikely that Jews would celebrate the introduction of their small boys into Jewish schooling by pronouncing the name of Christ unless it meant something other than an affirmation of the truth of Christianity. And indeed, there was special polemical significance to the Hebrew alphabet recited both forward and backward.

As Moshe Idel has pointed out,[32] a Jewish mystical tradition of R. Eleazar of Worms held that the Hebrew alphabet in reverse order was the name of God but in the normal order was not. Perhaps this premise and the fact that the four last letters in order spelled out QRST led to the custom of affirming that Christ was Not God at the time when Jews celebrated the entry of their sons into the Torah, the very Torah which Christians claimed that Christ had displaced. By reciting the last four letters of the alphabet, were Jews parodying "Christe eleison" in the Mass and thereby asserting that Christ is not God?

The child's initiation into Torah is a medieval reconfiguration of many traditions from within ancient and early medieval Judaism, and the shape that reordering took significantly resembles the Christian eucharistic rite, which was being given special prominence in the late twelfth and thirteenth centuries. One way of viewing the Jewish ritual is as a mock eucharistic ceremony expressing the Jewish conviction that the Torah, not Jesus, is the means of communion with God. Divine love was shown by a gift of milk and honey, the Torah, to the Jews, not his son Jesus. Moreover, every Jew is to "give" his own son to the study of Torah, and this act of sacrifice and self-sacrifice, not Jesus, will atone for the rest of Israel.

The delay of confirmation and first eucharist to age seven helped shape the Jewish initiation rite as a Jewish confirmation-eucharist ceremony. The heightened importance of the eucharist may also be a reason why the Jewish ritual that resembled it nearly disappeared. But before considering its demise, we need to look at a second aspect of the process of Ashkenazic inward acculturation that triggered its appearance.

Tosafist Innovation and German-Jewish Reaction

At the same time that Christians were emphasizing the importance of reason and consent, a struggle was going on within the rabbinic culture of Ashkenaz between the older culture of the Rhineland, based on customs, and newer intellectual forces in northern France, based on the scholastic inquiry of the Talmud — Tosafism. This process has been discussed as an important transformation within Ashkenazic culture. Only occasionally has an effort been made to relate these trends to the host culture of medieval Christian Europe and the dynamics that were at work there.[33]

The appearance of the school rite was a product of these larger processes. Whereas the late tenth and eleventh centuries saw the emergence in northern Europe of the beginnings of a Jewish culture grounded in local customs and independent of the textual authority of the Babylonian Talmud or the codified interpretation of that work by the Baghdadi Geonim,[34] a new school of Talmud glossators, the Tosafists, challenged it in the early twelfth century. One can look at this shift within a fairly narrow compass, such as a study of changes in the ways Jewish texts were studied or an analysis of how Jewish law developed from an aggregation of customs to a geometrically expansive scholastic progression of categories and new laws. This shift can also be viewed as a pedagogic change from learning earlier customs to relying on one's own intelligence and the application of logical analysis, contradiction, and distinction.

The Tosafists' innovative dialectical assault,[35] accompanied by the new focus on the interior life of the individual, did not go unchallenged. Among the reactions to the loss of rabbinic leadership in the riots of 1096, a family of rabbinic luminaries, Benei Makhir, great-grandnephews of the venerable Rabbeinu Gershom ben Judah of Mainz, set about collecting the earlier customs and laws of early Ashkenaz and compiling digests of traditions that had existed prior to the Tosafist revolution.[36] In addition, we see written for the first time the ancient traditions and customs of German-Jewish Pietists. Some of these were practiced in the early Middle Ages in the towns of Apulia and Calabria in Byzantine southern Italy; some were even more ancient. The German Pietists were members of a founding dynasty of Ashkenaz and claimed to retain traditions from ancient Babylonia passed down from father to younger son, even as Christian nobles dedicated their younger sons to monastic life. The timing of when they wrote their traditions down, not much after the Benei Makhir wrote down the Rhenish legal customs, indicates that they were part of a conservative response to the cultural shock of the Tosafists.[37]

Within the Jewish community the ancient elements of the school initiation ritual surfaced, in part as a response of the German-Ashkenazic subculture, with its insistence on the value of its ancestral customs, to a challenge from the northern French-Ashkenazic Tosafists and Hebrew Bible commentators, who stressed the individual scholar's intellectual acumen and direct, reasoned interpretation of the ancient texts rather than only received opinion and custom. This reaction, especially prominent with some of the German Pietists,[38] was true of twelfth-century German Judaism in general.

It is not fortuitous that the Jewish school initiation ceremony appeared in the late twelfth and early thirteenth centuries, the same time that early Rhenish-Jewish customs and the German Pietist traditions were being written down for preservation.[39] Indeed, the earliest version of the ceremony was recorded by the principal Pietist writer, R. Eleazar of Worms, whose defense of custom is his reason for preserving the ritual. The features of the ceremony that focused on Shavuot and the magical learning of Torah by eating foods inscribed with sacred words and alphabets, the early medieval Babylonian incantation against POTAḤ, and other magical features are all customs and practices that were associated with adults who studied Torah magically in the early medieval East and were now applied to the Ashkenazic European child.

The crystallization of this initiation in medieval Europe is another example of early Rhenish Ashkenaz's refusal to give up ancestral customs under the attack of textual standards newly imposed by the Tosafists.[40] As we have seen, in rabbinic times the onset of schooling took place at a certain age, not at a particular time of year. The Tosafists tried to impose as an authoritative Mishnah the ages-of-man text: "At age five (one begins studying) Scripture."[41] The appearance and defense of the German-Ashkenazic custom of starting on Shavuot, not just at the age of five or six, is a sign of their resistance to the new reliance on texts and their adherence to ancestral custom.[42] By insisting on Shavuot, with all its magical Torah gestures, as the time a small child should begin to study Torah, they were reasserting the local customs of Ashkenaz (minhag avoteinu) against innovations based on the arbitrary dictates of texts.

The Jewish school initiation, then, far from being the same as the deferment of confirmation to age seven, reflects the opposite process. It continued the ancient mode of both religious cultures, recently rejected by the Christian West, that small children can be acted upon and need not understand what they are undergoing for rituals to be effective. In short, a custom-oriented and external or magical culture persisted in Ashkenaz while it was fading in the France of the universities and such monastic orders as the Cistercians, which drew on new religious sensibilities. Eventually it was swept away in the changing cultural tides that affected both religious cultures.

Resistance to the School Initiation Rite

The disappearance of the Jewish initiation rite and its eventual replacement by the public rite of bar mitzvah are phenomena which also illustrate the acculturative processes that I have just described. Both Christian and Jewish sources of opposition were responsible for the ritual's disappearance. In the repressive climate of the thirteenth century especially, ecclesiastical authorities passed laws to prevent Christian children, among others, from mistreating the consecrated Host.[43] And it was at this time that a new accusation was made: that Jews desecrate the Host by stabbing it, thus reenacting the murder of Jesus. The heightened regulations and hysterical atmosphere surrounding the Jews and the Host probably made Jews restrain themselves from doing anything that might look like a mock communion. It was too dangerous to perform the ritual.[44]

One attempt to stop the custom emerged, ironically, within the circle of German Pietists that included R. Eleazar of Worms, who had advocated it. In fact, R. Judah b. Samuel the Pietist was R. Eleazar's teacher. Although R. Judah advocated following the ancient traditions of pietism, he sometimes opposed existing customs when they conflicted with his personal sense of religious norms. The case of the lettered cake is just such an example. In *Sefer ha-Asufot*, just before the text that describes the initiation rite, we read: "I found in the book of R. Judah the Pietist that he did not want children to be fed the cake because biblical verses are written on it. It is not proper to excrete (biblical verses)."[45]

We find a similar consideration discussed in connection with the eucharist. Concerning the digestion and elimination of the Host, Christian writers made clear that the bread was not bread but was entirely transformed, and it became, as James of Vitry put it, "not bodily food but food of the soul; not of the flesh but of the heart."[46] In another effort to deny the physicality of the Host and the implication that it is digested and excreted, Roland Bandinelli, who later became Pope Alexander III, wrote of someone who tried to live on the Host. Instead of being sustained by it, he in effect digested his own body and died in fourteen days. This proved that he was not digesting and excreting the eucharist.[47]

We do not know for certain that the Jewish school ceremony was observed in northern France, despite its being mentioned in the Champenois *Mahzor Vitry*. And R. Aaron ha-Kohen of Lunel, in the conclusion to his version of the rite in *Orhot Hayyim*, notes: "This custom was the custom of the ancients. The people of Jerusalem did it, and even today it is done in some places." Perhaps "in some places" means in Germany, but not in his native Provence.

But there was opposition to the Jewish reading ritual in the Jewish legal literature even in Germany. The custom was challenged by citing the authority of texts applied in a restrictive way. Since the rite in Germany took place on Shavuot, a religious festival on which certain types of behavior were forbidden, questions about certain parts of the rite arose in the late thirteenth century. Among the actions that a Jew may not do on a festival is to erase anything written (moḥeq). And yet in the ritual the child is required to lick letters off of a tablet and to eat written texts on both cakes and hard-boiled eggs.

And so R. Meir b. Barukh (Maharam) of Rothenburg (d. 1293) was asked "about the children's cakes ('ugot ha-tinoqot) on which letters and words are written. How do the children eat them on the festival (yom ṭov)?" And he replied: "If (you are concerned) because of the prohibition of erasing on a festival, the scriptural prohibition of erasing only refers to erasing in order to write something, as we learn in the Chapter (of the Talmud called) 'It is a general principle.' True, there is a rabbinically derived prohibition (for adults), but we are dealing in this case with small children, and there is no religious problem at all." [48]

This rabbinic responsum to a question of Jewish law is one indication that the ritual was still being practiced in Germany in the second half of the thirteenth century, and that some thought its practice involved a violation of Jewish law. The question also implies that the ritual was celebrated on a festival, that is, Shavuot, the holiday that all German-Jewish versions stipulate as the time when the ritual was to be observed.

A second responsum of Meir's mentions another feature of the ritual: ("Question: We eat peeled eggs inscribed with Hebrew letters. Why do we not fear the evil spirits that attack persons who eat peeled eggs? Is it because evil spirits are rare in this land? Answer:) Evil spirits are probably very rare in these parts, or possibly the holy writings on the eggs ward off spirits." [49]

The holy writings could themselves pose a problem. Elsewhere, Meir renders a decision that further confirms aspects of the ceremony but also indicates the problematic nature of writing certain things on foods that are then eaten: "And I say (the following). It is prohibited to write on a cake which is given to children (ne'arim) for opening the heart using names of the Holy One, blessed be He, which may not be erased. It is permitted (to write) the names of angels." [50]

Here a new issue is raised. May God's names (God, the Lord) be erased by a minor? This prohibition is altogether different from the question of whether a minor may erase any letters on a festival, in that no Jew is permitted to desecrate God's name by erasing it at any time. This last passage adds details that further support the existence of the rite in the late thirteenth century, and Meir even refers to the motive of the practice, "opening the heart," which re-iterates R. Eleazar of Worms's comment in *Sefer ha-Roqeah* that "it is good for the opening of the heart." The texts that the ceremony employs are filled with biblical verses that contain one or another form of the name of God. This reply by Meir, unlike his other one, could have seriously inhibited the ceremony's practice in Germany, where he was the most authoritative rabbinic figure in the second half of the thirteenth century.

Judah and other Jewish writers could not defend the ritual by distinguish-ing, as Christian theologians had done regarding the eucharist, between the visible Hebrew letters written on the physical cake and their spiritual status. To Judah and Meir, the ontological status of the divine name was all too physical. To eat the cakes meant that one was desecrating the name of God. So Judah and Meir agreed: it was wrong to eat cakes on which the names of God or other sacred words from the Hebrew Bible were written.

R. Eleazar of Worms, an advocate in the early thirteenth century of old Ashkenazic customs, vigorously disagreed with Judah: "They feed the boy the cake and the egg because it is good for the opening of the heart. Let no one de-viate from (following) this custom." [51] But his insistence was to no avail. It is likely that Judah's objections influenced R. Meir of Rothenburg to give them the force of Jewish law, and the children's initiation rite fell out of favor even in Germany, where it had begun. We know from the testimony of R. David b. Isaac (Ginzberg) of Fulda (ca. 1540s–1607) that by the late sixteenth cen-tury the rite was no longer practiced there. David discusses ways to "open the heart" to prevent forgetting what one learns, refers to the initiation ritual, and laments that he would have had his own children perform the rite had he been aware of it: "This was common practice in the days of the ancients and the days of the Geonim. It is a tested matter to open the heart. Had I known of the rite when my children were still young, I would have employed this remedy (*segu-lah*) for them. However, I was unaware of it until I recently received it, when I discovered it in a very old text." [52] The Lithuanian rabbi Shabbetai b. Meir Ha-Kohen (1621–1662), who was the author of *Siftei Kohen*, mentions the custom as a discontinued practice and remarks, "These customs are not practiced today." [53]

Child Oblation to Monasteries and Bar Mitzvah

Although the Jewish impetus to develop a child's school initiation ceremony derived more from conservative protests against dialectical ideas of the Tosafists than from the new emphasis in Christian culture on the importance of a child's consent and choice, the latter trend began to catch up with Ashkenazic culture by the end of the thirteenth century. This is reflected in two other children's initiation rites, which are signs in both Jewish and Christian culture of a new awareness of children's status and of the need to distinguish between children and adults.

The idea of sacrifice that the eucharist symbolically represented is crucial to another Christian children's rite of passage that was transformed in the central Middle Ages: child oblation, or the donation of small children to monasteries (figure 10).[54] From the early centuries of monastic life in the West, parents could devote, or give, a child at a very young age to a religious community. Bede was seven years old in 670 when he was oblated. Parents modeled their act on the biblical Hanna, who offered Samuel to Eli once the child was weaned.[55]

In the early centuries of monastic life in the West, the recipient community was invariably a Benedictine house. As organized religious life became more diversified in the eleventh and twelfth centuries, considerable opposition developed to the practice of child oblation. The newly founded house of Cîteaux, although committed to strict observance of the Benedictine rule, which permitted child oblation,[56] introduced the provision, before 1115, that oblation could not take place until a child had reached the age of twelve.[57] Theologians like Thomas Aquinas, himself an oblate at age six, argued that in the old way the child was denied consent, and increasingly an age of reasoned consent was demanded, usually twelve for girls and fourteen for boys.[58]

By delaying participation in religious adulthood, more time was created for being a child. The infant might be baptized for good theological reasons, but later in life an understanding of the meaning of being a Christian and consent in joining the community of Christians were required. The individual undergoing the ritual was now treated as an adult, not a child, and as a subject, not an object. To take the eucharist for the first time at age seven, one needed enough awareness to understand the seriousness of the rite. But to

genere · · · exortus fit · ac duodennif fco
tradituf Benedicto · &

10. The Oblation of St. Maurus, eleventh century. Photographie du manuscrit 2273 de la
Bibliothèque municipale de Troyes, f. 45b. Reprinted with permission.

enter the religious life, a person needed to understand much more and to
consent before, not after, experiencing years of regimented living.

The same process of forming a new boundary between childhood and
adulthood may be seen even more clearly in the case of the Jewish bar mitzvah rite. The idea that there should be a single age of majority is less explicit
in Judaism than it would at first appear. If anything, age twenty is biblically
mandated, and rabbinic sources continue to emphasize age twenty as well as
age thirteen for males.[59] What then are we to make of the rabbinic text that
was added to Mishnah Avot sometime in the central Middle Ages, stating that
the proper start of religious majority is "at thirteen, (fulfilling) the commandments"? That text seems to be an expression of a unified ancient view on the
subject.

Ironically, the opposite seems to be the case. In the late antique world of rabbinic Judaism, when that passage in Tractate Avot was not considered to be part of the Mishnah, considerable latitude obtained about when one might begin to observe certain rituals of adult Judaism. In the central Middle Ages, by contrast, the age of thirteen began gaining influence, at least in Germany, as the one and only defining age of religious majority.[60]

To understand better this unexpected situation, we need to look at rabbinic and early medieval sources about age and required religious behavior. The Talmud developed several categories of religious activities that adult male Jews were obligated to do and that boys might do if they understood what was involved.[61] Two of these were putting on tefillin in daily worship with adult males and receiving the honor of being called to read the Torah in the synagogue. There is abundant evidence from geonic and early medieval European sources that attaining age thirteen was not a prerequisite for doing these acts. Indeed, there does not seem to have been a strict rule concerning age thirteen at all.[62]

Prior to the thirteenth century, young boys who had not yet reached age thirteen were permitted to perform these and other religious obligations of adult Jews. The permissive view was an extension of the general practice that fathers should accustom their sons to behave like adult Jews as soon as they were ready and not at a specific age. The specified ages were merely guidelines. For example, on days requiring a full evening-to-evening fast, boys were to begin by fasting a half day at age eleven and a full day at age twelve, in anticipation of the religious requirement to fast a full day by age thirteen. Curiously, there is no ceremony to demarcate such an important transition to adulthood at age thirteen. None was observed by the Jews of Yemen, who preserved ancient talmudic customs and practices throughout the Middle Ages, according to S. D. Goitein.[63]

In the late twelfth and thirteenth centuries, signs of opposition to a number of these earlier practices began to appear. R. Isaac b. Abba Mari of Marseilles (ca. 1120–ca. 1190), the author of Sefer ha-ʿIṭṭur, objected in Provence to boys' putting on tefillin before age thirteen, despite the talmudic text that permits it.[64] This objection may be a consequence of the fact that the text "at thirteen, (fulfilling) the commandments" was now considered part of the ancient Mishnah, but much still remains unclear about these changes. Although a major German-Jewish authority, R. Mordecai b. Hillel ha-Kohen, like R. Jacob

b. Meir Tam, ignored Isaac's opinion and held to the talmudic view that a father may buy his son tefillin as soon as the boy can take proper care of them. The Provençal scholar's viewpoint was a harbinger of things to come.[65]

In the sixteenth century, the Sephardic codifier R. Joseph Karo (1488–1575) continued to uphold the plain sense of the talmudic text, but R. Moses Isserles (1525/30–1572) disagreed with Karo.[66] The Polish scholar adopted Isaac's view: "The custom (minhag) is in accord with the author of the 'Iṭṭur, that minors should not put on tefillin until bar mitzvah, that is, thirteen years and a day."[67] The fact that Isserles thought it necessary to define the term bar mitzvah as meaning a boy age thirteen and a day suggests that this understanding of the term was not yet well known to his readers there. The talmudic term bar mitzvah originally meant an adult Jew who was responsible for a particular religious obligation; now the term was coming to mean a boy who had reached the minimum age for performing all religious obligations, and that age is defined as thirteen years and a day.

Isserles' insistence on a restriction of adult religious behavior, such as putting on tefillin, to boys who become bar mitzvah at age thirteen years and a day indicates that he connected this restriction with that new moment of transition in a boy's life. Elsewhere Isserles cites R. Jacob b. Moses ha-Levi Moellin (Maharil) of Mainz (1375–1427) to support the limiting of another religious duty to that age. Wherever it is not already permitted, he writes, a boy may not lead synagogue services as a cantor on the night after the Sabbath unless he already is at least thirteen years and a day old on the Sabbath in question. Isserles makes this ruling despite the fact that in the Shulḥan 'Arukh R. Joseph Karo explicitly permits minors to do this.[68]

Isserles' adoption of Maharil's limitation of the religious activities of putting on tefillin or of leading a congregation in prayer to boys age thirteen years and a day suggests that changes were occurring in late medieval Germany. Adult religious activities were being restricted to boys who were at least that age, and this moment was being referred to as "becoming bar mitzvah." In a different comment on Karo's Shulḥan 'Arukh, Isserles seems familiar with the new usage of the term bar mitzvah, but he objects to another custom connected with that transition, one that had also been observed in Germany by Maharil, who in turn attributed it to R. Mordecai b. Hillel ha-Kohen. These authorities would recite a regular blessing when a boy "became bar mitzvah," that is, one introduced by the standard formula that mentions the name of God: "Blessed are You, Lord our God, King of the universe." [69]

A hint of such a custom is already found in the ancient Palestinian commentary on Genesis, *Midrash Bereishit Rabbah*: "Whoever has a son who has reached the age of thirteen years should say the blessing: Blessed (is the One) Who has exempted me from (responsibility for) this one's punishment." Whereas the midrash phrases this blessing without the standard formula, the German rabbis whom Isserles cited included the words referring to God's special name and kingship (*shem u-malkhut*), and Isserles objected to this, since, he writes, "I have not found this blessing in the Talmud." [70]

This comment is another sign that according to late medieval German custom only boys who were at least thirteen years and a day old could observe adult religious behaviors. According to the Polish rabbinical authorities who reported it, that age was being called *bar mitzvah*, when some type of rite was being observed, such as the father's recitation of a fully formulated blessing.

Although it was still permissible in Germany during the thirteenth century for young boys to read from the Torah, this would soon change. Concerning the custom of calling minors to read the Torah, R. Isaac b. Moses of Vienna (ca. 1180–ca. 1250) observed that they are theoretically permitted to be called to read the Torah in the synagogue (in Germany), but the northern French rabbis had limited them to reading it once a year, on the festival of Simhat Torah. [71]

By the late fourteenth century, however, becoming bar mitzvah is increasingly being associated in Germany with the boy reading the Torah at age thirteen for the first time. The German provenance of a rudimentary bar mitzvah rite is illustrated in Maharil's own lifetime. About him it is reported: "When his son became bar mitzvah (*na'asah bar mitzvah*) he read the Torah and (Maharil) would bless him: 'Blessed are You, Lord our God, King of the universe, who exempted me from (responsibility for) this one's (punishment).' And this blessing is also (mentioned) in the Great (Book) of Mordecai (b. Hillel ha-Kohen), with God's name and kingship." [72]

R. Meir of Rothenburg found fault with some adult religious practices being permitted to children. Meir strongly objected to a children's practice that had been permitted for centuries, namely, counting a minor holding a prayer book or Torah scroll as part of a quorum of ten adult males in prayer services. It was an established Ashkenazic custom, and Meir opposed it, saying that one should leave the synagogue rather than participate in such a service. The trend was growing in Germany to prohibit religious acts formerly permitted to minors until they reached age thirteen.[73]

An additional indication of the German origins of some kind of ceremony marking the transition of bar mitzvah, possibly even accompanied by some formal learning or sermon, is hinted at in the remarks of another leading Polish rabbi, R. Shlomo Luria (Maharshal, 1570–1637). He observed that when a boy reached age thirteen, "the German Jews make a bar mitzvah feast" and "there is no greater feast than this. . . . One offers praise and gratitude to God that the young boy (na'ar) has been able to become bar mitzvah (lihiyot bar mitzvah) . . . and that the father has been able to raise him until now and initiate him into the entire Torah covenant (le-hakhniso bi-verit ha-Torah bi-khelalah)."[74]

The last phrase echoes the response recited at the end of a Jewish infant's circumcision ceremony: "As he has entered the covenant, so may he enter the Torah, the marriage chamber, and (a life of) good deeds." The second phrase is now being interpreted as the time of the child's religious maturity at age thirteen. It is not likely that the phrase "initiate him into the entire Torah covenant" connotes simply the boy sight-reading the Torah, a skill small children had acquired for centuries. Rather, it suggests some demonstration by the boy of his learning, although there is no way of determining what this was, and this interpretation may be reading in too much based on later evidence of a bar mitzvah derashah (learned speech).[75]

Apart from the German and Polish sources, an apparently independent tradition of a bar mitzvah ceremony is preserved from Provence, where R. Isaac b. Abba Mari had argued that tefillin should be restricted to boys thirteen years and a day. In Sefer Orḥot Ḥayyim, one of the two Provençal books that preserve versions of the children's school initiation ceremony, R. Aaron b. Jacob ha-Kohen of Lunel quotes the passage from Midrash Bereishit Rabbah about a father blessing his thirteen-year-old son and continues: "There are those who say it the first time their son goes up ('oleh) to read the Torah. And the Gaon R. Yehudai, of blessed memory, stood up in the synagogue and recited this blessing the first time his son read from the Torah."[76]

This tradition from fourteenth-century Provence indicates that some Jews there were following the earlier precedent set by one of the great rabbinic authorities of the early Middle Ages, R. Yehudai b. Nahman, Gaon of Sura in mid-eighth-century Baghdad. Perhaps this custom was still new, as Aaron seems to be arguing in favor of observing it, when he adduces the precedent of the revered Baghdadi sage as strong support for doing so. Although the Provençal text connects a son's reaching age thirteen to the time when he reads the Torah in the synagogue for the first time, and his father recites the special blessing, it does not call this occasion *bar mitzvah*, as do the texts from late medieval Germany and Poland.[77]

What has happened? Although each source from late medieval Germany or Poland should be seen for what it actually states and not be assumed to imply all of the elements mentioned in any one of them, a new picture does emerge. Some bar mitzvah customs had developed in Germany and were being diffused to Poland and apparently to Renaissance Italy as well. A boy at age thirteen years and a day is now being referred to as "becoming bar mitzvah." At least in some cases, he reads the Torah in public for the first time. On the occasion of his reaching this age, his father recites the special blessing, with or without the name and kingship formula. Some "German Jews" hold a festive meal when a boy reaches this status, perhaps when he demonstrates his learning.

The Polish rabbinic sources point to late thirteenth-century Germany as the origin of at least some of these customs, and it is in medieval Germany, as well as in Provence, that we find evidence of the restriction of adult religious practices to boys who have reached age thirteen. We do not yet see the fully developed bar mitzvah rite that appears later, as in Renaissance Italy, but together there is enough evidence to posit a relationship between rabbinic restrictions of adult religious practices to boys who have reached age thirteen and the subsequent development of various rites of passage, however preliminary, to mark this transition from childhood to religious adulthood.[78]

This change also means that up to age thirteen a Jewish child was not required to act like "a man on a smaller scale," to use Philippe Ariès's phrase.[79] Positively, it meant that the young male was required to be a child. The result of this important cultural process was that a boundary was being created at age thirteen between childhood and adulthood, after that age. In practice, as well as according to sacred texts, age thirteen and a day now meant something. Only then and not before could males put on tefillin, get called up to the Torah in the synagogue for the first time, and be counted in a minyan.

It was to bridge this new gap that the bar mitzvah ritual seems to have gradually developed in Germany in the late Middle Ages.[80] It marked the new transition between childhood, when certain adult religious rites were no longer permitted, and religious adulthood, when they were expected. Coming of age was marked, appropriately enough, by the boy's putting on tefillin for the first time and receiving an ʿaliyah to read the Torah in the synagogue, two of the very practices that had begun to be forbidden in late medieval Germany, the same place where the bar mitzvah rite first emerged some two centuries later.

Another new custom that indicates that during the later Middle Ages bar mitzvah replaced the school ritual is the Ashkenazic custom of the wimpel (figure 11). In Germany, a child's swaddling cloth used during the circumcision ceremony was kept, and his new name and a Hebrew phrase were embroidered on it. The inscribed phrase was an ancient text recited by those present at the boy's circumcision: "As he has entered the covenant, so may he enter the Torah, the marriage chamber, and (a life of) good deeds." In antiquity and the early Middle Ages, the phrase "enter the Torah" probably referred in a general way to the entire process of acquiring a religious education, leading to religious maturity up to age thirteen and a day. But in medieval Ashkenaz, where the school initiation developed and gradually disappeared, to be followed by bar mitzvah, the phrase became linked specifically to the age of thirteen and the public bar mitzvah ceremony in the synagogue.

The cloth that had been put away after being embroidered was used in the bar mitzvah ceremony as a Torah binder. The gesture of wrapping the Torah scroll with the same cloth that had once wrapped the infant at his circumcision dramatically linked the Jewish child with the Torah scroll, and also linked the two rites of passage: the ritual of bar mitzvah became the child's second initiation after circumcision. The school initiation was no longer remembered: it had been replaced by the bar mitzvah ceremony in the synagogue. Other important symbolic and ritual connections developed in Judaism between the child and the Torah scroll.[81]

The fact that the age of thirteen was now marked by a public celebration shows that there was a new emphasis in Ashkenaz on voluntary acceptance of religious responsibility. Membership in the adult Jewish community could no longer be achieved by mechanically going through the rituals but had to be accompanied by commitment, reasoned consent, and maturity. The prohibition had created an expanded conception of childhood. Or, a new awareness of childhood had prompted the new prohibitions. In either case, the result

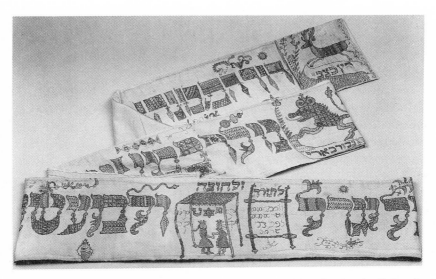

11. *Wimpel*/Torah binder, Schmalkalden, Germany, 1762. Linen embroidered with silk thread, 18 x 348 cm. © The Jewish Museum, New York, Gift of Dr. Harry G. Friedman, F 5096. Photo: John Parnell. Reprinted with permission.

was the emergence of a new stage of social maturation at age thirteen. It is not fortuitous, then, that a public ceremony, a new rite of passage, developed in Europe in the fifteenth century. Now, as the boy's thirteenth birthday approached, he was permitted to put on tefillin for the first time and to get used to doing so daily. On the Sabbath immediately following his thirteenth birthday, he was called to the Torah in the synagogue to read and recite the blessings in public. He was now recognized as an adult male in the synagogue, and a religious feast (se'udat mizvah) comparable to a wedding feast was held to mark this great occasion.

The new status accorded to childhood is reflected in other sources that speak not only of children but also of childhood, expressed as "the ways of children."[82] These are signs of a new consciousness of the separate state of being a child, not just the obvious fact of the existence of children.

The postponement of religious majority in Jewish culture to age thirteen is parallel to the deferral of oblation into a monastery in Cistercian houses and elsewhere, starting in the twelfth century, to age twelve or fourteen. Both practices reflect a conviction that maturity and mental consent are required of those entering the religious life. And acting like an adult Jew can be seen as similar to a Christian's following the rule of a religious order. For the adult Jew, the Torah is the rule that dictates appropriate behavior throughout the day and year, from the age of religious majority to death.

Of course, there was an important difference between the Jewish and Christian acceptance, even as a teenager, of religious obligations. In the Jewish community, every Jewish male became a bar mitzvah by virtue of his age, not because his parents singled him out. Christian parents, on the other hand, had to offer their child to a religious community. The question facing the Jewish child was whether he could practice adult religious gestures prior to age thirteen and a day, not, as in the Christian culture, whether he was being coerced into a life he had not freely chosen for himself.

The delay of the privileges of Jewish bar mitzvah to age thirteen and the postponement of Christian oblation to ages twelve or fourteen both express the attitude that membership in a religious community filled with rules and difficult regimens should be undertaken only by a person of sufficient maturity to be able to express consent in advance of doing them. The deferral of oblation in the Christian community and the deferral of adult religious obligations, including tefillin and public Torah honors, in the Jewish community, both reflect the cultural shift in the central Middle Ages from acts to reason.

In this regard, the history of initiations adds a new perspective on the way that children of different ages were viewed in medieval Europe. Ariès's controversial thesis that the idea of childhood is a product of the eighteenth century and that prior to this time children were regarded without special emotional attachment but as miniature adults is not substantiated in the Hebrew or other medieval materials.[83] But the issue of what view of childhood did obtain, where and when, can benefit from a cross-cultural analysis, especially when Jews and Christians lived side by side in medieval Europe.

What became of the medieval initiation ceremony? Elements of it persisted in schools, but not in most localities. It broke up into its constituent parts. The children's ancient pedagogic traditions remained in the school—the alphabet, the sweet foods as an enticement, and the waxed tablet. The ancient adult Shavuot traditions were separated from the child's entrance into schooling and continued as adult practices on Shavuot—special Torah study and the eating of Torah foods such as those made from flour, milk, oil, honey, or sugar.[84] If anyone continued to eat letters baked on cakes or written on eggs on Shavuot, it was adults, as reflected in the magical formularies, not children beginning school.

Children tended to enter school, as in ancient rabbinic times, whenever they were ready, not just on Shavuot. Adults continued to associate special foods with the holiday. The incantation against POTAH, the prince of forgetfulness, continued, not in the child's initiation, but in the weekly havdalah ceremony practiced in the home by the family and in the synagogue by the entire community at the end of the Sabbath. Its pedagogic function in schooling, like its namesake, forgetfulness, was forgotten.

One element in the medieval initiation ceremony persisted down to modern times but migrated to a different time of the year. The custom of giving schoolchildren honey cakes is no longer associated with the Shavuot holiday in the spring but now comes at Rosh Hashanah, the Jewish New Year, in the fall. This custom is a merging of two separate sets of food symbols.[85] Since in Jewish tradition the New Year is thought to be the anniversary of the day the world was created, marking it by eating honey was understood to represent that the entire cosmos was a divine gift. But honey need not be given to children in the form of a sweetened cake. In Ashkenaz, adults customarily eat red apples and honey.[86] The honey cake is a faint trace of the medieval school initiation rite. And since children begin their studies in September, the associations of honey with school and with the Jewish New Year have been merged — a contemporary equation of honey cakes and Torah.

Notes

Abbreviations

B.   Babylonian Talmud
b.   ben, son of
M.   Mishnah
Migne, PL   *Patrologiae cursus completus.* Series Latina. Edited by J. P. Migne. 221 vols. Paris, 1844–64.
MGH   Monumenta Germanica Historiae
QS   Qumran Scroll
R.   Rabbi
T.   Tosefta
Y.   Yerushalmi (Palestinian) Talmud

Notes to Chapter One Introduction

1. Earlier written traditions encourage a father to begin to teach his son Torah "once an infant begins to talk" (*Sifre on Deuteronomy*, Eiqev 11, sec. 46, Finkelstein, 104; Hammer, *Sifre*, 98; T. Ḥagiga 1,2, Lieberman, 375; B. Sukkah 42a and parallels; *Shulḥan ʿArukh*, Yoreh Deʿah, par. 245:5). All of the medieval texts and the illumination about the ceremony, presented in more detail in chapter 2, take for granted that the child will be initiated into schooling no earlier than age five. Compare *Midrash Tanḥuma* on Leviticus 19:23; Buber, 3:79; and see chapter 3. We lack any anecdotal information, independent of the texts, about how old the children were when they underwent the ceremony, and it is possible that they did so anywhere from age three to age six.

2. In the Hebrew Bible, what was called Shavuot in rabbinic Judaism was the festival of the wheat harvest (Lev. 23:9–22; Num. 28:26); its identification as the date when the Torah was given to Israel is postbiblical. See B. Shabbat 88a, and compare the Book of Jubilees 1:1–6, 6:17–20. Pentecost was the occasion in the New Testament when the Holy Spirit descended upon the apostles, thereby founding the early church. See Acts 2:1–4 and the discussion below.

3. On *lev* as mind, see Ginsberg, "Heart."

4. Davis, "Rites of Violence," 152–87. I am writing a separate study about Jews and Christians imagining the other and themselves. It will treat the ways Jews and Christians repre-

sented the other and themselves by making use of the symbols and imagery of the other's religious culture while inverting and subverting them. See Bonfil, *Jewish Life in Renaissance Italy*, 1–15, and Marcus, "Jews and Christians."

5. Jacob Katz applied a sociological methodology to the historical interpretation of Jewish legal sources in *Exclusiveness and Tolerance, Tradition and Crisis*, and *The "Shabbes Goy."* A cultural anthropology of Jewish law would be a demanding but worthwhile study. On polemics, see Cohen, "Towards a Functional Classification," 93–114, which includes the study of the symbolic rhetoric of narratives (98–99). Cf. Schechter, "Nachmanides," 104.

6. I refer to Carlo Ginzburg's important discussion of "circular, reciprocal influence between the cultures of subordinate and ruling classes" in *The Cheese*, xvii. The use of the term *elite* implies that popular culture is the alternative. I am suggesting that we aim for a way to understand cultures whole. See Scribner, "Is a History of Popular Culture Possible?" 175–91. The classical statement is Geertz, "Religion as a Cultural Symbol," 1–46, reprinted in his *Interpretation of Cultures*, 87–125.

7. The journal *Annales* has been in the forefront of historical anthropology since its founding by Marc Bloch and Lucien Febvre in 1929. See Le Goff, "Préface" to Marc Bloch, *Les rois thaumaturges*, ii, who refers to Bloch as "le fondateur de l'anthropologie historique." For an important collection of studies from this journal in translation, see Forster and Ranum, *Ritual, Religion, and the Sacred*. In addition, the approach has been fostered by important studies such as Thomas, *Religion and the Decline of Magic*; Ladurie, *Montaillou*; Ginzburg, *The Cheese*, esp. xiii–xxvi, *Night Battles*, and *Ecstasies*, which all belong to a growing canon. See, too, Burke, *Historical Anthropology*, esp. his introduction, which addresses the question "What is historical anthropology?" Among American historians, see Davis, *Society and Culture*, *The Return of Martin Guerre*, and *From the Archives*, as well as her important theoretical essay "Some Tasks and Themes," 307–36; also Darnton, *Great Cat Massacre* and "The Symbolic Element in History," 218–34.

8. The literature on ritual is vast and has been used selectively. Of special importance is Leach, "Ritual," 520–26; Zuesse, "Ritual," 405–22, with extensive bibliography; "Meditation on Ritual," 517–30; Turner, *Ritual Process* and *Dramas, Fields and Metaphors*; and Smith, *To Take Place*.

9. Boon, *Other Tribes, Other Scribes*, 7–9. See, too, Clifford, "On Ethnographic Authority," 118–46; Feeley-Harnik, "Is Historical Anthropology Possible?" 99; and Clifford and Marcus, *Writing Culture*.

10. For a recent discussion of anthropological methods and the study of Judaism, see Eilberg-Schwartz, *Savage in Judaism*, chapters 1–4, who calls for "the conception of Judaism as a religious culture" (237), and "Voyeurism, Anthropology and the Study of Judaism"; Marcus, "Medieval Jewish Studies," 113–127, and "History, Story and Collective Memory," 365–88, esp. 365–68, which contrasts positivist and folklore approaches to that of anthropological history; Horowitz, "The Way We Were," 75–90, and "Coffee, Coffee Houses, and the Nocturnal Rituals of Early Modern Jewry," 17, esp. his reference there to "a social history of piety"; Goldberg, Introduction, 1–43; Bonfil, "Myth, Rhetoric and History?" 107n29; Epstein, " 'The Ways of Truth,' " 225n4.

11. See Eilberg-Schwartz, *Savage in Judaism*, and Goldberg, Introduction. Most of the studies are ancient and modern in Eilberg-Schwartz, *People of the Body*. A successful ethnographic account, using the fieldwork approach in a contemporary synagogue, is Heilman, *Synagogue Life*.

12. On narratives, see esp. Bonfil, "Between the Land of Israel and Babylonia," "Myth, Rhetoric and History?" and "Can Medieval Storytelling Help Understanding Midrash?"; Marcus, "History, Story and Collective Memory" and "Une communauté pieuse et le doute."

The 1096 Hebrew First Crusade narratives especially lend themselves to an analysis of Jewish-Christian social polemic. See Marcus, "From Politics," 40–52; Abulafia, "Invectives against Christianity," 66–72; Cohen, "Towards a Functional Classification," 98–99, " '1096 Persecution Narratives' "; and Chazan, European Jewry.

13. A model of a new type of medieval European cultural history is Rubin, Corpus Christi. See also Bonfil, Jewish Life in Renaissance Italy.

14. For some of the problems using rabbinic legal sources for the history of Jewish law, see Soloveitchik, "Can Halakhic Texts Talk History?" and She'eilot u-Teshuvot ke-Maqor Histori. Even when scholars discuss folklore, they sometimes privilege those customs that are legal in character and dismiss others as "just folklore." See Ta-Shema, Minhag Ashkenaz ha-Qadmon, 39. On p. 21: "The 'minhag' that concerns us here is any religious behavior that has halakhic [legal] or quasi-halakhic force but no source in the Talmud," to which he contrasts "folk behavior lacking religious value ('asiyyah 'amamit ḥasrat 'erekh dati)." See 21n15 and 39–42.

15. For a survey of these genres, see Marcus, "Jews in Western Europe," 31–66, and "Jews in the Medieval World," 70–91.

16. On ceremony as a secular and conservative type of ritual, see Alexander, "Ceremony," 179–83. The term will be used interchangeably with ritual and rite.

17. Zuesse, "Meditation on Ritual," 518. On symbolism, see Sperber, Rethinking Symbolism, 85–113.

18. Price, Rituals and Power, 7.

19. See Elbogen, Jewish Liturgy, and Zimmer, "Body Gestures during Prayer"; Trexler, The Christian at Prayer; and, more generally, Schmitt, "Introduction and General Bibliography" and La raison des gestes. For a preliminary effort to study Jewish prayer gestures in relation to a group's religious worldview, see Marcus, "Prayer Gestures in German Hasidism."

20. There is important material in the often neglected masterly cultural history of Güdemann, Geschichte des Erziehungswesens; and see Abrahams, Jewish Life in the Middle Ages. Many gestures are described as Jewish "magic" in Trachtenberg, Jewish Magic and Superstition, and abundant data about gestures, clothing, and other realia are available in Metzger and Metzger, Jewish Life in the Middle Ages; but see Horowitz, "The Way We Were." Two basic historical studies of Jewish customs which include rites of passage are the still definitive Löw, Lebensalter, and the more popular compendium, Schauss, Lifetime.

21. See Fernandez, "Performance of Ritual Metaphors" and "Persuasions and Performances."

22. See Crocker, "My Brother the Parrot"; Smith, "I am a Parrot (Red)"; and Turner, " 'We are Parrots,' 'Twins are Birds.' "

23. For the idea of an Ashkenazic self-image of Temple holiness and piety, see Baer, Yisrael ba-'Amim, and Mintz, Ḥurban, 93–98. Applied to the medieval Ashkenazic religious legal tradition, see Soloveitchik, "Religious Law and Change" and Halakhah, Kalkalah, ve-Dimui 'Azmi; and Marcus, "From Politics" and "Dynamics of Ashkenaz." Among the most important biblical sources for this idea, see Ezra 9:2, Isaiah 62:12 and 63:18, and Ezekiel 11:16. Gerson D. Cohen

developed the late biblical idea of the Jewish people being viewed as holy from a comparison of Ezra 9:2 (ma'al)–10:11 and Joshua 7:2 (ma'al)–26 in seminars that he taught in 1969.

24. See Eilberg-Schwartz, *Savage in Judaism*, chapters 5–7, and Goldberg, *Jewish Life in Muslim Libya*, chapter 6. Worth considering are the various ways in which customs can be related to texts. In addition to acting out metaphors found in canonical texts, rituals may be based on puns and word plays, such as the talmudic traditions that recommend eating specific foods on Rosh Hashanah (B. Keritot 6a; B. Horayot 12a) because their Aramaic names are homophones of significant words associated with the festival mood. For example, one should eat beets (Aramaic: *silqa*) and recite, "May it be (Your) will that our enemies disappear (Hebrew: *yistalqu*)"; or eat pumpkin (Aramaic: *qera'*) and say, "May (You) tear up (Hebrew: *yiqra'*) our adverse judgment (in the New Year) and may our virtues call out (*yiqre'u*) before You." See R. Joseph Karo, *Shulhan 'Arukh, Orah Hayyim*, par. 583:1, and Goldberg, "Anthropology and the Study of Traditional Jewish Societies," 15–16 and references.

In a private communication (30 January 1994), Goldberg proposes further that one might even look at the reverse phenomenon, the "metaphorization of ritual," in which a custom is transferred from its original setting to a new, "metaphoric" one. For example, "blowing the shofar [mandated for Rosh Hashanah] on Hoshanah Rabbah [the conclusion of the Sukkot festival three weeks later] . . . organizing *sedarim* [Passover eve ritualized meals] for various occasions—Hoshanah Rabbah eve or Tu Bishvat [the fifteenth of the month of Shevat]." One might also study how Jewish wedding customs—lifting the person on a chair in dance, throwing candies at the person in the synagogue, songs about bride and groom—have been transferred to bar mitzvah celebrations, at least in the United States.

25. See Rubin, *Corpus Christi*, and Schmitt, *La raison des gestes*.

26. See Cohen, "Messianic Postures," 36–38; Chazan, *European Jewry*; and Marcus, "From Politics," as well as Riley-Smith, *Crusades*, 16–20.

27. For an influential early medieval Hebrew account of Jews killing their own families at Masada, see *Sefer Yosippon*, 430: "On the morn, they took their wives, sons, and daughters and slaughtered them." Although the men who kill their families at Masada die in battle and not by their own hands, another medieval Italian text describes suicidal martyrdom, again using the verb *slaughter*. See Mann, *Texts and Studies*, 1:24 lines 8–9.

28. The three Hebrew texts were published in Neubauer and Stern, *Hebräische Berichte*, with a German translation, and again in Hebrew in Habermann, *Sefer Gezeirot Ashkenaz ve-Zarfat*. All three are available in English in Eidelberg, *Jews and the Crusaders*, and two of them are translated in appendices to Chazan, *European Jewry*.

29. See Spiegel, *Legend*, 482–83, 497, 510, 527–28; Goldin, *Last Trial*, esp. 26–27, 60, 86, 118–119; Cohen, "Philosophical Exegesis," 135–42nn13,14 and the bibliography cited there. The significance in Christian exegesis of the sacrificed Isaac as Christ also shaped the Jewish narrative: the many Jewish sacrifices exceeded the single earlier sacrifice of Isaac/Jesus. See Vermes, "Redemption and Genesis XXII." Compare Cohen, "'1096 Persecution Narratives.'"

30. See Graetz, "The Structure of Jewish History," 117–19, 138–39, 267–68.

31. Most nineteenth-century German Jewish scholars who accepted this dichotomy also expressed a preference for Muslim Spain to Christian Ashkenaz. The value-laden framework of each camp suggests that the interpretation itself was a construct by which scholars pro-

jected the present onto the medieval past. Exceptions to the pro-Spain bias were Leopold
Zunz, who wrote the first biographical sketch of R. Solomon Yiẓḥaqi or Rashi of Troyes
(ca. 1040–1105) and Moritz Güdemann, who explained that Ashkenaz was more authentically
Jewish because it did not slavishly imitate non-Jewish cultural models. See Zunz, "Salomon
ben Isaac genannt Raschi," 277–385; Güdemann, *Geschichte des Erziehungswesens*, 1:13–14; and
Schorsch, "From Wolfenbüttel to Wissenschaft," 124–25, "Moritz Güdemann," 42–66, and
"The Myth of Sephardic Supremacy," 47–66. For a balanced assessment, see Cohen, *Under
Crescent and Cross*.

32. The notion of symbiosis is closely identified with S. D. Goitein, but the overall historical argument goes back to the nineteenth century. See Goitein, *Jews and Arabs*, 6 and
index under "Symbiosis, Arab-Jewish." It is illustrated throughout Goitein's masterpiece,
A Mediterranean Society. See, too, G. D. Cohen, Introduction, xiii–xlii.

33. See Schirmann, "Samuel the Nagid," and Stern, "Life of Shmuel ha-Nagid."

34. See Marx, "Moses Maimonides," 87–111; Twersky, *Introduction*; Pines, Introduction,
xi–cxxxiv. For 1138 as the year of Maimonides' birth instead of the conventional 1135, see
Havlin, "Moshe ben Maimon," 536, and Goitein, "Moses Maimonides, Man of Action," 155.

35. This view may be inferred from the work of four generations of scholars who have
written collective rabbinic biographies in Christian Europe. See Aptowitzer, *Mavo*; Urbach,
Ba'alei ha-Tosafot; Grossman, *Ḥakhmei Ashkenaz*; and Yuval, *Ḥakhamim*.

36. See Grossman, *Ḥakhmei Ashkenaz*. The aside in E. E. Urbach's encyclopedic *Ba'alei ha-
Tosafot*, 17–21, concerning the parallel twelfth-century phenomenon of scholastic analysis
in the University of Paris and the simultaneous development of dialectic applied to canon
and Roman legal corpora in Bologna has not been pursued systematically as part of the
"renaissance of the twelfth century." But see Ben-Sasson, "On Chronographical Tendencies,"
393–401, and chapter 6, note 1.

37. Among the significant earlier exceptions are Güdemann, *Geschichte des Erziehungswesens*,
Yizhak Baer's studies, such as his comparison of the piety of St. Francis of Assisi to that in
the Hebrew Rhenish work *Sefer Ḥasidim*, and his study of Rashi's historical context. See Baer,
"Religious-Social Tendency," "Rashi," and "Mystical Teachings." See, too, Ben-Sasson, "Assimilation." Robert Chazan, *European Jewry*, 5, 193–97, 324, notes the persistence of the general
historiographic trend and observes that Baer was a complex exception to the rule. Among
other studies that hint at Ashkenazic integration, see Soloveitchik, "Three Themes," Kanarfogel, *Jewish Education*, 70–72. For studies that stress how Ashkenazic culture was aware of and
responded to Christian cultural symbols, see Marcus, "From Politics," and Cohen, "'1096
Persecution Narratives,'" 175, where Cohen contrasts a newer approach to the persisting
consensus: "Ashkenazic Jewry was integrated (mushreshet) in the Christian world in which it
lived much more than is usually thought to be the case"; and see below.

38. For medieval French, see Banitt, "Une langue phantôme"; for Jews using the Latin term
dialectica, see Baer, "Religious-Social Tendency," 11. Also see Marcus, "Judeo-Latin," 176–77.
On Jewish customs influenced by Christian practices, in addition to Güdemann, *Geschichte des
Erziehungswesens*, see Gutmann, "Christian Influences."

39. See the polemical remarks found only in the early printings of E. E. Urbach's edition
of R. Abraham b. Azriel's medieval Ashkenazic liturgical commentary *Sefer 'Arugat ha-Bosem*,

1:12–13, against Yitzhak Baer's argument, in "Religious-Social Tendency," that there was a dependent relationship between medieval German-Jewish pietist ideas and contemporary Christian influence. Cf. Cohen, "Messianic Postures," 38.

40. Scheindlin, *Wine, Women, and Death* and *The Gazelle*.

41. Of course, there were courts in Christian Europe, and some Jews played roles in them in Carolingian times and later in the German empire, as well as in England and Christian Spain, but historians have paid less attention to them than the more famous Muslim-Sephardic examples. On Jews in the court of Charlemagne's son Louis the Pious, see Cabaniss, "Bodo-Eleazar," and Bonfil, "Evidence of Agobard of Lyons"; on Frederick Barbarossa's court, Urbach, *Ba'alei ha-Tosafot*, 362, 414; on England, Roth, *History of the Jews in England*, 29–31, 111–13; and for Christian Spain, Baer, *History of the Jews in Christian Spain*, 1:50–51, 112–13, 120–26, 130–47, 162–71, 307–11, 325–27, 362–64.

42. See Smalley, *Study of the Bible*, and the exaggerated claims of Shereshevsky, "Hebrew Traditions," 268–89, and Touitou, "Quelques aspects," 35–39. More balanced is Graboïs, "The *Hebraica Veritas*," 613–34, and "L'exégèse rabbinique," but see the revision by Langmuir, "AHR Forum: Comment," 622, and Jordan, *French Monarchy*, 11–22.

43. For an introduction to the literature, see Cohen, "Towards a Functional Classification" and the copious notes in *Nizzahon Vetus*.

44. See Rosenthal, "The Study of the Bible," 2:252–79, and the classic study of northern French Jewish biblical exegesis, Poznanski, Introduction.

45. For important connections between a polemical agenda and plain-sense biblical exegesis in northern France, see Grossman, "The Jewish-Christian Polemic" and "Exile and Redemption," and the assessment by Cohen, "Towards a Functional Classification," 98–99. Grossman argues elsewhere that part of the stimulus for northern French Jewish Bible exegetes to stress the plain sense was the influence of Spanish-Jewish models. See Grossman, "Between Spain and France," 84–88.

46. See Bonfil, *Jewish Life in Renaissance Italy*, esp. 2–3, 6–9, 102–3, 105, 208.

47. Roth, *Jews in the Renaissance*.

48. Butterfield, *Whig Interpretation of History*.

49. It should be remembered that Jewish borrowings of Christian motifs need not presuppose Jews' ability to read Latin, which was much more limited than their Arabic fluency in Muslim societies. For case studies of modern acculturation, see Katz, *Tradition and Crisis*; Hyman, *Emancipation*, Index, under "acculturation" in the modern sense. Compare Bonfil, *Jewish Life in Renaissance Italy*, 6–7. A premodern exception would be Jews who flirted with Christianity or were ambivalent but did not convert.

50. See Marcus, "From Politics"; Gutmann, "Christian Influences"; Cohen, "'1096 Persecution Narratives'"; Malkiel, "Infanticide in Passover Iconography"; Epstein, "Elephant and the Law," *Dreams of Subversion*, and "'Ways of Truth'"; and Horowitz, "'And It Was Reversed'" and "The Rite to Be Reckless."

51. Van Gennep, *Rites of Passage*. On circumcision, see Marcus, "Circumcision, Jewish"; on marriage, Schauss, *Lifetime*, 156–57, 161–65; on mourning, Schauss, *Lifetime*, 234, 253.

52. Schauss, *Lifetime*, 112–15; Weinstein, "Rites of Passage," 82. One can ask if the prescription, in *Midrash Bereishit Rabbah*, par. 63, Theodor-Albeck, 2:693, for a father to recite a special

benediction when his son reaches age thirteen is not a ritual marker of some kind, but the text is suggestive rather than probative. See also the discussion in chapter 6.

53. The shock of this encounter may be compared with the worldview of Menocchio, the miller of Friuli, whom Carlo Ginzburg has suggested came to his ancient views under the shock of Counter-Reformation pressures. See *The Cheese*, 20–21.

54. For the expression, see Jordan, *French Monarchy*, 10.

Notes to Chapter Two *The Initiation Rite*

1. For a study of this custom in Eastern European Jewish schools and the Yiddish phrase, see Roskies, "Alphabet Instruction," 25. The expression is mentioned in the *Brantspiegel*, 178a, a Yiddish book of Jewish customs compiled by Moses b. Henikh (d. 1633); see also Yudlov, "Italian Alphabet Charts." For later examples, without the illustration, see Roskies, "Alphabet Instruction," 38. The historical relationship between the visualization of the angel motif in the Italian-Jewish alphabet charts and the Yiddish expression is unclear.

2. See Spamer, "Sitte und Brauch," 2:165, fig. 181: "Mädchen am ersten Schultag mit Zucker-tüte. Dresden, 1930"; Schmidt, *Volksglaube und Volksbrauch*, 260–74; Pilgram, "Geschenke an Schulanfänger," 56–69.

3. There are examples of teaching children the alphabet in antiquity by feeding them cakes shaped as the letters of the alphabet or imprinted on alphabets. See Horace, *Serm.*, 1.1.25–26, and Marrou, *History of Education in Antiquity*, 367; Bonner, *Education in Ancient Rome*, 165–66. On alphabet cakes in Ireland, see Gaidoz, "Les gâteaux alphabétiques," 1–8.

4. Moses b. Maimon (Maimonides), *Peirush ha-Mishnah*, Introduction to Sanhedrin, chapter 10, 2:134.

5. Abraham b. Moses Maimuni, "Iggrot Qena'ot," f. 18a. The word *qaliyot* refers to parched grains of wheat that were mixed with nuts and given to children as a delicacy. See B. Pesahim 109a, where there is a tradition that this combination was given to children to keep them up late on the eve of Passover. Its exact meaning in thirteenth-century Egypt, when Abraham Maimuni wrote, is not clear.

6. R. Judah b. Samuel, the Pietist, *Sefer Hasidim*, Parma MS, par. 764, 193. On the hundreds of exempla in the book, see Dan, *Ha-Sippur ha-'Ivri*, chapter 18, and Yassif, "*Exempla* in *Sefer Hasidim*," 217–55. Some of the more elaborate narratives are discussed in Alexander-Frizer, *Pious Sinner*, and several are translated in Judah b. Samuel, he-Hasid, "Narrative Fantasies from *Sefer Hasidim*," 215–38.

7. Canetti, *Tongue Set Free*, 85.

8. Addison, *Present State of the Jews*, 83–84.

9. See Horowitz, "'A Different Mode of Civility,'" 309–25.

10. The name is written first in Hebrew characters and then in Roman letters.

11. See Buxtorf, *Synagoga Iudaica*, 153, translated in A[lexander] R[oss], *A View of Jewish Religion*, 90.

12. Meir b. Isaac Aldabi, *Shevilei Emunah* (Paths of Faith). The passage, which I have not located in the first edition, is quoted in chapter 46 of the *Brantspiegel*, f. 175a–175b. The excerpt from the *Brantspiegel* about the child being fed sweets before going to school was published

in Assaf, *Meqorot*, 1:58, and also appeared in Twersky, "Jewish Education in Medieval Europe," 4:256.

13. Briggs and Guède, *No More For Ever*, 28–31.

14. Although the kittab takes place in the spring, it is not connected with Shavuot. The Moroccan water feast is a Shavuot custom that takes place during the afternoon of the second day of the festival, when people pour water on well-dressed members of the community or select a member to atone for the community's sins by being dunked in the river. No one knows the origins of this practice, but the local explanation is that it is because the Torah is compared to water, and Shavuot marks the giving of Torah. See Davis, "Moroccan Water-Feast," 4; Hirschberg, *History of the Jews in North Africa*, 1:169–70, and Mordechai Hakohen, *Book of Mordechai*, 110.

15. The phrase "ḥatan ha-simḥah" connotes bridegroom (ḥatan) but may mean just "birth-day boy," since ḥatan can mean "young child" (tinoq). The word ḥatan for "child" is ancient, was used in medieval Hebrew, and has a cognate, "HaTaN," in Arabic. The Hebrew is de-rived from the biblical phrase ḥatan damim (bridegroom of blood) (Exod. 4:24–25), asso-ciated with the circumcision of Moses' son. For talmudic and Arabic examples, see Kohut, *'Arukh ha-Shalem*, 2:522, based on R. Natan b. Yehiel, *'Arukh*. The usage of ḥatan as "guest of honor" or recipient of an honor is a common contemporary Israeli idiom, as in the win-ner of an important prize, who is called ḥatan peras. . . . It may be closer to "laureate," and for the same reason. The ancient Greeks and medieval Jews and Muslims placed a garland of laurel or flowers on the honoree's head. A related contemporary example is the Israeli kindergarten birthday party ceremony held in school on the child's birthday. A garland of flowers is placed on the child's head, and children offer blessings: May you grow up to be a good soldier, get promoted to first grade, etc. See Shamgar-Handelman and Handelman, "Celebrations of Bureaucracy," 293–312, esp. 298, "the garland"; and Weil, "Language and Ritual of Socialization," 329–41.

16. In a brief conversation (17 April 1988) about the ethnographic or literary source of the song, the composer and performer Shlomo Bar said that it was based on a custom and not taken from a written source.

17. It was also a custom in southeastern Morocco. See Briggs and Guède, *No More For Ever*, 29.

18. The names Todga and Tudra could refer to the same place. The Arabic letters ra' and ghain are gutterals and can be pronounced alike. On the location, see Bartholomew, *Times Atlas of the World*, 4, plate 88.

19. B. Qiddushin 29a, quoted in chapter 3.

20. On Shavuot and the wedding motif between God and Israel at Sinai celebrated in Morocco, see Wasserteil, *Minhagei Yisrael*, 265; Dobrinsky, *Treasury of Sephardic Laws and Customs*, 288. There is such a tradition in the *Zohar*, III, 97a–98b, which was probably part of ancient Judaism. See Liebes, "Messiah of the Zohar," 74–82. On the term ḥatan Torah, see Sperber, *Minhagei Yisrael*, 135–37.

21. See Zafrani, "Traditional Jewish Education in Morocco," 126.

22. Although this precise age is strange, the child is not yet five, as in the kittab ceremony in Gharaia.

23. Goldman, *Search for God at Harvard*, 232. Professor Schimmel replied to my letter, which was prompted by Goldman's reference, as follows: "I am not aware of early written sources

such as *hadith*, but I have come across the custom in various parts of the Islamic world, as the Arabic letters of the *basmala*, and in fact all letters, are considered to be filled with *baraka*, which can be acquired by drinking the water or honey which was in touch [with] them. Very frequent are therefore the metal bowls with Arabic inscriptions—in part seemingly meaningless letters—from which a sick person would drink water in order to be healed. Such bowls, which are preserved in many museums, are known from the Middle Ages. . . . I know the custom basically from my own experience in India and from accounts of Islamic folklore from various times, but not from Arabic texts." Letter of 7 July 1991.

24. Daiches, *Babylonian Oil Magic*, 26; *Greek Magical Papyri*, 13; similar rituals are mentioned in *Heikhalot Zuṭarti*, quoted in Schäfer, "Jewish Magic Literature," 90, and discussed below in chapter 5. Ethnographic evidence of a Kurdish initiation combines writing the alphabet and smearing honey on it, as in Ashkenaz, but motivating the ceremony by the formula, typical of the Sephardic variations, "Oh, God, as the honey is sweet, so may the Torah be sweet in this boy's mouth." See Brauer, *Yehudei Kurdistan*, 200, cited in Goldberg, "Torah and Children," 114.

25. There was a debate in geonic times, that is, when *geonim* or rabbinic masters in medieval Baghdad were dominant (eighth–eleventh centuries), about whether Genesis or Leviticus should be the first book Jewish children studied after they learned the alphabet. In tenth-century North Africa the practice still was to begin with Leviticus, although popular tales circulated there which assumed that Genesis was studied first. See Yassif, "Hebrew Narrative in Eastern Lands," 58–61. The text is in Nissim b. Jacob Ibn Shahin, *Ḥibbur Yafeh mei-ha-Yeshu'ah*, 51; Brinner, *Elegant Composition*, 86–87 and 88–89.

26. Compare the illustration in figure 1, which portrays this contrast. In the Kurdish ceremony, after the child licks the honey, those who brought the boy to school say to the teacher, "The flesh is yours; the bones are ours," that is, discipline is permitted but should be restrained. See Brauer, *Yehudei Kurdistan*, 200, and B. Bava Batra 21a: "When you punish a pupil, hit him only with a shoelace." See, too, Guibert de Nogent, *Memoirs*, bk. 1, ch. 5–6, pp. 48–50.

27. Fano, 1505; Cremona, 1557; Jerusalem, 1960, with paragraph numbers added after the first edition. The translation follows ed. Fano. The book is a collection of customs and laws that Eleazar wrote down in the late twelfth- or early thirteenth-century Rhineland. The ceremony is described in par. 296. On Eleazar, see Kamelhar, *Rabbeinu Eleazar b. Yehudah*; Marcus, *Piety and Society*, esp. chapters 7 and 8.

28. See B. Berakhot 16b.

29. B. Pesaḥim 50b; *Midrash Bereishit Rabbah*, Va-Yeira, sec. 48, Theodor-Albeck, 2:491; Y. Ta'anit 1:6, 64c; Y. Pesaḥim 1:1, 30c.

30. So MS Paris, ed. Fano and ed. Cremona. Later editions, such as ed. Jerusalem, 1960, read "*Aggadat Shir ha-Shirim*." I have not found this phrase in *Aggadat Shir ha-Shirim*, which Solomon Schechter published from defective manuscripts, or in *Midrash Shir ha-Shirim*, ed. Lazar Grünhut, or in *Shir ha-Shirim Rabbah*, and it may refer to a different text or be missing from the manuscripts of one of those.

31. This important book of Jewish law and tradition from medieval Germany has never been published in its entirety. It survives in a single manuscript, London, Jews College 134 (Montefiore 115). The passage is found on f. 67a and was published a number of times; see

Assaf, *Meqorot*, 4:11–12, and Stern, "Torah Education Rite," 20–21. Heinrich Gross noted that the compiler refers to Eleazar of Worms as one of his teachers, and this may explain the identical beginnings of the description in *Sefer ha-Roqeaḥ* and *Sefer ha-Asufot* and suggests that priority should be assigned to the former. See Gross, "Das Handschriftliche Werk Assufot," 64–87.

32. See Amir, "Place of Psalm 119," 56–81.

33. The name of this figure (POTAḤ or PURAH) has been disputed but seems likely to be related to the Hebrew verb PTḤ ("open") and to have been assimilated to the biblical word *purah* in Isaiah 63:3. See Heller, "Le nom divin de vingt-deux lettres," 69–70, and Krauss, "Note sur le nom divin de vingt-deux lettres," 253–54; cf. "Havdalah de-Rabbi Aqivah," 278–79, where Gershom Scholem argues that *poteh* (seducer) is the original name. I tend to think that *poteh*, like *purah*, is secondary to *potaḥ* (opener), but it is impossible to determine this.

34. The names are found in the so-called magical *Havdalah de-Rabbi ʿAqiva* as well as *Seder Rav ʿAmram Gaon*, both from approximately ninth-century Babylonia, but they were also incorporated into the classical Jewish legal codes that describe the ceremony with which the Jewish Sabbath concludes, even though they are omitted in later printed editions. In addition to Scholem, "Havdalah de-Rabbi ʿAqiva," see *Seder Rav ʿAmram Gaon*, 83; R. Isaac b. Judah Ibn Giyyat, *Meʾah Sheʿarim*, 15; and R. Jacob b. R. Asher, *Arbaʿah Ṭurim*, par. 298, both of whom quote the text from *Seder Rav ʿAmram*.

35. Hamburg, Staats- und Universitätsbibliothek, Hebrew MS 17 (Steinschneider Cat. no. 152), f. 81a–82b, reprinted in a facsimile edition in Roth, Cod. hebr. 17. Moritz Steinschneider noted that Zunz had identified a reference to "my brother Abraham" in this manuscript as the brother of R. Meir b. Barukh of Rothenburg (d. 1293). See Steinschneider, *Catalog der hebräischen Handschriften*, 56–58. This attribution remains uncertain but probable. If reliable, it would place this text chronologically after *Sefer ha-Roqeaḥ* (early thirteenth century) and *Sefer ha-Asufot* (mid-thirteenth century). The passage was published by Roth, "Educating Jewish Children on Shavuot," 9–12, and Stern, "Torah Education Rite," 17–19.

36. Psalm 19 is the special Psalm recited on Shavuot.

37. The presence of three eggs and three cakes is also a feature of the ritual as described in the northern French *Maḥzor Vitry*. See below.

38. Leipzig, Universitätsbibliothek, Hebrew MS V. 1102, vol. 1, f. 131a. The manuscript is from southern Germany, ca. 1320. See Narkiss, Introduction, and facsimile plate 29.

39. See Davidson, *Oẓar ha-Shirah ve-ha-Piyyuṭ, aleph*, #484, 1:24.

40. See Narkiss, Introduction, 97, who missed the reference to this part of the illumination in *Sefer ha-Asufot*. For other meanings of the prominence of the river scene, see chapter 5.

41. On this book, generally attributed to R. Simḥa of Vitry, Rashi's student's contemporary (early twelfth century), see Ta-Shema, "On Some Aspects of 'Maḥzor Vitry,' " 81–89, and Immanuel, "On 'Maḥzor Vitry,' " 129–30. The Reggio Manuscript of the book is now New York, JTS Mic. 8092, and it may be dated 1204 based on a marginal note on f. 37a. The ceremony is described on f. 164b and continues on f. 165a. The description of the ceremony is followed by a table of alphabets written in large square letters arranged in various permutations (see figure 3). Since f. 165 is torn, part of the table is missing. Possibly, it served as a children's primer or as a talisman. Compare the beginning of R. Isaac b. Moses of Vienna, *Sefer Or Zaruʿa*, Amsterdam, Rosenthaliana Library MS 1, printed in ed. Zhitomir, that begins with a mne-

monic Hebrew alphabet modeled on B. Shabbat 104a. On the Reggio/JTS manuscript, see Goldschmidt, "Text of the Prayers," 63–75, and Ta-Shema, "On Some Aspects of 'Mahzor Vitry,' " 83. In light of the manuscript evidence, the history of the Mahzor Vitry needs to be reassessed.

The printed edition of Horowitz is based on the thirteenth-century manuscript in the British Library, Add. 27200/01 (Catalogue Margalioth 655) and does not contain the table of alphabets. Additional versions of the ceremony appear in other manuscripts of the Mahzor Vitry, but it is likely, according to Avraham Grossman, that the Reggio/JTS manuscript is the earliest Mahzor Vitry manuscript. For this reason, I have dated the French version to the thirteenth century and not to the first or second half of the twelfth, as would follow from the attribution to a R. Simha.

42. Note that this public chanting of verses from the Torah, followed by a festive meal, reminds one of what was done at the bar mitzvah celebration starting in the late Middle Ages (see chapter 6). Here the requirement is educational and preparatory: the boy is learning from a book how to chant the text of the Torah out loud with the proper musical cantillation modes used in the synagogue when adults read from the scroll. Even learning to read is partly motivated by his need to read and learn the prayers that adult Jewish males could be expected to lead. On the practical and liturgical motivation of Jewish elementary education for boys, see Goitein, Sidrei Hinukh, 36. This does not diminish the significance of the religious obligation Jewish fathers had to educate their sons in Torah.

43. I discuss this metaphor in chapter 5.

44. See R. Aaron b. Jacob ha-Kohen of Lunel, Sefer Orhot Hayyim, 1–2:24; and Kol Bo, sec. 74.

Notes to Chapter Three *Ancient Jewish Pedagogy*

1. On ancient Jewish literacy, see Demsky, "Writing"; Josephus, Contra Apionem, II, 25; B. Menahot 29b; B. Hagiga 15a-b. Eusebius, Praepar. evan. X, 5; XI, 6, 519, notes that Jewish children knew the meanings of the names of the letters of their alphabet, cited in Dornseiff, Das Alphabet, 27. See, too, Hallo, "Isaiah 28:9–13 and the Ugaritic Abecedaries," 324–38, and B. Shabbat 104a, where letters are given moralistic associations. A medieval Latin comment by a student of Peter Abelard is often cited in connection with universal Jewish literacy, among girls as well as boys, in medieval Europe. It is more a Christian's perceptions about Jews and his desire to change Christian behavior than it is a mirror of Jewish literacy, but it is suggestive. See Graboïs, "Hebraica Veritas," 633.

For schooling in late antiquity, see Bacher, "Das altjüdische Schulwesen," 48–81; Krauss, Talmudische Archäologie, 3:199–239, 336–358; Perlow, L'éducation et l'enseignement; Schwabe, "Jewish and Greco-Roman Schools," 112–23; Arzt, "The Teacher in Talmud and Midrash," 35–47; Aberbach, "Educational Institutions," 107–20; Safrai, "Elementary Education," 148–69; Goldin, "Several Sidelights of a Torah Education," 1:176–91; and Gafni, Mosedot ha-Qehillah. Isaiah Gafni's sourcebook, syllabi, and conversations have been very helpful.

For Jewish schooling in medieval Muslim lands, see Goitein, Sidrei Hinukh and A Mediterranean Society, 2:171–211. On medieval Europe, see Marcus, "Schools, Jewish," 11:69–72, and Kanarfogel, Jewish Education. Many sources are included in Assaf, Meqorot, passim. See, for example, R. Eleazar of Worms's outline of a curriculum that starts with letters and words in

Sefer ha-Roqeaḥ, 11, and the thirteenth-century *Ḥuqqei ha-Torah ha-Qadmonim.* See Kanarfogel, *Jewish Education,* 114, lines 174–76; Güdemann, *Geschichte des Erziehungswesens* 1:272; Assaf, *Meqorot,* 1:15; Jacobs, *Jew of Angevin England,* 249.

On the father's obligation, see Deut. 4:9 and B. Qiddushin 30a; Deut. 11:19 as interpreted in *Sifre on Deuteronomy,* Eiqev 11, Finkelstein, 104; Hammer, *Sifre,* 98; B. Qiddushin 29b; and Maimonides, *Mishneh Torah,* Hilekhot Talmud Torah, ch. 1.

2. B. Yevamot 22a and B. Bekhorot 47a.

3. B. Shabbat 31a. Compare *Avot de Rabbi Natan,* A, chapter 15, 61; Goldin, *Fathers,* 80. This text may be talmudic (ca. 200–500 C.E.) or even later, but it contains earlier traditions. See Cohen, "Significance of Yavneh," 40. For an early Christian example of learning the forward alphabet, see *Infancy Gospel of Thomas* 6:13–21, in Miller, *Complete Gospels,* 373–74.

4. The Zionist leader and author Dr. Shemaryahu Levin (1867–1935), born in Belorussia, recalls in his autobiography, *Childhood in Exile,* 70–71, a reflex of this ancient practice with a contemporary twist:

About this time, I remember—that is, round my first Pentecost as a *cheder* boy—my grandfather took me up one evening for an impromptu examination, and in the presence of a houseful of guests played a trick on me. He asked me whether I could repeat the Hebrew alphabet forward and then "back to front." I answered yes. Forward it went easily enough. But backward was another business. I stammered, found myself stuck, and had to repeat the whole alphabet forward again in order to remember which letter preceded which.

My grandfather did not wait for the end. "I'll show you how simple it is," he said, smiling. He rose from his seat, faced the company, and repeated the alphabet forward. Then he turned his back to the company and repeated the same thing. "That," he said, while everybody laughed at me, "is the way to say the alphabet back to front easily."

5. See Demsky, "Sheshakh," and below.

6. *Avot de-Rabbi Natan,* A, chapter 6, 28–29; Goldin, *Fathers,* 41. Compare a different first curriculum in a story included in *Pirqei Derekh Erez,* 23n52, published as a supplement to *Seder Eliahu Rabba.*

7. See Quintilian, *Inst. or.* I, 1, 25, quoted in Dornseiff, *Das Alphabet,* 17n2. Jerome (ca. 342–420) notes in his commentary to Jeremiah 25:26, Migne, PL 24, 838, that Greek children learned letter pairs as did the Jews, and that this was called *atbash:* "propter memoriam parvulorum solemus lectionis ordinem vertere et primis extremas miscere ut dicamus a[lpha], o[mega], b[eta], p[si]. sic et apud Hebraeos primum est a[leph], secundum b[et], usque ad vigesimam secundam et extremam literam t[av], cui penultima est b legimus itaque *atbash.*" See Epstein, "Studies in *Sefer Yezirah,*" 179–80.

8. See Demsky, "Writing," 12; Demsky, "Sheshakh"; and Fishbane, *Biblical Interpretation in Ancient Israel,* 464. For the use of this technique in early medieval liturgical poetry (piyyut) created in Byzantine Palestine, see Fleisher, *Shirat ha-Qodesh,* 127.

9. See *Ben Sira* 24:23.

10. B. Sukkah 42a. See *Sifre on Deuteronomy,* Eiqev 11, sec. 46, Finkelstein, 104; Hammer, *Sifre,* 98. R. Mordecai b. Hillel ha-Kohen (ca. 1240–1298), a German rabbinic authority, quotes this tradition but attributes to the Palestinian Talmud a different verse. Instead of Deuteronomy 33:4, he says, "In the Palestinian Talmud, it concludes, 'his father teaches him the verse, "My son, heed the discipline of your father (and do not forsake the instruction [*torah*] of

your mother)" ' " (Prov. 1:8). See Mordecai to B. Sukkah, par. 763. There is also evidence from the Geniza fragments of children's primers that Proverbs 1:8 as well as Deuteronomy 33:4 was used. See Narkiss, "Illuminated Hebrew Children's Books from Medieval Egypt," 62. An example is Cambridge, University Library, T-S. 16.378.

11. B. Bava Batra 14a.

12. Tosafot to B. Baba Batra 14a, s.v. "dilma"; see B. Sukkah 42a.

13. The numerical value of the Hebrew letters of a word. See Lieberman, *Hellenism in Jewish Palestine*, 69, 72–73.

14. B. Makkot 23b–24a.

15. M. Avot 1:1.

16. *Sifre on Deuteronomy*, Eiqev 11, sec. 48, Finkelstein, 112; Hammer, *Sifre*, 104; and below. See, too, *Midrash Alpha Beta de-Rabbi ʿAqiva*, 3:50, which portrays each letter of the alphabet as asking God to begin the Torah with it. As a justification of its importance, the last letter, *tav*, says that it begins Deuteronomy 33:4: "When Moses charged us . . ." (*Torah zivah lanu . . .*).

17. *Midrash Vayyiqra Rabbah*, 9:3, Margalioth, 178.

18. Ibid., in the variant readings.

19. *Avot de Rabbi Natan*, A, ch. 15, 61; Goldin, *Fathers*, 81.

20. *Midrash Vayyiqra Rabbah*, 7:3, Margalioth, 156. For later opposition to this ancient practice, see Yassif, "Hebrew Narrative in Eastern Lands," 58, and sources cited there.

21. See Finkelstein, *Mavo le-Masekhtot Avot*, 108, and Bickerman, *Jews in the Greek Age*, 170. For other prerabbinic evidence, see the privileged role of Priests and Levites in study at Qumran, as in 1QS (The Scroll of the Rule) 5.8–10 and related passages cited and discussed by Fraade, "Interpretive Authority," 46–69.

22. See below, chapter 5. For Origen, see Migne, PG 13:63–64; Alexander, Introduction to "3 (Hebrew Apocalypse of) Enoch," 1:231. This is also noted by Jerome (Migne, PL 22: 547 and 25:17). Christians continued to discourage young students from studying Genesis in medieval Europe. See Guibert of Nogent, *Memoirs*, bk. 1, ch. 17, p. 91, and Migne, PL 178:731.

23. On AYQ BKHR, see Trachtenberg, *Jewish Magic and Superstition*, 264; for other examples of mnemonic made-up sentences, see Assaf, *Meqorot*, 4:16 (no. 21), from the Cairo Geniza. These are equivalent to such ditties as, "The quick brown fox jumped over the lazy dogs," used to teach typing.

24. The central mandatory prayer in the Jewish liturgy is known as the Prayer (*ha-tefillah*) or *ha-ʿamidah* (literally, "standing") or *shemoneh ʿesreh* (the eighteen [benedictions]). See Elbogen, *Jewish Liturgy*, 24–66. Together with the biblical texts that are called the Shema (Deut. 6:4–9; Deut. 11–21; Num. 37–41), it constitutes the core of the daily synagogue liturgy. For the Shema, see Elbogen, *Jewish Liturgy*, 16–24.

25. B. Berakhot 16b.

26. B. Shabbat 11a.

27. B. Qiddushin 29a. For the redemption of the firstborn (*pidyon ha-ben*), see Klein, *Guide to Jewish Religious Practice*, 430–32.

28. It is not clear how old this is. For an example, see Birnbaum, *Daily Prayer Book*, 1–2.

29. For the rituals associated with Passover and Sukkot, see Klein, *Guide to Jewish Religious Practice*, 103–40, 155–73.

30. The antiquity of so much of the ceremony suggests that ancient examples may yet be

found linking Shavuot and children (as well as adults) studying Torah in magical ways. See chapter 4. Thus, to say that it seems to appear for the first time in Europe is not to say that it was created there.

31. *Sifre on Deuteronomy*, Eiqev 11, sec. 46, Finkelstein, 104; Hammer, *Sifre*, 98; T. Ḥagiga 1,2, Lieberman, 375; B. Sukkah 42a and parallels.

32. See *Midrash Tanḥuma* on Lev. 19:23, Buber, 3:79; and compare B. Nedarim 32a: "Abraham was three years old when he recognized that God was his Creator."

33. B. 'Eiruvin 82a. R. Sherira Gaon of Baghdad (ca. 906–1006) cites this text to justify awarding custody of a six-year-old boy to his father against the counterclaim of his deceased wife's mother. He reasons that if the child's own living mother would not have had a claim on the boy after age six, how much less does his grandmother! See *Teshuvot ha-Ge'onim*, no. 553, quoted in Assaf, *Meqorot*, 2:5.

34. 1QSa 1.6–8, translated and discussed in Fraade, "Interpretive Authority," 55–56.

35. See Y. Ketubot 8:11, 32c, and Goodblatt, "Sources," 83–103.

36. Compare B. 'Eiruvin 82a.

37. This text resembles another attributed to Abaye in B. Ketubot 50a. Other Jewish ages-of-man texts that do not deal explicitly with schooling are in *Midrash Qohelet Rabbah*, to Ecclesiastes 1:1, translated and discussed by Kraemer, "Images of Jewish Childhood," 76–77, and the formula adults recite at the conclusion of the circumcision ritual, discussed below. On the subject in the West, see Sears, *Ages of Man*, and Burrow, *Ages of Man*.

38. Compare the requirement of having reached age ten before studying the sectarian laws, just cited from the Rule of the Congregation, as Fraade points out.

39. (M.) Avot 5:21.

40. See, too, the passage in *Midrash Tanḥuma*, on Leviticus 19:23, Buber, 3:79, the date of which is not clear. The author of the midrash introduces our text, "at age five (one begins studying) Scripture," with the formula "shanu" used of mishnaic passages. See, too, a twelfth-century magical text, *Shimmusha Rabba*, quoted in Maḥzor Vitry, 645, and in Assaf, *Meqorot*, 2:2, which introduces the tannaitic tradition as part of the Mishnah. On the date of this text, see Scholem, "Sidrei de-Shimmusha Rabba," 196.

41. See Tosafot on B. Bava Batra 21a s.v. "Bi-vezir" and on B. Ketubot 50a, s.v. "Bar." This scholastic resolution is also found in R. Judah b. Qalonimos of Spires' *Yiḥusei Tanna'im ve-Amora'im*, who posits that the "Mishnah" refers to preschool learning at home with the father, who teaches the child and gets him ready to begin Scripture at age six with a teacher. The passage is in Oxford, Bodleian Library, Hebrew MS Opp. 391–393, Neubauer 2199, f. 37a, quoted in Assaf, *Meqorot*, 4:2, and in New York, Library of the Jewish Theological Seminary, MS R 2348 = Mic. 9624, f. 99b.

42. For a different Jewish tradition, possibly from Normandy, about beginning school in the mid-spring, on the new moon of Nissan, see *Ḥuqqei ha-Torah ha-Qadmonim*, Kanarfogel, *Jewish Education*, 113, line 172; Güdemann, *Geschichte des Erziehungswesens*, 1:272; Assaf, *Meqorot*, 1:15; Jacobs, *Jews of Angevin England*, 249, and compare Guibert of Nogent, *Memoirs*, bk. 1, ch. 4, pp. 44–45.

43. Halperin, *Faces of the Chariot*.

44. The dating and character of these texts as a whole have been the subject of considerable controversy. See Scholem, *Jewish Gnosticism, Merkabah Mysticism, and Talmudic Tradition*; Gruen-

wald, *Apocalyptic and Merkavah Mysticism*, 169–73; Halperin, *Merkavah in Rabbinic Literature*; Chernus, *Mysticism in Rabbinic Judaism*; Dan, *Three Types of Ancient Jewish Mysticism*, 24–31; "Theophany of Sar ha-Torah"; Halperin, *Faces of the Chariot*, 428–46; Idel, *Kabbalah: New Perspectives*; Schäfer, *Hekhalot-Studien*, esp. 277–95; Schäfer, *Synopse*, *Hidden and Manifest God*, 150–57; Morray-Jones, "Heikhalot Literature," 1–39; and Swartz, "'Like the Ministering Angels.'"

45. On the antiquity of these practices of a mystical Shavuot and the relationship to Pentecost and Shavuot in what follows, see Liebes, "Christian Influences on the Zohar," 160–61, and below.

46. On the ritualization of this analogy in relation to purity rites, see below; for the myth of Israel's exodus and approach to Sinai and the initiation rite, see chapter 5.

47. See Fisher, *Christian Initiation*, 2; Cramer, *Baptism and Change*, 137–38.

48. For the important research documenting the path of Jewish cultural transmission from ancient Palestine via Italy to northern Europe, see Bonfil, "Evidence of Agobard of Lyons."

Notes to Chapter Four Food Magic and Mnemonic Gestures

1. See Bonner, *Education in Ancient Rome*, 39–40.

2. Quintilian, *Institutio oratoria*, 11.2, 17–22; Cicero, *De oratore*, 2.86, 351–54; *Rhetorica ad Herennium*, 3.16–24.

3. Yates, *Art of Memory*, 1–26; Hajdu, *Mnemotechnische Schriftum des Mittelalters*; Carruthers, *Book of Memory*. See, too, the fascinating study by Spence, *Memory Palace of Matteo Ricci*.

4. Yates, *Art of Memory*, 1–2.

5. Cicero, *De oratore*, 2, 86, 351–54, quoted in Yates, *Art of Memory*, 2.

6. See Zlotnick, *Iron Pillar—Mishnah*, 51–71. Compare Eickelman, "Art of Memory," 485–516.

7. Judah Messer Leon, *Book of the Honeycomb's Flow*, book 1, chap. 13, 131–39. See Bonfil, Introduction, 38. See Leon Modena, *Autobiography*, 216, c; Margalit, "On Memory," 759–72, and Sermoneta, "Aspetti del pensiero moderno," 2:17–35, both cited in Cohen.

8. See Zlotnick, "Memory," and Neusner, *Memorized Torah*, which deals with mnemonic compositional patterns, not theory or technique per se. For the style of mishnaic composition based on phrase lengths that facilitate memorization, see Friedman, "Shortest Go First."

9. *Avot de-Rabbi Natan*, A, chap. 6, 28–29; Goldin, *Fathers*, 41. Compare the mystical image of Akiva's turning from a rock into a fountain as a metaphor for his enlightenment. See Idel, *Kabbalah: New Perspectives*, 77–78.

10. See, for example, Psalm 119:32, "ki tarhiv libbi" ("you broaden my heart [i.e., understanding]"), a positive meaning, compared to Psalm 101:5, "u-rehav levav," and Proverbs 21:4 "u-rehav lev," where the figurative meaning becomes "pride." The English phrases "broad-minded" and "swell-headed" are roughly equivalent, allowing for the shift from the heart to the head. For a postbiblical example of the heart as container of wisdom, see Ben Sira 21:14: "The heart of a fool is like a broken dish; it will hold no knowledge." For initiation ceremony texts, see chapter 2.

11. See Fraade, *From Tradition to Commentary*, 19, 111, 244.

12. M. Avot 2:8 and Sifre on Deuteronomy, Eiqev 11, sec. 48, Finkelstein, 110; Hammer, *Sifre*, 102. For an earlier example, see 2 Maccabees 1:4: "May He open your heart (*dianoixai tēn kardian humōn*) with the Law."

13. The rabbis in the Talmud did make use of magic, but rarely for mnemonic purposes. See Blau, *Das altjüdische Zauberwesen*, and below.

14. See Fraade, *From Tradition to Commentary*, 92–94.

15. See Schäfer, *Synopse*, par. 292, which he translates in Schäfer, *Hidden and Manifest God*, 51: "Let them toil with the Torah, just as they toiled with the Torah all [previous] generations." For the meaning of crowns and the technical magical term "to use the crowns" hinted at in M. Avot 1:13, ascribed to Rabbi Akiva, see Gaster, *Tittled Bible*.

16. Additional suggestions include thinking about what one has learned to prevent forgetting it. See Y. Berakhot 5:1, 9a: "R. Tanhum taught: One who understands (*sover*) what he has learned will not quickly forget it." S. D. Goitein reports that a Jewish Yemenite teacher commented about this view: "Don't you know that 'understanding' prior to 'memorization' harms the child's mind?" See his "Jewish Education in Yemen," 247.

17. M. Avot 3:8.

18. *Avot de-Rabbi Natan*, A, chapter 24, 78; Goldin, *Fathers*, 104. The metaphor of the mind as container is clear.

19. B. Ḥagiga 9b.

20. B. Sanhedrin 99a, and notice the comment immediately preceding, which compares not studying Torah to idolatry.

21. See Parry, *L'Epithète traditionelle dans Homère*; Parry, *Making of Homeric Verse*, 1–190; Lord, *Singer of Tales*; Goody, *Literacy in Traditional Societies*, and Ong, *Orality and Literacy*, 57–67.

22. The question of which Torah texts were studied in late antiquity by verbatim memorization needs to be explored further.

23. There are rabbinic statements that sight aids memory, but in reference not to memorizing sacred text but to remembering the commandments by means of numerical and other associations. For example, see B. Menahot 43b: "seeing leads to remembering; remembering leads to doing." Rashi glosses: "seeing" (means) "the fringes" (*zizit*, of the talit); "doing" (means) "the commandments" (*mizvot*).

24. See Schäfer, *Hekhalot-Studien*, 291.

25. Halperin, *Faces of the Chariot*, 437–39.

26. On the wealth of the *tanna'im*, the earliest rabbinic masters in Palestine, see Cohen, "Place of the Rabbi," 169–70 and notes. In this regard, one should recall the encomium to the scribe, the lay student of Torah, described in *Ben Sirah* 38:24–34, which emphasizes the requisite of leisure (Greek *skhole*), which is the etymological origin of "scholar" and "school." On the magical study of Torah, see Schäfer, *Hekhalot-Studien*, 293, and Swartz, " 'Like the Ministering Angel.' " On the pagan aristocracy, see Brown, *World of Late Antiquity*, 11–48.

27. Halperin, *Faces of the Chariot*, 17–19, and Liebes, "Messiah of the Zohar," 79. That the rabbis were not in control of the synagogues in ancient Palestine, see Cohen, "Epigraphical Rabbis," 1–17, and Levine, "Sages and the Synagogue," 207, 211–18.

28. A different ancient Jewish practice, of making one-year-old children fast half a day and two-year-olds all day on the Day of Atonement, also was opposed by the Mishnah (M. Yoma 8:4) with less than complete success. See *Masekhet Soferim* 18:7, and note Saul Lieberman's objections to the editor's choice of readings, in Lieberman, Review, 56–57, and the discussion in Gilat, "Age Thirteen for the Commandments?" 44–45. See, too, R. Aaron b. Judah ha-

Kohen of Lunel, *Orḥot Ḥayyim*, 1:25. These are but two examples of pre-mishnaic Palestinian customs which can be reconstructed from rabbinic and medieval sources.

29. There were clear mnemonic uses made of alphabets and other letter combinations that were thought to be the names of God. See, for example, the twelfth-century text from southern France, R. Jacob of Marvège's *She'eilot u-Teshuvot Min ha-Shamayim*, 53–56. Other magical uses of alphabets for memory enhancement are preserved in texts like *Sefer ha-Meishiv* from fourteenth-century Spain. See Idel, "On the Method of the Author of *Sefer ha-Meishiv*," 223–24, esp. n. 198, where Idel quotes from R. Eleazar of Worms's *Sefer ha-Ḥokhmah* (thirteenth century) that the reverse Hebrew alphabet is the Name of God. In general, see Tambiah, "Magical Power of Words," 175–208.

30. Ingesting honey is found in Greek magical papyri in rituals designed to preserve the memory. See Betz, *Greek Magical Papyri*, 13 ("add a sufficiency of honey, and anoint your lips with the mixture"), 27. Compare the tale in the Yiddish *Mayseh Bukh*, which contains medieval traditions about the Rhineland Pietists, about R. Judah the Pietist, who tried to teach a R. Eliezer the mystical names of God by writing them in the sand. R. Eliezer would learn them, but when R. Judah covered them up with the sand, R. Eliezer would forget them. Finally: "The fourth time R. Judah again wrote some words in the sand and told R. Eliezer to lick them up with his tongue. R. Eliezer did so and as soon as he had swallowed the words with the sand, he knew as much as the pious man and never forgot it again." See *Ma'aseh Book*, 366.

31. See Curtius, *European Literature and the Latin Middle Ages*, 134–36.

32. See Bickerman, *Jews in the Greek Age*, 170–76: "The study of the law by laymen was a Hellenistic innovation in Jerusalem" (173), and Cohen, *From the Maccabees*, 43.

33. Jeremiah also uses similar language elsewhere: "I will put My Torah into their inmost being and inscribe it upon their hearts" (31:32). The image is also implied in Isaiah 6:7, another call to prophecy, which does not explicitly mention putting words into the prophet's mouth. See Fishbane, *Biblical Interpretation in Ancient Israel*, 326–29, 373–74, and chapter 5 below.

34. Compare *Ben Sira* 24:20: "For the memory of me (wisdom) is sweeter than honey, and the possession of me than the honeycomb." Cf. *Ben Sira* 49:1. Revelation 10:8–10 plays on Ezekiel and modifies it: "And I took the little scroll from the hand of the angel and ate it; it was sweet as honey in my mouth, but when I had eaten it my stomach was made bitter" (10:10). Cf. *Midrash Shemot Rabbah*, 5:9, 161, "the gentiles tasted it as bitter," which suggests an awareness of Revelation 10:10. On manna, see Fishbane, *Biblical Interpretation in Ancient Israel*, 423, and chapter 5 below.

35. B. Bava Batra 12a.

36. Compare *Ben Sira*, where "the man who . . . studies the Torah of the Most High" (39:1) requires not only "water and fire and iron and salt" but also "wheat flour and milk and honey, the blood of the grape, and olive oil and clothing" (39:26); compare 2 Esdras 14:4a (drink and memory) and B. Yoma 83b ("honey and very sweet food enlighten the eyes of man"); and see Leclercq, *Love of Learning*, 259, quoting an early medieval poem: "listen, boys, how sweet the letters are (*audite pueri, quam sunt dulces litterae*)."

37. See, too, B. Horayot 13a (end).

38. See Klein, *Guide to Jewish Religious Practice*, 74–75.

39. See *Joseph and Aseneth*, 16:15–16 (ca. first-century B.C.E.–second-century C.E.), 2:228–29, and Chestnutt, *Conversion in Joseph and Aseneth*. Compare Hesiod, *Theogony*, 83–84, and the use of honey in numerous magical rites in the Greek papyri, as cited in Betz, *Greek Magical Papyri*.

40. See Bonner, *Education in Ancient Rome*, 175 (fig. 20), 176 (fig. 21). It continued in medieval Europe.

41. The Hebrew word for writing tablet, luah, is also used to describe the tablets on which the Ten Commandments were written: luhot.

42. See Riché, *Education and Culture in the Barbarian West*, 115, 459–62; Walafried Strabo, "The School-Life of Walafried Strabo," 156; Shahar, *Childhood in the Middle Ages*, 189; Moran, *Growth of English Schooling*, 40–41; Grendler, *Schooling in Renaissance Italy*, 142–43. Compare Guibert of Nogent, *Memoirs*, bk. 1, ch. 17, p. 91, and his twelfth-century reflections on his studies as a young man: "I did not prepare a draft on the wax tablets, but committed them to the written page in their final form as I thought them out."

43. Or Qilir. See "Kallir, Eleazar," 713–15, and esp. Fleisher, "New Light on Qiliri."

44. See *'Arukh ha-Shalem*, s.v. "QLR."

45. Zunz, *Zur Geschichte und Literatur*, 168.

46. Michaelis, *Lexicon Syriacum*, 801 [803]: "Crustum panis, super quod oratiunculam quandam scribunt Jacobitae, quae in Psalterio eorum exstat, tum pueris tradunt comedendum." In his *A Compendius Syriac Dictionary*, edited by R. Payne Smith, the term *kalyra* is defined as "a flat round loaf, small cake of bread."

47. See Oxford, Bodleian, Syriac MS Pococke 10, f. 4a, quoted in Smith, *Catalogi codd. MSS. Bodleianae*, no. 16 (= Pococke 10), 59: "oratio pro puero, quum parentes eum in librum ediscendum incumbere velint: adducant eum ad sacerdotum, qui hanc orationem super panis crustum exscriptam ei comedendam tradet."

48. I am grateful to Dr. Sebastian Brock for transcribing and translating this passage for me from Poc. 10.

49. Private communication, 8 April 1987.

50. For example, "wisdom and understanding" (Prov. 1:2), "wisdom, knowledge, and understanding" (Exod. 31:3), "eheyeh asher eheyeh" (Exod. 3:14), "El Shaddai" (Gen. 17:1).

51. Edited by Scher, *Patrologia Orientalis*, 4:327–97; the passage is at 352–53, on which see Murray, *Symbols of Church and Kingdom*, 23. My appreciation to Robert Bonfil for calling this important text to my attention.

Thus far I have found only one sign of a text to be recited in medieval Europe when a Christian boy learns his letters. In a twelfth-century Latin manuscript from the Austrian monastery of Saint Florian, a rubric introduces a brief prayer: "quando puer litteras discit: Deus, qui in sapientia hoc est coaeterno filio omnia condidisti, da, quaesumus, huic famulo docibilem mentem, ut et in exterioribus studiis proficiat; et aeternae mereatur fieri capax doctrinae." See Library of Saint Florian, codex 467, folio 111b, cited in Specht, *Geschichte des Unterrichtswesens*, 150, and examined from a photocopy kindly made for me from the microfilm located at the Hill Monastic Manuscript Library, Saint John's Abbey and University, Collegeville, Minnesota. I inspected the original manuscript in Austria.

52. *Halikhot Qedem*, 63–64.

53. See Fleisher, *Shirat ha-Qodesh*, 214.

54. *Mahzor Vitry*, 363–64.

55. Despite the trend to accept this tradition as a historical fact, Robert Bonfil has argued cogently that it is a fiction. See Scholem, *Major Trends*, 41, 84; Dan, *Torat ha-Sod*, 14–20; Grossman, *Hakhmei Ashkenaz*, 29–44; and compare Bonfil, "Evidence of Agobard of Lyons," 346–48, and "Between Eretz Israel and Babylonia," 1–30.

56. *Toratan shel Rishonim*, 58–59, from Parma, Biblioteca Palatina, Heb MS 2785 (De Rossi 327), f. 118a. Compare the talmudic statement B. Berakhot 40a; B. Sanhedrin 70b, that "a baby does not know how to call out Mommy or Daddy until it tastes grain," on which Rashi comments: "This is called the Tree of Knowledge."

57. Dan, *Torat ha-Sod*, 22–24, Keiner, "Hebrew Paraphrase," 22–25, and *Hebrew Paraphrase*.

58. *Sefer Razi'el*, 42a; see also 45a.

59. New York, Library of the Jewish Theological Seminary Hebrew MS Mic. 8128, f. 33a; Scholem, *Jewish Gnosticism*, 111–12; Schäfer, *Synopse*, par. 572.

60. The emendation of *ant* (You are) instead of *anah* (O! [vocative]) or *ana(h)* (I) was suggested by Itamar Gruenwald.

61. For the image, see Sabbath Morning liturgy, "Yismah Moshe," in *Seder 'Avodat Yisrael*, 219, and Davidson, *Ozar ha-Shir'ah*, 2:447.

62. Schäfer, *Synopse*, par. 578; translated in Halperin, *Faces of the Chariot*, 429, and in Schäfer, *Hidden and Manifest God*, 94.

63. See *Harba de-Moshe*, 3:87, translation 1:328: "To remember immediately all thou learnest, write on a new-laid egg"; 3:94, trans. 1:337: "write upon a new-laid egg."

64. See Dan, *Torat ha-Sod*, 207–10.

65. Among the many objects on which amulets may be written, the egg plays a prominent role. It is found in many cultures. For example, the amulets are written in Morocco on hardboiled eggs, a bean, an oleander leaf, and the jawbone of a sheep. See Westermarck, *Ritual and Belief in Morocco*, 1:217, 219. In Germany, mixtures of eggs and alphabets were fed to small children. See Dornseiff, "ABC"; Andree, "ABC-Kuchen," 94–96, with illustration of a writing tablet made out of *Lebkuchen*, Christmas ginger cookies made with honey; and Beitl, *Wörterbuch*, 16–17.

66. Halperin, *Faces of the Chariot*, 414–36, and see Liebes, "Messiah of the Zohar," 78–82, who proposes that mystical Torah study on Shavuot eve, later described in the *Zohar*, is ancient.

67. See Ta-Shema, "Havdalah," 7:1481–82.

68. See Havlin, "Hadran," 7:1053–54; Sperber, *Minhagei Yisrael*, 128–34. The name is an Aramaic translation of the phrase *yofi lakh*, in M. Sukkah 4:5, meaning "farewell to you," from the noun *hadar*, but the word was later interpreted as a verb to mean "let us return to you" in the sense of "let us study you again." See Lieberman, "Qelas Qillusin," 439n33. The custom of reciting the ten sons of Rav Pappa when Talmud scholars complete "chapters" (*peraqim*) of text is mentioned in a question asked of R. Hai Gaon (939–1038), preserved in R. Abraham b. Isaac, *Sefer ha-Eshkol*, 159.

69. The custom of celebrating the occasion with a festive meal is mentioned already in the Talmud: B. Shabbat 118b–119a.

70. See Douglas, *Purity and Danger*; Turner, "Betwixt and Between," 93–111.

71. Hai Gaon is already said to have approved the custom of not drinking water at the solstice or equinox; see Trachtenberg, *Jewish Magic and Superstition*, 257.

72. See *Seder R. 'Amram*, 83. There is a medieval mystical tradition that R. Amram wrote this incantation under divine influence. See New York, Library of the Jewish Theological Seminary Hebrew MS, Mic. 1851, f. 1a, quoted in Idel, "On the Method," 239n287.

73. Scholem, *Havdalah de-Rabbi 'Aqiva*, 278–80.

74. On the invocation of POTAH (Opener) at the end of the Sabbath, Harvey Goldberg observed the following in a private communication (7 August 1993). Some Jews in North Africa refer in Arabic to "closing" a fast, at the beginning of the day, and of "opening" (Hebrew *poteah*) a fast at the end. He further speculates that this might be an awareness that Jews "are closed in upon themselves during these days and open themselves up to the wider world at the end of the special Jewish day."

75. First edition: Piove di Sacco, 1475, Orah Hayyim, par. 298. It is omitted in recent editions.

76. See the elaborate ritual of the transmission of the divine names, discussed in Scholem, "Tradition and New Creation," 135–36, where the text is translated from R. Eleazar of Worms, *Sefer Ha-Shem*, a book of divine-name letter combinations that has never been published. See, too, Dan, *Torat ha-Sod*, 74–75, and Swartz, "'Like the Ministering Angels,'" 153–66.

77. M. Yoma 1:1; Scholem, *Origins of the Kabbalah*, 240–42.

78. See Klein, *Guide to Jewish Religious Practice*, 512–15.

79. *Baraita de-Niddah*, 1 ff. See, too, *Geschichte von den Zehn Märtyrern*, 28* (version I), lines 33–44, 30*, lines 2–44.

80. *Baraita de Niddah*. Compare *Sefer Hasidim*, Wistinetzki, par. 799: "when a man is seated in front of a window writing or concentrating on Torah, he should not look out at pigs or feces."

81. Riché, *Education and Culture in the Barbarian West*, 455, citing Gregory of Tours, *Vitae Patrum* VIII, MGH, SRM, I-2, 692.

82. Isidore of Seville, *Etymologiae*, XI, 2.10, and others who cite him. See Shahar, *Childhood*, 17; McLaughlin, "Survivors and Surrogates," 136.

83. *Midrash Pesiqta Rabbati* 10, Friedman, 39b; *Pesiqta Rabbati*, Braude, 1:188; and Levine, *Rabbinic Class*, 52n41.

84. The child's ritual purity before entering school is further related to a woman's ritual purity. See chapter 5.

85. For water as Torah in rabbinic Judaism, see Fraade, *From Tradition to Commentary*, 111, 244n112; Fraade, "Interpretive Authority," 59n40; and Fishbane, "Well of Living Water," 3–16.

86. B. Horayot 12a. Cf. B. Keritot 6a, where "water" replaces "river."

87. *Seder Eliyahu Rabbah*, 116–17. See *Sefer Hasidim*, Wistinetzki, par. 1509, based on B. 'Avodah Zarah 3b (bottom): "one who stops studying Torah is like a fish out of water," and compare this simile to the portrayal of the fish in the river in the *Leipzig Mahzor* illumination discussed in chapter 5.

88. Bacher, "Das altjüdische Schulwesen," 54. See, too, II Chron. 17:7–9.

89. Zlotnick, "Memory," 231–33.

90. T. Ohalot 16:8; T. Parah 4:7, and compare B. Sanhedrin 99b, cited in Zlotnick, "Memory," 213.

91. B. Megillah 32a. The theme is found in R. Eleazar of Worms, *Sefer ha-Roqeah*, Introduction, passim.

92. Tosafot to B. Megillah 32a, s.v. "ve-ha-shoneh be-lo zimrah"; B. 'Avodah Zarah 3b. See Balogh, " 'Voces Paginarum.' "

93. The phrase here is taken to mean the Torah.

94. B. 'Eiruvin 53b (bottom)–54a, cited in Zimmer, "Body Gestures," 118.

95. Ong, *Orality and Literacy*, 67.

96. See Zimmer, "Body Gestures," 118.

97. From the Ashkenazic sources Zimmer cites, the custom is derived from heikhalot midrashic texts and then ritualized. See Zimmer, "Body Gestures," 120. Harvey Goldberg noted in a private communication (24 August 1993) that aside from bows, "the older generation of Moroccan Jews stand perfectly still throughout the 'Amidah. The ones educated here [in Israel] have picked up shukkeling to one degree or another."

Notes to Chapter Five *Symbolic Readings*

1. Geertz, "Thick Description," 3–30.

2. See Löw, *Lebensalter*; Schauss, *Lifetime*; Geffen, *Celebration and Renewal*.

3. Van Gennep, *Rites of Passage*, 10–11. See also Weckman, "Understanding Initiation," 62–79.

4. On the use of the concepts of Jewish and Christian space, see Jordan, "Jews on Top," 39–56, and Stow, "Jewish Family in the Rhineland," 1085–1110. See, too, Metzger and Metzger, *Jewish Life in the Middle Ages*, 79–109, and Duby, "Portraits." On parents hiring tutors, see Kanarfogel, *Jewish Education and Society*, 19–27, and Guibert de Nogent, *Memoires*, bk. 1, ch. 6, p. 49: "the school being no other than the dining hall of our house."

5. On the *mohel*, see Klein, *Guide to Jewish Religious Practice*, 426–27. The comparison between circumcision and the school initiation is made explicit in the French texts which locate the latter right after the former.

6. *Sefer ha-Roqeah*, par. 296. The standard edition (Jerusalem, 1960) only has "dog"; the first edition (Fano, 1505) has *go va-kekev*, which is a corruption of the correct reading in Paris, Bibliothèque Nationale MS hébreux 363, f. 96a, and ed. Cremona, 1557: *goy va-kelev* (Gentile, i.e., Christian, or dog). On the use of the dog motif in Jewish-Christian polemical writings, see Berger, "Christians, Gentiles, and the Talmud," 129, and *Piyyutei Rabbi Ephraim*, 229, 284. For a medieval Christian anti-Jewish example, see Wells, "Attitudes to the Jews," 38–43.

7. *Mahzor Vitry*, 629; Hebrew MS New York, Jewish Theological Seminary Mic. 8092, f. 165a: "to teach him modesty, humility, and the fear (of God)"; MS Hamburg 17, f. 81b. Compare the Greek *paedagogos*, a trusted slave who carried and protected a young boy to and from elementary school. See Bonner, *Education in Ancient Rome*, 38–46, and his figures 2–4. For a rabbinic usage of the term *pedagogue*, see *Sifrei 'al Sefer Be-Midbar*, sec. 87, Horowitz, 87, Neusner, *Sifré*, 86.

8. See Turner, "Betwixt and Between," and Douglas, *Purity and Danger*. An analogous situation in Jewish rites of passage is the night prior to an infant boy's circumcision, which led to the custom of guarding him all night (*Wachnacht*). See Schauss, *Lifetime*, 32–33, and Trachtenberg, *Jewish Magic and Superstition*, 170–71. Cf. Wuttke, *Der deutsche Volksaberglaube*, 386–87.

9. See Marcus, "From Politics."

10. Eliade, *Rites and Symbols*, xii–xv, and van Gennep, *Rites of Passage*, 91–115.

11. See Shahar, *Childhood*, 77–120, 162–82.

12. See Jeremiah 20:17: "Because he did not kill me before birth so that my mother might be my grave, and her womb big [with me] for all time"; and compare the talmudic idiom, "One who teaches his neighbor's son Torah, it is as though he gave birth to him (*yelado*)." See B. Sanhedrin 19b, and compare the parallel in B. Sanhedrin 99b: "as though he made him ('*asa'o*)"; and Sallust, *De diis et mundo*, 4, who reports a Phrygian rite in which new initiates were fed on milk as if they were reborn. Judaism also compares a new proselyte to a newborn. See B. Yevamot 22a, B. Bekhorot 47a.

13. See Shahar, *Childhood*, 85–87, and illustrations in Forsyth, "Children in Early Medieval Art," 39–44. For examples of symbolically wrapping an initiate, as in the child's ceremony, see van Gennep, *Rites of Passage*, 77–78, and Eliade, *Rites and Symbols*, 53. See *Sefer Ḥasidim*, Wistinetzki, par. 1778.

14. Heschel, *Earth Is the Lord's*, 47: "When taken for the first time to the ḥeder, the child is wrapped in a prayer shawl like a scroll." In a documentary about the Lubovitcher Hasidim, a man rushes into a synagogue carrying something wrapped in a ṭalit. At first, I assumed it was a Torah. It turned out to be his son, being taken to his first Torah lesson.

15. Goldberg, "Torah and Children," 107–30. A few years ago on Shavuot, a guest who had the honor of lifting the Torah scroll (*hagbah*) raised it but then nearly dropped it. When someone caught it before it tore or fell, my loquacious seventy-six-year old neighbor immediately said, "Just like a baby."

16. In Ashkenaz, see the description in the Solomon b. Samson narrative about the 1096 Crusade riots. After the Christians tore the Torah scroll "to shreds," "all the women said in one voice: Alas, the Holy Torah . . . our little children would kiss it." See Habermann, *Sefer Gezeirot Ashkenaz ve-Ẓarfat*, 35; *Jews and the Crusaders*, 37; Chazan, *European Jewry*, 260. See, too, R. Isaac b. Moses of Vienna, *Sefer Or Zaru'a*, part 2, par. 48, f. 11a: "and all the young children (ha-tinoqot) go over and kiss the wrapped Torah scroll." Lifting a small child to kiss the wrapped Torah is done to this day. In addition, the child, like the Torah scroll in the synagogue, is wrapped and then unwrapped for the purpose of reading.

17. The text is from T. Berakhot 6:12, ed. Lieberman, 36–37; B. Shabbat 137b; it is recited at the end of the circumcision ceremony. See Klein, *Guide to Jewish Religious Practice*, 428. See also figure 11.

18. See Kirshenblatt-Gimblett, "The Cut That Binds," 138–39; Goldberg, "Torah and Children," 112.

19. See Bynum, *Holy Feast and Holy Fast*, 279–80; Davis, "Women on Top," 124–51; Maranda, "Dialectic of Metaphor," 197–202. A modern example of inversion is the ironic use that Franz Kafka makes of the phrase "enters the Torah," which is part of the liturgy of the circumcision rite. At the end of the ceremony (discussed in more detail in Chapter 6) the assembled say, "As he has entered the covenant (brit) so may he enter the Torah. . . ." Kafka's parable "Before the Law" ("Vor dem Gesetz") in his novel *The Trial* may allude to this phrase, according to Harry Steinauer: "Before the law stands a doorkeeper. To this doorkeeper there comes an ordinary man and requests entry into the law," which he cannot enter. See Kafka, "Before the Law."

20. Although the use of the number three is multivalent within Judaism, it includes the interpretation of being anti-Trinitarian.

21. B. Avodah Zarah 5b.

22. See *Mekhilta de-Rabbi Yishmael*, Yitro 3, 212.

23. For Jewish purity rituals in water, see Scholem, "Tradition and New Creation," 135–36; Dan, *Torat ha-Sod*, 74–75; Gruenwald, *Apocalyptic and Merkava Mysticism*, 135; Idel, "Development of an Ancient Technique," 1–7; Lauterbach, "Tashlik"; Swartz, "'Like the Ministering Angels,'" 152, 157. On baptism, see Fisher, *Christian Initiation*, 13. In 1096, Jews in Germany were forcibly baptized in rivers. See *Jews and the Crusaders*, 67. See Yuval, "Vengeance and Curses," 84–86, who points to the connection between Jewish martyrdom in rivers and Christian views that rivers are "potential baptismal fonts." The initiated boy may also be protected from any potential harm by the talismanic power of the Torah he has just ingested.

24. The analysis of the Jewish school initiation shows the transition to be highly structured even when it provides opportunities for communal bonding during the Shavuot festival.

25. For evidence that it took place on the festival itself and not just before or after it, see the legal opinions rendered about erasing (by eating) letters on a festival, discussed in chapter 6.

26. The "counting" (Hebrew *sefirah*) of seven weeks from the time the barley sheaf was waved on the second day of Passover. See Lev. 23:9–21; Klein, *Guide to Jewish Religious Practice*, 142–47.

27. On the different periods marked by German and East European Jews because of the Crusade experience of the former, see Sperber, "Mourning Customs in the Period of Counting the Omer," 361–69.

28. See Marcus, "From Politics," and G. Cohen, "The Hebrew Chronicles and the Ashkenazic Tradition," 36–53.

29. For an analogous literary and possibly ritual representation, see *Zohar* III, 96a–98b where biblical Israel and the spring holiday cycle are compared to a woman about to be married. Passover marks the stay in Egypt, where Israel was impure (the woman has her menses); following the days of flow, she counts seven "white days," which correspond to the seven weeks of sefirah (counting). Finally she is purified before the wedding on Shavuot. See Liebes, "The Messiah of the Zohar," 75–76. Note the addition of studying the Torah the night before and the analogy of the impure woman who needs to be purified and the pure child who needs to be protected from sources of impurity when carried to the school. It is possible that the Zoharic myth and the Ashkenazic initiation ceremony drew on related ancient sources. On the Ashkenazic antecedents of the earliest kabbalistic text, *Sefer ha-Bahir*, see Scholem, *Kabbalah*, 315–16. One should recall that R. Isaac Luria of Safed, who is credited with the creation of the all-night ritual study of Torah on the night of Shavuot, was from Ashkenaz.

30. Gen. 47:27; Exod. 1:11–22, 2:23–24.

31. See Exod. 16:3; Num. 11:4–6.

32. Exod. 16:14–16; Exod. 19:10–11; Deut. 34:1–4.

33. See Blumenkranz, *Le juif au miroir*; Seiferth, *Synagogue and Church*.

34. In this German-Jewish illumination the child is wrapped in a cloak, not a ṭalit, which the French *Maḥzor Vitry* mentions.

35. A partial solution to this problem has been offered by Katz, "Torah Study on the Mountain and by the Water," 4–8. Evelyn Cohen has also noted the aesthetic balance of the three parts of the school illumination taken by itself as a program of three scenes. See Cohen, "The Teacher, the Father and the Virgin Mary in the *Leipzig Maḥzor*," 71–76.

36. See Mark 14:22; Luke 22:20; cf. I Cor. 10:16, 11:23–26, and Feeley-Harnik, *The Lord's Table*, 107–48; Bynum, *Holy Feast and Holy Fast*, 31–69; and Rubin, *Corpus Christi*, 12–82.

37. See Lev. 23:20 and Num. 28:26.

38. *Sifre on Deuteronomy*, Eiqev, 48; Finkelstein, 113; Hammer, *Sifre*, 104.

39. *Sifre on Deuteronomy*, Eiqev, 45; Finkelstein, 103–4; Hammer, *Sifre*, 97–98.

40. B. Shabbat 120a.

41. B. Ḥagiga 14a.

42. B. Horayot 14a; B. Berakhot 64a.

43. *Sifre on Deuteronomy*, Eiqev, 48; Finkelstein, 109–10; Hammer, *Sifre*, 102.

44. *Mekhilta de-Rabbi Yishmael*, Vayyisa 2, 161. See, too, *Midrash Shemot Rabbah*, 5:9, 160–61, and Flusser, "Society and Religion in the Second Temple Period," 14.

45. See Bynum, *Holy Feast and Holy Fast*, 59, 74, 77, 114–16, 145–46, 228; Rubin, *Corpus Christi*, 20, 119, 143. Compare Stephan Langton, who observes in his sermon on manna, delivered in Paris in 1180, that "manna est sacra scriptura." See *Selected Sermons of Stephen Langton*, 23. For a Jewish example from Spain, see Joseph Ibn Ẓadiq (d. 1149) in Schirmann, *Ha-Shirah ha-ʿIvrit*, 2: 553. For an anti-Judaism polemic, see Bernard of Clairvaux, who says that Jews are "literary" because they gnaw "as on a dry crust the letter of the divine writings," cited in Leclercq, *Love of Learning*, 259, from Saint Bernard, Epist. 106.2 (PL 182.242).

46. Water well: Num. 20:2–11, 16–18. Quail: Exod. 16:13.

47. Jerusalem, Jewish National and University Library, MS Hebrew Quarto 781/1, f. 169b. See Narkiss, *Hebrew Illuminated Manuscripts*, 92, for information about the manuscript but no reproduction. The baking scene resembles one in *The Laud Maḥzor*, Oxford, Bodleian Library, Laud Or., 321, f. 127b, which Narkiss, *Hebrew Illuminated Manuscripts*, 94, plate 27, labels "baking of the *maẓẓah*" but is more likely, again, a depiction of the Shavuot leḥem bikkurim.

48. On these gestures, see Narkiss, "Iconography," 99–100.

49. See 1 Cor. 3:2 (milk versus meat), B. Yoma 75a (manna is like breast milk); Shahar, *Childhood*, 79; Boswell, *Kindness*, 211–12. Compare *Midrash Shir ha-Shirim*, 10a–10b, on Song of Songs 1:8–9, which states that an angel took the Jewish babies from the Nile and covered them with honey and oil; Fildes, *Breasts, Bottles, and Babies*, 60–61.

50. See Lincoln, "Beverages," 120, and his reference to *Odyssey* 10.519.

51. On the gift of the Holy Land, see Exod. 3:8, 13:5; Num. 13:27; 16:13, 14; Deut. 31:20; Jer. 11:5; Ezek. 20:6, 15. The connection to the Torah is based on an interpretation of such verses as Song of Songs 4:11 as referring to Torah, as discussed below. See, too, *Midrash Shir ha-Shirim*, on that verse.

52. See Cook, "Bee in Greek Mythology," 1–24, esp. 2, 7–8, 15–17; Haupt, "Manna, Nectar and Ambrosia," 227–36; Gaster, *Thespis*, 222–23, 304–9; Waszink, "Biene und Honig," 5–38. Compare Saint Ambrose's being fed by the bees, a bas-relief of an altar in the Basilica of Saint

Ambrose, Milan (in Lopez, *Birth of Europe*, plate 10); Solomon Ibn Gabirol's poem "The Bee," in Schirmann, *Ha-Shirah ha-'Ivrit*, 1:220; and for the bee as Christlike, see Cramer, *Baptism and Change*, 177–78.

53. B. Pesaḥim 112a.

54. For the new cultural emphasis on Mary and the Christ Child in the central Middle Ages, see Southern, *Making of the Middle Ages*, 238–40, and plates 1 and 4; McLaughlin, "Survivors and Surrogates," 132–33; Lasareff, "Studies in the Iconography of the Virgin," 42–65; Werner, *Alone of All Her Sex*, 177–269.

55. See Urbach, "Homiletical Interpretations," 247–75; Kimelman, "Rabbi Yohanan," 567–95.

56. *Midrash Shir ha-Shirim* on Song of Songs 4:11.

57. *Midrash Bemidbar Rabbah*, Nasso 13.

58. Vulgate: "ubera tua." See Pope, *Anchor Bible Song of Songs*, 298–99; Bynum, *Jesus as Mother*, 128, 147–48. See, too, Gruber, "Motherhood of God in Second Isaiah," 351–59.

59. Y. Sanhedrin 11:4. Compare the folk lyric "kisses sweeter than wine."

60. B. 'Avodah Zarah 35a.

61. See, however, the tale in B. Shabbat 53b: "The Rabbis taught: It once happened that a man's wife died and left a sucking son, and the father had not the means to pay for a wet-nurse; then a miracle happened to him and he developed breasts like the two breasts of a woman, and he suckled his son. Rav Joseph said: Come and see how great is this man that such a miracle was wrought for him. Said Abaye to him: On the contrary, how inferior is this man, that the natural order was changed for him." See, too, *Midrash Zuṭa* on Song of Songs, 8 and 11; Urbach, *The Sages*, 110 and 728n34; R. Eleazar of Worms, *Peirush Shir ha-Shirim*, 102. Compare the maternal images in Bernard of Clairvaux's commentary to Song of Songs, discussed in Bynum, *Jesus as Mother*, 115–20.

62. For a fifteenth-century example from Alsace, see Ben-Sasson, "Social Views of R. Yohanan Luria," 170: "I have much wheat to grind and to interpret in the Talmud and much milk, but no one (wants to) suck." See, too, B. Berakhot 63b; B. Niddah 45a.

63. Compare *Midrash Shir ha-Shirim*, 34a, on the same phrase: "Just as breasts flow with milk, so Moses and Aaron flowed with wisdom."

64. B. Pesaḥim 87a.

65. Rashi to B. Pesaḥim 87a, s.v. "ve-shadai."

66. See Bynum, *Holy Feast and Holy Fast*, plates 13–25.

67. Cohen, "The Teacher, the Father, and the Virgin Mary," 73. Cohen mentions two examples of the *mater amabilis*: the Virgin and Child of the south façade of Amiens Cathedral (ca. 1260); a wooden diptych from Cologne ca. 1325 in the Gemäldegalerie, Staatliche Museen, Berlin (no. 1627). For the throne motif, see Forsyth, *Throne of Wisdom*, esp. 26–27. There are also striking similarities between the child and teacher scene and an Adoration of the Magi from Arezzo. See Forsyth, *Throne of Wisdom*, illustration 1.

68. See the depictions of the cocooned Christian infant in Boswell, *Kindness*, plates 14–15, and compare them to the semi-cocooned image in the Schocken Bible, Jerusalem, Schocken Library, Hebrew MS 14840, frontispiece, reproduced in Narkiss, *Hebrew Illuminated Manuscripts*, 102, plate 31, eighth row, first picture on right ("Pharoah's daughter gives Moses to his mother Jocheved").

69. See Levin, *Childhood in Exile*, 49–50. For other sacrificial imagery associated with the initiation of circumcision, see Wolfson, "Circumcision and the Divine Name," 99–104.

70. See Sinanoglou, "Christ Child as Sacrifice," 491–509; Walter, *Art and Ritual*, 209–11; Berthold of Regensburg's sermon in *Predigten*, edited by F. Pfiffer (Vienna, 1880), 2:270, cited in Trachtenberg, *Devil and the Jews*, 110, 240n2: "Who would like to bite off the little head, or the little hands, or the little feet of a little child?" For an important study on the theme of sacrifice in ancient religions, see Burkert, *Homo Necans*.

71. *Maḥzor Vitry*, Reggio, JTS Mic. 8092, f. 164b, middle column, bottom.

72. Ibid., last column.

73. *Midrash Vayyiqra Rabbah*, 7:3, Margalioth, 156: "R. Isi."

74. *Maḥzor Vitry*, MS Reggio JTS mic. 8092, f. 165a.

75. *Maḥzor Vitry*, ed. Horowitz, 630.

76. *Midrash Vayyiqra Rabbah*, 7:3, Margalioth, 156; B. Menaḥot 110a; B. Megillah 31b; B. Ta'anit 27b, all cited in Cohen, "Temple and the Synagogue," 162–63; see, too, *Pesiqta de-Rav Kahana*, "et qorbani laḥmi," Buber, 60b; Mandelbaum, 117–18; Braude, *Pesikta*, 133.

77. B. Berakhot 17a, cited in Cohen, "Temple and the Synagogue," 167.

78. B. Shabbat 119b. See Y. Ḥagiga 1:7, 76c; *Midrash Eikhah Rabbah*, introduction, 2 ("if the children are chirping with their voices, you will not be able to destroy this people").

79. Cf. B. Berakhot 63b.

80. *Midrash Shir ha-Shirim*, 13a.

81. *Midrash Tehillim*, 68:9, 318; Braude, *Midrash*, 1:544. The image is based on the requirement to pinch off some kneaded dough for the priest before baking bread. See Num. 15:20.

82. A similar comparison to Jews and Temple priests is made in the narratives about the acts of ritual sacrifice Jews performed on their children and spouses and on themselves in 1096. See Marcus, "From Politics."

83. See *Midrash Tehillim* 12:1, Buber, 104; Braude, *Midrash*, 168.

84. See Kanarfogel, *Jewish Education and Society*, 106–7, lines 1–41; Güdemann, *Geschichte des Erziehungswesens*, 1:267–68; Assaf, *Meqorot*, 1:9–10. In his introduction Kanarfogel, 104, points to an important parallel in *Sefer Ḥasidim*, ed. Wistinetzki, par. 1474, which also accords a special role to children of priests (*kohanim*) and Levites and suggests that this may be part of a Jewish adaptation of the Christian monastic ideal. I would add that it illustrates the twofold process of Ashkenazic inward acculturation which this book describes. On the one hand, the emphasis on priests and Levites as Torah students is an ancient Jewish strain of piety that persisted in Ashkenaz. On the other, the medieval Pietists (*hasidei Ashkenaz*) recast it in a contemporary Christian environment. They could do so because they sensed, correctly, that these patterns were Jewish *before* they were Christian. See Fraade, "Interpretive Authority," 53–65. The single extant manuscript of this text is Oxford, Bodleian Library, Hebrew MS Opp. 342, Neubauer no. 873, f. 196a–198a; it is also printed in Güdemann, *Geschichte des Erziehungswesens*, 1:92–106, 264–72, and in Assaf, *Meqorot*, 1:6–16.

85. For the quotation, see B. Berakhot 17a. Cf. Golb, *Toledot ha-Yehudim*, 38–40.

86. Thomas de Eccleston, "De adventu fratrum minorum in Angliam," *Monumenta Francescana*, Rolls Series 4 (1858): 67–68, cited by Sinanoglou, "Christ Child as Sacrifice," 492.

87. For the 1096 martyrs, see Marcus, "From Politics"; Chazan, *European Jewry*; and Cohen,

"'1096 Persecution Narratives.'" For the Host desecration accusation, see Rubin, *Corpus Christi*, 116–29. On the blood libel, in particular, see Hsia, *Myth of Ritual Murder*, 27–31, 51–52, 190–95, 201–2; Langmuir, *Toward a Definition*, 263–81; and cf. Sanday, *Divine Hunger*.

88. Yuval, "Vengeance and Curses," 70–90; Marcus, "Hierarchies, Religious Boundaries," 25n27. In several replies to Yuval's provocative study, scholars did not deal with the issue of the blood libel and the Christian factors that might be more likely sources of explanation than the precedent of Jewish ritual killings during the First Crusade riots in the Rhineland.

89. For some indications that Jews were aware of the eucharistic sacrifice, see Tosafot to B. 'Avodah Zarah 2a, s.v. "asur," where the ancient term tiqrovet ("offering," as in T. Bava Batra 6:14, B. 'Avodah Zarah 32b) is applied to contemporary Christian worship; Rashi on B. Berakhot 41b, s.v. "pat ha-ba'ah be-khesnin," refers to a type of spiced bread ancient Jews used to eat after dessert, like "our oublies." See Kohut, *'Arukh Completum*, s.v. "lehem," 3:34; Shareshevsky, *Rashi the Man and His World*, 235n37. Rashi uses the French word for the Latin *oblatus* "offering," a term Christians used for the eucharistic wafer and for children offered to monasteries, i.e., oblates. See Latham, *Revised Medieval Latin Word-List*, 318, and Boswell, *Kindness*, 297n2. In the record of a Jew who converted to Christianity and reverted to Judaism, he tells a French inquisitor in the thirteenth century that "he is not a Christian but a Jew named Samuel and that Christians eat their God." See Hidiroglou, "Les juifs dans la littérature historique latine," 413, 448, and Jordan, *French Monarchy*, 293n3.

In a letter to the archbishop of Sens and the bishop of Paris, written on July 15, 1205, Pope Innocent III complains that the Jews who have Christian wetnurses in their homes make them "pour their milk into the latrine for three days" after they "take in the body and blood of Jesus Christ" on Easter. See Grayzel, *Church and the Jews*, 114–17. In 1275, in Bristol, several Jews were excommunicated by the archbishop because of their "iniquitous insults, blasphemies, and injuries and . . . [their] assault upon a chaplain of St. Peter's who had administered the holy Eucharist to a sick person in the Jewry." See Jordan, "Christian Excommunication of the Jews," 34.

90. An example of how Christians imagined Jews is reflected in a story told by Caesarius of Heisterbach (thirteenth century, Rhineland). They hired "the house of a knight" and "entered together at the time of the evening sacrifice" (*tempore sacrificii vespertini*). This language places the Jewish religious behavior of reciting the evening prayers (*ma'ariv*) within the conceptual framework of Christian eucharistic symbols. Ironically, the talmudic rabbis understood Jewish daily prayers to be substitutes for the ancient Temple sacrifices, as noted earlier. See Caesarius of Heisterbach, *Dialogus miraculorum*, X.69, 263–64; Scott and Bland, *Dialogue on Miracles*, 2:227; Grayzel, *Church and the Jews*, 329, doc. no. 32. On the magical uses to which Christians put the eucharist, see Browe, "Die Eucharistie als Zaubermittel im Mittelalter," 134–54, and Rubin, *Corpus Christi*, 338–41.

91. I agree with Moore, *The Formation of a Persecuting Society*, 100–101, following Mary Douglas, that power inversions played a part as well. A beleaguered majority projected onto the more powerful minority that they ate the children of the majority. For strong evidence that Christians were aware that Jews killed their own children as martyrs, see Minty, "*Kiddush ha-Shem* in the Eyes of Christians"; Malkiel, "Infanticide in Passover Iconography"; and Despres, "Cultic Anti-Judaism and Chaucer's Litel Clergeon."

Notes to Chapter Six Childhood Initiations into Religious Cultures

1. The literature on the transformation is vast. See Haskins, *Renaissance of the Twelfth Century*; Southern, *Making of the Middle Ages*; Chenu, *Nature, Man, and Society*; Radding, *World Made by Men*; and the essays in Benson and Constable, *Renaissance and Renewal*. A number of scholars have applied the notion of "the renaissance of the twelfth century" to the European Jewish Middle Ages, but a synthetic treatment remains to be done. See, for example, Ben-Sasson, "On Chronographical Tendencies," 34–49; Marcus, *Piety and Society*, 1–2; "History, Story and Collective Memory," 386n46; Chazan, *European Jewry*, 193–95; Idel, *Kabbalah: New Perspectives*, 251; and Ta-Shema, *Minhag Ashkenaz ha-Qadmon*, 20.

2. Lopez, *Commercial Revolution*, 27–122; Radding, *World Made by Men*, 186–254.

3. Southern, *Medieval Humanism*, 81–82, 86–104; Le Goff, *Intellectuals in the Middle Ages*, 35–48.

4. This is clear from Soloveitchik, "Three Themes in the *Sefer Ḥasidim*," 311–57.

5. See Bonfil, "Between Eretz Israel and Babylonia," 19–22; Ta-Shema, *Minhag Ashkenaz ha-Qadmon*, 98–105; Kanarfogel, *Jewish Education and Society*, 63, 70–72.

6. Many have pointed to the Palestinian source of Ashkenazic custom. See, recently, Ta-Shema, *Minhag Ashkenaz ha-Qadmon*, esp. 61, 74, 82, 98–99; Bonfil, "Evidence of Agobard of Lyons."

7. See Kanarfogel, "Attitudes toward Childhood," 6–9, and passages such as *Sefer Ḥasidim*, par. 820, which refers to children's imaginations.

8. The main patterns are discussed in Löw, *Lebensalter*; Schauss, *Lifetime*; Fisher, *Christian Initiation*; and Cramer, *Baptism and Change*.

9. Fisher, *Christian Initiation*, 1–46; Cramer, *Baptism and Change*, 131–266.

10. See Cohen, "Rabbinic Conversion Ceremony," 194 and n48.

11. Fisher, *Christian Initiation*, 20, 27; Cramer, *Baptism and Change*, 179–84.

12. See Lynch, *Godparents and Kinship*, 129, citing Augustine's letter 98.2; Pelikan, *Christian Tradition*, 1:317–18; Cramer, *Baptism and Change*, 87–129.

13. See Dyck, "Anabaptism," 1:247.

14. Lynch, *Godparents and Kinship*, 210–18.

15. Löw, *Lebensalter*, 84.

16. Lynch, *Godparents and Kinship*, 6.

17. See Klein, *Guide to Jewish Religious Practice*, 427–28; Marcus, "Circumcision, Jewish," 410–12.

18. See Fisher, *Christian Initiation*, 101–8; Cramer, *Baptism and Change*, 179–84; Shahar, *Childhood*, 109.

19. Fisher, *Christian Initiation*, 2; Cramer, *Baptism and Change*, 181.

20. Canon 21; Hefele and Leclercq, *Histoire des conciles*, 5:1350, translated in Fisher, *Christian Initiation*, 104n7; Rubin, *Corpus Christi*, 54–55, 86–87.

21. Rubin, *Corpus Christi*, 164–212.

22. Rubin, *Corpus Christi*, 122–31; Grayzel, *Church and the Jews*, 329.

23. See Krauss, *Leben Jesu*; Cohen, "Towards a Functional Classification," 98–99; Basser, "Acts of Jesus."

24. See Marcus, "From Politics," 49.

25. See Chazan, *European Jewry*.

26. See Eidelberg, *Jews and Crusaders*, 37, 130.

27. See Thurston, "Alphabet," 621–31, which describes an ancient church dedication ceremony in which an attendant sprinkles ashes on the floor of the church in the form of a cross from corner to corner. The bishop then takes his crozier and marks out in the ashes the Greek alphabet, from the northwest corner to the southeast corner, and the Latin alphabet, from southwest to northeast. For Jewish mystical tradition equating the alphabet and God's name, see Dornseiff, *Das Alphabet*, 69–80; Scholem, *Origins*, 29n48; Idel, "On the Method," 223–24.

28. See R. Moses b. Naḥman, *Peirushei ha-Torah*, Introduction, 1:6.

29. Lévi, "Commentaire biblique," 237–38, reprinted in Assaf, *Meqorot*, 1:1. The second text is found just before the description of the initiation rite in *Sefer ha-Asufot*, f. 67a.

30. Although Israel Lévi identified this R. Leontin as the late tenth-/early eleventh-century Rhenish teacher of Rabbeinu Gershom of Mainz (d. 1028), it is more likely, as Abraham Epstein concluded, that he is a twelfth-century figure. See Epstein, "Leontin und andere Namen," 557–70.

31. The Hebrew: *ToRah zivah lanu moSHe moRaSHah QehillaT yaʿaQov*. Other letters are doubled in this verse, such as h[eh], l[amed], v[av], and m[em], but they are not included in the custom. The attachment of the custom to the verse is forced. Compare the use of the name "QRISTOS" in the ancient Jewish magical text *Sefer ha-Razim*, 73, and compare the use of other Christian names—"Maria" and "Parakletos"—in other Jewish magical formulas in Trachtenberg, *Jewish Magic and Superstition*, 103.

32. Idel, "World of the Angels," 2–3, 6.

33. See esp. Soloveitchik, "Three Themes in the *Sefer Ḥasidim*."

34. Bonfil, "Between Eretz Israel and Babylonia," passim, and Grossman, *Ḥakhmei Ashkenaz*, 157–58, 424–40.

35. It should be remembered that the Tosafists were returning to the dialectical methods of the Babylonian Talmud itself, without the leveling effect of the geonic codifiers who had successfully suppressed commentary and dialectic in the Muslim-Jewish world for centuries. See Soloveitchik, "Three Themes in the *Sefer Ḥasidim*." It was an innovation in twelfth-century Ashkenaz, which had relied until recently on its unwritten customs from a Byzantine-Palestinian-Italian past.

36. Grossman, *Ḥakhmei Ashkenaz*, 361–99.

37. See Bonfil, "Between Eretz Israel and Babylonia," 22; Abrams, "Literary Emergence."

38. See Marcus, *Piety and Society*, chapters 7 and 8. I would add that the German Pietists drew on ancient customs and traditions but that R. Judah the Pietist was more idiosyncratic and unpredictable about following them, a direction suggested by Israel Ta-Shema, in a conversation. In contrast, R. Eleazar of Worms was more conservative in presenting them as valid customs. Their different attitudes toward the children's initiation rite is indicative of this general difference. See *Piety and Society*, 113–14, and Marcus, "Historical Meaning."

39. *Sefer ha-Roqeaḥ* is itself a prime example. See Urbach, *Baʿalei ha-Tosafot*, 392–99.

40. A hint of this major transformation from living custom to the newer book learning is preserved in a comment by the brothers R. Moses and R. Samuel of Evreux, in Normandy, that "Talmuds, commentaries and novellae and (other) compositions are our teachers, [not] men." See R. Aaron b. Jacob ha-Kohen of Lunel, *Orḥot Ḥayyim*, 64b, quoted in Kanarfogel, *Jewish Education and Society*, 153n6.

41. See chapter 3, where I discuss how the text became part of the Mishnah not much earlier than the twelfth century. Once the Tosafists considered it to be mishnaic, they accorded it authority over other competing views, including the German-Jewish custom of beginning on Shavuot; the authors of the German-Jewish tradition affirmed their custom's validity and wrote it down in part as a conservative response to the Tosafist's position.

42. For the clash in the twelfth century between newly assertive written authority and older customs, see Clanchy, *From Memory to Written Record*, and Stock, *Implications of Literacy*. Ironically, it is memory that permits adaptation and transpositions that written texts freeze. See Clanchy, "Remembering the Past," 169–72.

43. See Boswell, *Christianity*, 269–302; Jordan, *French Monarchy*, 56–238; Rubin, *Corpus Christi*, 43–48.

44. My appreciation to Robert Bonfil for this suggestion.

45. See f. 67b. Had he wanted to, he could have compared the honeyed cakes to manna and adopted the rabbinic view that the manna was not excreted. See *Sifrei Be-Midbar*, Baha'alotekha, sec. 88, (p.) 87; Neusner, *Sifré*, 2:87, B. Yoma 75b, and Swartz, " 'Like the Ministering Angels,' " 159.

46. James de Vitry, "de sacramentis," p. 214, quoted in Rubin, *Corpus Christi*, 38.

47. Roland Bandinelli, "Sentences," in Gietl, *Die Sentenzen Rolands nachmals Papste Alexander III* (Freiburg, 1891), 232, cited in Rubin, *Corpus Christi*, 37.

48. See R. Meir b. Barukh of Rothenburg, *Teshuvot Pesaqim u-Minhagim*, 1:99–100. Cf. *Shulhan 'Arukh*, Orah Hayyim, Hilekhot Shabbat, 340:3, where R. Moses Isserles adds: "It is forbidden to break a cake on which letters have been written even though one only intends to eat it, since this constitutes erasing (on the Sabbath and is forbidden)."

49. *Sefer ha-Mordecai* on Shabbat, par. 369 and notes; B. Niddah 17a.

50. R. Meir b. Barukh, *Teshuvot, Pesaqim, u-Minhagim*, 2:264, par. 217.

51. *Sefer ha-Roqeah*, par. 296.

52. Assaf, *Meqorot* 4:12n5, quotes R. David's *Migdal David* from a Jerusalem manuscript. See Zimmer, "R. David b. Isaac of Fulda," 223 and n49, quoted from R. David b. Isaac, *Migdal David*, Jerusalem, National Library, Hebrew MS Octavo 397; no. 43, in Scholem, *Catalogus*, 111–12.

53. *Siftei Kohen* on *Shulhan 'Arukh*, Yoreh De'ah, 245:8. Some traces did persist as in the case of R. Jacob Emden (1697–1776). See Cooper, *Eat and Be Satisfied*, 118, and Levin, *Childhood in Exile*, 49–50.

54. See Boswell, *Kindness*, 228–55; 296–321; Quinn, *Benedictine Oblation*.

55. 1 Sam. 1; Boswell, *Kindness*, 147, 442–43; Shahar, *Childhood*, 191–92. For Bede, see his *Ecclesiastical History*, vol. 24, "Autobiographical Note," 329. See Guibert of Nogent, *Memoirs*, bk. 1, ch. 3, p. 42.

56. See *St. Benedict's Rule for Monasteries*, chapters 58–59. The latter includes the following ritual: "If anyone of the nobility offers his son to God in the monastery and the boy is very young, let his parents draw up the petition which we mentioned above (c. 58); and at the oblation let them wrap the petition and the boy's hand in the altar cloth and so offer him." A text that describes the ritual from the late eleventh century is part of *The Monastic Constitutions of Lanfranc*, 110–11. As the editor points out, about this very time Ordericus Vitalis and Suger of St. Denis were child oblates.

57. Radding, *World Made by Men*, 231, 107.

58. Boswell, *Kindness*, 314–15.

59. See Kraemer, "Images of Jewish Childhood," 68–78.

60. For evidence that some Jews in Renaissance Italy continued the earlier patterns, see Weinstock, "Ad Ya'avor Za'am ha-Na'arut," "Rites of Passage"; Bonfil, *Jewish Life in Renaissance Italy*.

61. See B. Sukkah 42a, Gilat, "Age Thirteen," and Goldin, "Beziehung," 211–56.

62. On tefillin, see Klein, *Guide to Jewish Religious Practice*, 7, who points to the discrepancy between the Talmud's provision (when ready) and contemporary practice (age thirteen). Tefillin are leather boxes in which biblical texts are written. They are wrapped around the arm and placed on the head, and are ancient. See Rabinowitz, "Tefillin," 898–904. On Torah, see B. Megillah 23a; R. Joseph Karo, *Shulḥan 'Arukh*, Oraḥ Ḥayyim 282:3; cf. Goitein, *Mediterranean Society*, 2:556n9, and *Sidrei Ḥinukh*, 36.

63. On fasts, see Schechter, "Child," 306–12, and Gilat, "Age Thirteen," 44–45; on Yemen, see Goitein, "Jewish Education in Yemen," 241–48.

64. B. Sukkah 42a and *Sefer ha-'Iṭṭur*, 26c.

65. See Mordecai b. Hillel ha-Kohen, *Sefer ha-Mordecai* on Berakhot, par. 60, which includes R. Jacob Tam's view as well.

66. Karo, *Beit Yosef* on Ṭur, Oraḥ Ḥayyim, 37:4; Isserles, *Darkhei Moshe* on Ṭur, Oraḥ Ḥayyim, 37. See Tal, "Isserles, Moses ben Israel," 9:1081–85. By the seventeenth century in Poland, it was accepted that boys could begin to put on tefillin three or four months before their bar mitzvah. See R. Abraham Gombiner (ca. 1637–1683), *Magen Avraham* on *Shulḥan 'Arukh*, Oraḥ Ḥayyim 37:4.

67. On the talmudic usage of the term *bar mitzvah* (obligated), see, for example, B. Bava Batra 96a. Referring to a boy age thirteen years and a day, the term was an innovation and replaced such earlier terms for a boy of majority as *gadol* (adult) or *bar 'oneshin* (culpable/responsible); see Löw, *Lebensalter*, 211.

68. See Isserles on Karo, *Shulḥan 'Arukh*, Oraḥ Ḥayyim 54:10; Karo, loc. cit. For the custom of letting minors lead only the Sabbath night service, see Ta-Shema, "Some Matters Relating to Mourners' Qaddish," 566–68.

69. Isserles, *Darkhei Moshe* on Ṭur, Oraḥ Ḥayyim, 225:1, and Isserles on Karo, *Shulḥan 'Arukh*, Oraḥ Ḥayyim, 225:1. See, too, Isserles on Karo, *Shulḥan 'Arukh*, Oraḥ Ḥayyim, 55:10: "when he becomes bar mitzvah," without any elaboration.

70. *Midrash Bereishit Rabbah*, sec. 63, Theodor-Albeck 2:693. Traditional Jews recite this text today, after a son has read from the Torah at his bar mitzvah, as Isserles prescribed it, without mention of God's name and kingship.

71. Isaac b. Moses of Vienna, *Or Zaru'a* II, par. 43, 20; I, par. 753, 215–16.

72. Jacob b. Moses ha-Levi Moellin (Maharil), *Minhagei Maharil*, Sabbioneta, 81a.

73. Meir b. Barukh of Rothenburg, *Sefer She'eilot u-Teshuvot*, no. 268, 21a.

74. *Yam shel Shlomo* on Bava Qama 7, 37, cited in Löw, *Lebensalter*, 411n82, and see Freehof, "Ceremonial Creativity," 220n6.

75. See Freehof, "Ceremonial Creativity," 220.

76. Aaron b. Jacob ha-Kohen of Lunel, *Sefer Orḥot Ḥayyim*, I, 40c, par. 58.

77. Arnaldo Momigliano, "Medieval Jewish Autobiography," 35–36, suggests evidence of a

bar mitzvah rite in the twelfth-century Latin memoir of the Jewish convert Hermannus, but this is farfetched.

78. The differences between these preliminary signs of a new rite in medieval Germany and Provence are clearly not yet the fully developed bar mitzvah rite of passage. Still, one should not give too little weight to several indications that something new has occurred. See the important studies of Weinstock, cited earlier. The anthropological-historical development of Jewish rites of passage, framed in a comparative manner, would be an important project.

79. Ariès, Centuries of Childhood, 10.

80. Schauss, Lifetime, 115.

81. See Goldberg, "Torah and Children."

82. See Sefer Hasidim, ed. Wistinetzki, par. 820.

83. See Ariès, Centuries of Childhood, chapters 1–2; Shahar, Childhood, introduction; Kanarfogel, Jewish Education and Society, introduction.

84. The persistence of the associations of these foods and the Torah is reflected in the instructions for preparing Shavuot dishes, reported by Joselit, New York's Jewish Jews, 112. Jewish Home Beautiful, 72, suggests that when one prepares the traditional blintzes, they can be arranged "like the two Tablets of the Law," and by sprinkling cinnamon on their surface in two parallel lines one can even "suggest the Ten Commandments themselves."

85. Various Jewish communities eat an elaborate set of symbolic foods, such as pumpkin, leek, beet, and dates, as well as honey, on Rosh Hashanah, based on B. Keritot 6a, which refers to eating them, and B. Hor. 12a, which refers to looking at them.

86. The first reference to honey and red apples is in Mahzor Vitry, par. 323, 362. The custom persists to this day.

Bibliography

Primary Sources

Manuscripts

[Anonymous Commentary on Piyyuṭim.] Hamburg. Staats- und Universitätsbibliothek.
  Hebrew MS 17 = Steinschneider Catalogue no. 152, 81a-82a. See Roth, Ernst.
Eleazar ben Judah of Worms. *Sefer ha-Roqeaḥ.* Paris. Bibliothèque Nationale. Hebrew MS 363
  [1452], f. 96a.
Judah ben Qalonimos of Spires. *Yiḥusei Tanna'im ve-Amora'im.* Oxford. Bodleian Library, Hebrew
  MS Opp. 391–93; Neubauer no. 2199.
————. *Yiḥusei Tanna'im ve-Amora'im.* New York. Library of the Jewish Theological Seminary of
  America. MS R 2348 = Mic. 9624, f. 99b.
Leipzig Maḥzor. Leipzig, Universitätsbibliothek, Hebrew MS V. 1102, vol. 1, f. 131a. See Published
  Sources, *Machsor Lipsiae.*
Maḥzor Vitry, "MS Reggio." New York, Library of the Jewish Theological Seminary of America.
  MS Mic. 8092, f. 164b-165a.
Sefer ha-Asufot. London. Jews College 134 (Montefiore 115), f. 67a.

Published Sources

Aaron b. Jacob ha-Kohen of Lunel. *Sefer Orḥot Ḥayyim.* I, Oraḥ Ḥayyim. Florence, 1751.
————. *Sefer Orḥot Ḥayyim.* II. Yoreh De'ah. Edited by M. Schlesinger. Berlin, 1902.
Abraham b. 'Azriel. *Sefer 'Arugat ha-Bosem.* Edited by Ephraim E. Urbach. 4 vols. Jerusalem,
  1939–63.
Abraham b. Isaac. *Sefer ha-Eshkol.* Edited by Hanokh Albeck. Jerusalem, 1935.
Abraham b. Moses (Maimuni). *Iggrot Qena'ot.* In A. A. Lichtenberg, ed., *Qovez Teshuvot ha-Rambam
  ve-Iggerotav.* Leipzig, 1859.
Addison, Lancelot. *The Present State of the Jews (More particularly relating to those in Barbary.) Wherein is
  contained an exact Account of their Customs, Secular and Religious. To which is annexed a Summary Discourse
  of the Misnah [sic], Talmud, and Gemara.* London, 1675.
Aggadat Shir ha-Shirim. Edited by S[olomon] Schechter. Cambridge, 1896.
'Arukh ha-Shalem. Edited by Alexander Kohut. Vienna, 1926. Based on R. Natan b. Yehiel, *'Arukh.*
Assaf, Simha, ed. *Meqorot le-Toledot ha-Ḥinukh be-Yisrael.* 4 vols. Tel Aviv, 1925–48.
Augustine. *Confessions.* Translated by R. S. Pine-Coffin. 1961. Reprint. New York, 1987.

Avot de-Rabbi Natan. Edited by Solomon Schechter. Vienna, 1887. Translated by Judah Goldin as *The Fathers according to Rabbi Nathan*. New Haven, 1955.

Baraita de-Niddah. In *Uralte Tosefta's*. Edited by Chaim Horowitz. Frankfurt am Main, 1889.

Barhadbsabba Arbaya. "Cause de la fondation des écoles." Syriac. Edited by Addai Scher. *Patrologia Orientalis* 4:327–97.

Bede. *Ecclesiastical History of the English People*. Translated by Leo Sherley-Price. Revised by R. E. Latham. London, 1990.

Buxtorf, Johannes. *Synagoga Judaica*. Basel, 1603.

Caesarius of Heisterbach. *Dialogus miraculorum*. Edited by Joseph Strange. 2 vols. Cologne, 1851. Translated by H. von E. Scott and C. C. Swinton Bland as *The Dialogue on Miracles*. 2 vols. London, 1929.

Canetti, Elias. *The Tongue Set Free*. New York, 1979.

Chazan, Robert. Appendices to *European Jewry and the First Crusade*. Berkeley, 1987.

Cicero, *De oratore*. Translated by Edward William Sutton and H. Rackham. 2 vols. Cambridge, Mass., 1942–48.

Daily Prayer Book. Edited by Philip Birnbaum. New York, 1949.

Eleazar b. Judah. *Peirush ha-Roqeah 'al ha-Megillot: Esther, Shir ha-Shirim, Ruth*. Bnai Brak, 1985.

———. *Peirush Shir ha-Shirim*. In *Peirush ha-Roqeah 'al ha-Megillot*. Bnai Brak, 1985.

———. *Sefer ha-Roqeah*. Fano, 1505; Cremona, 1557; Jerusalem, 1960.

Geschichte von den Zehn Märtyrern. Edited by Gottfried Reeg. Tübingen, 1985.

Grayzel, Solomon, ed. *The Church and the Jews in the Thirteenth Century*. 1933. New York, 1966.

The Greek Magical Papyri in Translation, Including the Demotic Spells. Edited by Hans Dieter Betz. Chicago, 1986.

Guibert of Nogent, Abbot. *The Memoirs of Abbot Guibert of Nogent*. Translated and edited by John F. Benton as *Self and Society in Medieval France*. Toronto, 1984.

Habermann, Avraham M. *Sefer Gezeirot Ashkenaz ve-Zarfat*. Jerusalem, 1945.

Harba de-Moshe. Edited by Moses Gaster. 1928. Reprint. 3 vols. New York, 1970, 3:68–103.

Havdalah de-Rabbi 'Aqivah. Edited by Gershom Scholem. *Tarbiz* 50(1981): 243–81.

The Hebrew Paraphrase of Saadia Gaon's Kitab Al-Amanat W'al-I'tiqadat. Edited by Ronald Charles Keiner. Ann Arbor, 1984.

Huqqei ha-Torah ha-Qadmonim (The Ancient Rules of the Torah). Transcribed from Oxford, Bodleian Library, Hebrew MS Opp. 342, Neubauer no. 873, f. 196a–198b, in Kanarfogel, *Jewish Education and Society*, 101–15. Also printed in Güdemann, *Geschichte des Erziehungswesens*, 1:92–106, 264–72, and Assaf, *Meqorot*, 1:6–16. An abbreviated English translation appears in Jacobs, *Jews of Angevin England*, 243–51.

Isaac b. Abba Mari of Marseilles. *Sefer ha-'Ittur*. Lemberg, 1860.

Isaac b. Judah Ibn Giyyat. *Me'ah She'arim*. Fürth, 1861.

Isaac b. Moses of Vienna. *Sefer Or Zaru'a*. 2 parts in 1 vol. Zhitomir, 1882.

Jacob b. Asher. *Arba'ah Turim*. Piove di Sacco, 1475.

Jacob b. Moses ha-Levi Moellin (Maharil). *Minhagei Maharil*. Sabbioneta, 1556.

Jacob of Marvège. *She'eilot u-Teshuvot Min ha-Shamayim*. Edited by Reuven Margaliot. Jerusalem, 1957.

Jacobs, Joseph, ed. *The Jews of Angevin England: Documents and Records*. 1893. Reprint. Westmead, 1969.

Jewish Home Beautiful. Edited by Betty Greenberg and Althea O. Silverman. New York, 1941.

The Jews and the Crusaders. Edited and translated by Shlomo Eidelberg. Madison, 1977.

Joseph and Aseneth. Translated by C. Burchard. In James H. Charlesworth, The Old Testament Pseudepigrapha, 2:177–247. New York, 1985.

Joseph Karo. Shulḥan ʿArukh. Venice, 1564–65; Jerusalem, 1967.

Judah b. Samuel, he-Ḥasid. "Narrative Fantasies from Sefer Ḥasidim. Edited and translated by Ivan G. Marcus. In Rabbinic Fantasies, edited by David Stern and Mark Mirsky, 215–38. Philadelphia, 1990.

———. Sefer Ḥasidim. Edited by Jehuda Wistinetzki. Frankfurt am Main, 1924.

Judah Messer Leon, Book of the Honeycomb's Flow. (Sefer Nofet Ẓufim). Edited and translated by Isaac Rabinowitz. Ithaca, N.Y., 1983.

Kafka, Franz. "Before the Law." In German Stories, edited by Harry Steinauer. New York, 1984.

Kol Bo. Naples, 1490.

Leon Modena. The Autobiography of a Seventeenth-Century Venetian Rabbi, Leon Modena's Life of Judah. Translated and edited by Mark R. Cohen. Princeton, 1988.

———. Lev ha-Aryeh. Venice, 1610.

Levin, Shemaryahu. Childhood in Exile. New York, 1929.

Maʿaseh Book. Edited by Moses Gaster. Philadelphia, 1934.

Machsor Lipsiae. Edited by Elias Katz. Leipzig, 1964.

Maḥzor Vitry. Edited by S. Horowitz. Berlin, 1889–97.

Masekhet Soferim. Edited by Michael Higger. New York, 1937.

Mayseh Bukh. Basel, 1602.

Meir b. Barukh of Rothenburg (Maharam). Sefer Sheʾeilot u-Teshuvot. Edited by N. Rabinowitz. Lemberg, 1860.

———. Teshuvot, Pesaqim u-Minhagim. Edited by Yitzhaq Zeev Kahana. 3 vols. Jerusalem, 1957–63.

Meir b. Isaac Aldabi. Shevilei Emunah. Riva di Trento, 1559.

Mekhilta de-Rabbi Yishmael. Edited by H. S. Horowitz and I. A. Rabin. 1930. 2d ed. Jerusalem, 1970.

Midrash Alpha Beta de-Rabbi ʿAqiba. In Beit ha-Midrash, edited by Adolf Jellinek, 3:12–64. 6 parts in 2 vols. Jerusalem, 1967.

Midrash Bereishit Rabbah. Edited by J. Theodor and H. Albeck. 1903–36. Reprint. 3 vols. Jerusalem, 1965.

Midrash Pesiqta Rabbati. Edited by Meir Friedmann. Vienna, 1880. Translated by William G. Braude as Pesikta Rabbati. 2 vols. New Haven, 1968.

Midrash Shir ha-Shirim. Edited by Lazar Grünhut. Jerusalem, 1897.

Midrash Tanḥuma. Edited by Solomon Buber. Vilna, 1885.

Midrash Tehillim. Edited by Solomon Buber. 1891. Reprint. Jerusalem, 1965–66. Translated by William Braude as The Midrash on Psalms. 2 vols. New Haven, 1959.

Midrash Vayyiqra Rabbah. Edited by Mordecai Margalioth. 1956–58. Reprint. New York, 1993.

Midrash Zuta ʿal Shir ha-Shirim, Rut, Eikhah, ve-Qohelet. Edited by Solomon Buber. 1894. Reprint. Tel Aviv, 1964.

Miller, Robert J., ed. The Complete Gospels. San Francisco, 1992.

The Monastic Constitutions of Lanfranc. Edited by David Knowles. London, 1951.

Mordecai b. Hillel ha-Kohen. Sefer ha-Mordecai. In Vilna edition of Babylonian Talmud.

Mordecai Hakohen, The Book of Mordechai. Edited and translated by Harvey Goldberg. Philadelphia, 1980.

Moses b. Henikh. Brantspiegel. Basel, 1633.

Moses b. Maimon (Maimonides). Peirush ha-Mishnah (Commentary to the Mishnah). Edited by Joseph Kafih. 3 vols. Jerusalem, 1965.

Moses b. Nahman (Nachmanides). Peirushei ha-Torah. Edited by Chaim B. Chavel. 2 vols. Jerusalem, 1967.

Neubauer, A[dolph], and M. Stern, eds. Hebräische Berichte über die Judenverfolgungen während der Kreuzzüge. Berlin, 1892.

Nissim b. Jacob Ibn Shahin, Hibbur Yafeh mei-ha-Yeshu'ah. Edited by Haim Hirschberg. Jerusalem, 1970. Translated by William M. Brinner as An Elegant Composition Concerning Relief after Adversity. New Haven, 1977.

Nizzahon Vetus. Edited and translated by David Berger as The Jewish-Christian Debate in the High Middle Ages. Philadelphia, 1979.

Ozar ha-Ge'onim. Edited by Benjamin M. Levin. 13 vols. Haifa, 1928; Jerusalem, 1929–.

Pesikta: Die älteste Hagada redigiert in Palästina von Rab Kahana. Edited by Solomon Buber. Lyck, 1868.

Pesikta de Rav Kahana. Edited by Bernard Mandelbaum. 2 vols. New York, 1962. Translated by William G. (Gershon Zev) Braude and Israel J. Kapstein as Pesikta de-Rab Kahana. Philadelphia, 1975.

Piyyutei Rabbi Ephraim b. R. Yaaqov mi-Bonna. Edited by A. M. Habermann. In Studies of the Research Institute for Hebrew Poetry in Jerusalem, 7:217–302. Jerusalem–Tel Aviv, 1958.

Quintilian, Institutio oratoria. Translated by H. E. Butler. 1920–22. Reprint. Cambridge, Mass., 1969.

Rhetorica ad Herennium. Translated by Harry Caplan. Cambridge, Mass., 1968.

R[oss], A[lexander]. A View of Jewish Religion. London, 1656.

Roth, Ernst. Cod. hebr. 17 und 61 Hamburg. Facsimile edition. Jerusalem, 1980.

St. Benedict's Rule for Monasteries. Translated by Leonard J. Doyle. Collegeville, Minn., 1948.

Schäfer, Peter, ed. Synopse zur Hekhalot-Literatur. Tübingen, 1981.

Scheindlin, Raymond P. The Gazelle: Medieval Hebrew Poems on God, Israel and the Soul. Philadelphia, 1991.

———. Wine, Women, and Death: Medieval Poems on the Good Life. Philadelphia, 1986.

Schirmann, Haim. Ha-Shirah ha-'Ivrit bi-Sefarad u-ve-Provence. 4 vols. Jerusalem, 1961.

Seder 'Avodat Yisrael. Edited by S. Baer. Rödelheim, 1868.

Seder Eliahu Rabbah and Seder Eliahu Zuta (Tanna d'be Eliahu). Edited by Meir Friedmann. Vienna, 1902.

Seder Rav 'Amram Gaon. Edited by Daniel Goldschmidt. Jerusalem, 1971.

Sefer Ben Sira ha-Shalem. Edited by Moshe Zvi Segal. Jerusalem, 1959.

Sefer Ha-Razim. Edited by Mordecai Margalioth. Jerusalem, 1966.

Sefer Razi'el. Amsterdam, 1701.

Sefer Yosippon. Edited by David Flusser. Jerusalem, 1978.

Selected Sermons of Stephen Langton. Edited by Phyllis B. Roberts. Toronto, 1980.

"Sidrei de-Shimmusha Rabba." Edited by Gershom Scholem. Tarbiz 16 (1944–45): 196–209.

Sifra. Edited by I. H. Weiss. Vienna, 1862. Reprint. New York, 1947.

Sifre ʿal Sefer Be-Midbar. Edited by H. S. Horowitz. 1917. Reprint. New York, 1947. Translated by Jacob Neusner as *Sifré to Numbers.* 2 vols. Atlanta, 1986.

Sifre on Deuteronomy. 1939. Edited by Louis Finkelstein. Reprint. New York, 1993. Translated by Reuven Hammer as *Sifre: A Tannaitic Commentary on the Book of Deuteronomy.* New Haven, 1986.

"The Sword of Moses." In *Texts and Studies,* edited by Moses Gaster, 1:312–37. 1928. Reprint. 3 vols. New York, 1970.

Talmud Bavli. Vilna, 1886.

Talmud Yerushalmi. Venice, 1523–24.

Teshuvot ha-Geʾonim. Edited by Abraham Harkavy. Berlin, 1887.

Toratan shel Rishonim. [*Halachische Schriften der Geonim,* I]. Edited by Chaim Horowitz. Frankfurt am Main, 1881.

Tosefta. Edited by Saul Lieberman. New York, 1955–93.

Walafried Strabo, "The School Life of Walafried Strabo." Translated by James Davie Butler. In *The Bibliotheca Sacra,* 40:152–72. Andover, 1883.

Secondary Sources

Aberbach. M. "Educational Institutions and Problems during the Talmudic Ages." *Hebrew Union College Annual* 37 (1966): 107–20.

Abrahams, Israel. *Jewish Life in the Middle Ages.* 1896. Reprint. New York, 1975.

Abrams, Daniel. "The Literary Emergence of Esotericism in German Pietism," *Shofar* 12:2 (Winter 1994): 67–85.

Abulafia, Anna Sapir. "Invectives against Christianity in the Hebrew Chronicles of the First Crusade." In *Crusade and Settlement,* edited by Peter W. Edbury, 66–72. Cardiff, 1985.

Alexander, Bobby C. "Ceremony." In *Encyclopedia of Religion,* edited by Mircea Eliade, 3:179–83. New York, 1987.

Alexander, P[hilip]. Introduction to "3 (Hebrew Apocalypse of) Enoch." In *The Old Testament Pseudepigrapha,* edited by James H. Charlesworth, 1:223–315. New York, 1983.

Alexander-Frizer, Tamar. *The Pious Sinner: Ethics and Aesthetics in the Medieval Ḥasidic Narrative.* Texts and Studies in Medieval and Early Modern Judaism, vol. 5. Tübingen, 1991.

Amir, Yehoshua. "The Place of Psalm 119 in the History of Judaism." Hebrew. In *Teʿudah* 2 [= ʿIyyunim ba-Miqra, The Y. M. Grints Memorial Volume, ed. Benjamin Uffenheimer], 56–81. Tel Aviv, 1982.

Andree, Richard. "ABC Kuchen." *Zeitschrift für Volkskunde* 15 (1905): 94–96.

Aptowitzer, Avigdor. *Mavo le-Sefer Raviah.* Jerusalem, 1938.

Ariès, Philippe. *Centuries of Childhood: A Social History of Family Life.* Translated by Robert Baldick. New York, 1962.

Arnold, Klaus. *Kind und Gesellschaft in Mittelalter und Renaissance.* Munich, 1980.

Arzt, Max. "The Teacher in Talmud and Midrash." In *Mordecai M. Kaplan Jubilee Volume,* 35–47. New York, 1953.

Bacher, Wilhelm. "Das altjüdische Schulwesen." *Jahrbuch für jüdische Geschichte und Literatur* 6 (1903): 48–81.

Baer, Yitzhaq. *A History of the Jews in Christian Spain.* 2 vols. Philadelphia, 1961–66.

———. "The Mystical Teachings in Abner of Burgos's Christology." Hebrew. Gershom Scholem Festschrift. *Tarbiz* 27 (1958): 278–89.

———. "Rashi and the Historical Reality of His Times." Hebrew. *Tarbiz* 20 (1949): 320–32.

———. "The Religious-Social Tendency in *Sefer Ḥasidim.*" Hebrew. *Zion* 3 (1937): 1–50.

———. *Yisrael ba-'Amim.* Jerusalem, 1955.

Balogh, Josef. "'Voces Paginarum': Beiträge zur Geschichte des lauten Lesens und Schreibens." *Philologus* 82 (1927): 84–109, 202–40.

Banitt, Menahem. "Une langue fantôme: le judéo-français." *Revue de linguistique romane* 27 (1963): 245–94.

Basser, Herbert W. "The Acts of Jesus." In *The Frank Talmage Memorial Volume, I,* edited by Barry Walfish, 273–82. Haifa, 1993.

Beitl, Richard, ed., *Wörterbuch der deutschen Volkskunde.* 3d. ed. Stuttgart, 1974.

Ben-Sasson, Haim Hillel. "Assimilation in Jewish History." Hebrew. 1976. Reprinted in Haim-Hillel Ben-Sasson, *Rezef U-Temurah,* edited by Joseph Hacker, 53–69. Tel Aviv, 1984.

———. "On Chronographical Tendencies in the Middle Ages." Hebrew. In *Historiyonim ve-Askolot Historiyot.* Jerusalem, 1963.

———. "The Social Views of R. Yohanan Luria." Hebrew. *Zion* 27 (1962): 166–98.

Benson, Robert L., and Giles Constable, eds. *Renaissance and Renewal in the Twelfth Century.* Cambridge, Mass., 1982.

Berger, David. "Christians, Gentiles, and the Talmud: A Fourteenth-Century Jewish Response to the Attack on Rabbinic Judaism." In *Religionsgespräche im Mittelalter,* edited by Bernard Lewis and Friederick Niehwöhner, 115–30. Wiesbaden, 1992.

Bickerman, Elias. *The Jews in the Greek Age.* Cambridge, Mass., 1988.

Bischoff, Bernhard. "Elementarunterricht und *Probationes Pennae* in der Ersten Hälfte des Mittelalters." In *Classical and Mediaeval Studies in Honor of Edward Kennard Rand,* edited by Leslie Webber Jones, 9–20. New York, 1938.

Blau, Ludwig. *Das altjüdische Zauberwesen.* Budapest, 1898.

Blumenkranz, Bernhard. *Le juif au miroir de l'art chrétien.* Paris, 1966.

Bonfil, Reuven. "Between the Land of Israel and Babylonia." Hebrew. *Shalem* 5 (1977): 1–30.

———. "Can Medieval Storytelling Help Understanding Midrash? The Story of Paltiel: A Preliminary Study on History and Midrash." In *The Midrashic Imagination: Jewish Exegesis, Thought and History,* edited by Michael Fishbane, 228–54. Albany, 1993.

———. "The Evidence of Agobard of Lyons about the Cultural World of the Jews in His Town in the Ninth Century." Hebrew. In *Meḥqarim be-Qabbalah, Be-Filosophiah Yehudit, u-ve-Sifrut ha-Musar ve-ha-Hagut, Mugashim le-Yeshayah Tishby,* edited by Joseph Dan and Joseph Hacker, 327–48. Jerusalem, 1986.

———. Introduction to Judah Messer Leon, *Sefer Nofet Zufim.* Hebrew. Jerusalem, 1981.

———. *Jewish Life in Renaissance Italy.* Translated by Anthony Oldcorn. Berkeley, 1994.

———. "Myth, Rhetoric and History? An Inquiry into *Megillat Aḥima'az.*" Hebrew. In *Tarbut ve-Hevrah be-Toledot Yisrael bimei ha-Beinayim* [Haim Hillel Ben-Sasson Memorial Volume], edited by Menahem Ben-Sasson et al., 99–135. Jerusalem, 1989.

Bonner, Stanley F. *Education in Ancient Rome.* Berkeley, 1977.

Boon, James A. Other Tribes, Other Scribes: Symbolic Anthropology in the Comparative Study of Cultures,
    Histories, Religions and Texts. Cambridge, 1982.
Boswell, John. Christianity, Social Tolerance, and Homosexuality. Chicago, 1980.
———. The Kindness of Strangers. New York, 1988.
Boyarin, Daniel. Carnal Israel: Reading Sex in Talmudic Culture. Berkeley, 1993.
Brauer, Erich. Yehudei Kurdistan. Edited by Raphael Patai. Jerusalem, 1947.
Briggs, Lloyd Cabot, and Norina Lami Guède. No More for Ever: A Saharan Jewish Town. Papers of
    the Peabody Museum of Archaeology and Ethnology, Harvard University, vol. 55, no. 1.
    1964. Reprint. Millwood, N.Y., 1978.
Brill, Moshe. "The Age of the Child When He Enters School." Hebrew. Tarbiẓ 9 (1938): 350–74.
Browe, Peter. "Die Eucharistie als Zaubermittel im Mittelalter." Archiv für Kulturgeschichte 20
    (1930): 134–54.
Brown, Peter. The World of Late Antiquity. London, 1971.
Burke, Peter. The Historical Anthropology of Early Modern Italy. Cambridge, 1987.
Burkert, Walter. Homo Necans: The Anthropology of Ancient Greek Sacrificial Ritual and Myth. Translated
    by Peter Bing. Berkeley, 1983.
Burrow, J. A. The Ages of Man. Oxford, 1986.
Butler, James Davie. "Medieval German Schools." In The Bibliotheca Sacra, vol. 39, edited by
    Edward A. Park, 401–17. Andover, Mass., 1882.
Butterfield, Herbert. The Whig Interpretation of History. London, 1931.
Bynum, Caroline Walker. Fragmentation and Redemption: Essays on Gender and the Human Body in Medieval
    Religion. New York, 1991.
———. Holy Feast and Holy Fast: The Religious Significance of Food to Medieval Women. Berkeley, 1987.
———. Jesus as Mother: Studies in the Spirituality of the High Middle Ages. Berkeley, 1982.
Cabaniss, A. "Bodo-Eleazar: A Famous Jewish Convert." Jewish Quarterly Review 43 (1952–53):
    313–28.
Carruthers, Mary. The Book of Memory. Cambridge, 1990.
Chazan, Robert. European Jewry and the First Crusade. Berkeley, 1987.
Chenu, M.-D. Nature, Man and Society in the Twelfth Century. Chicago, 1968.
Chernus, Ira. Mysticism in Rabbinic Judaism. Berlin, 1982.
Chestnutt, Randall D. Conversion in Joseph and Aseneth. Ph.D. diss., Department of Religion, Duke
    University, 1986.
Clanchy, M. T. From Memory to Written Record: England, 1066–1307. Cambridge, Mass., 1979.
———. "Remembering the Past and the Good Old Law." History 55, no. 184 (June 1970):
    165–76
Clifford, James. "On Ethnographic Authority." Representations 1, no. 2 (Spring 1983): 118–46.
Clifford, James, and George E. Marcus, eds. Writing Culture: The Poetics and Politics of Ethnography.
    Berkeley, 1986.
Cohen, Evelyn M. "The Teacher, the Father, and the Virgin Mary in the Leipzig Maḥzor." Proceed-
    ings of the Tenth World Congress of Jewish Studies. Division D, vol. 2: Art, Folklore and Music, 71–76.
    Jerusalem, 1990.
Cohen, Gerson D. "The Hebrew Chronicles and the Ashkenazic Tradition." In Minḥah le-Naḥum
    [Nahum Sarna Jubilee Volume], edited by Marc Brettler and Michael Fishbane, 36–53.
    London, 1993.

————. Introduction to Abraham Ibn Daud, *Sefer Ha-Qabbalah*. Philadelphia, 1967.

————. "Messianic Postures of Ashkenazim and Sephardim." *Studies of the Leo Baeck Institute*, edited by Max Kreutzberger, 3–42. New York, 1967.

Cohen, Jeremy. *The Friars and the Jews*. Ithaca, N.Y., 1982.

————. "Philosophical Exegesis in Historical Perspective: The Case of the Binding of Isaac." In *Divine Omniscience and Omnipotence in Medieval Philosophy*, edited by Tamar Rudavsky, 135–42. Dordrecht, 1985.

————. "The '1096 Persecution Narratives'—the Events and the Libels: Martyrological Stories in Their Social-Cultural Contexts." Hebrew. *Zion* 59:2 (1994): 169–208.

————. "Towards a Functional Classification of Jewish Anti-Christian Polemic in the High Middle Ages." In *Religionsgespräche im Mittelalter*, edited by Bernard Lewis and Friedrich Neiwöhner, 93–114. Wiesbaden, 1992.

Cohen, Mark R. *Under Crescent and Cross: The Jews in the Middle Ages*. Princeton, 1994.

Cohen, Shaye J. D. "Epigraphical Rabbis." *Jewish Quarterly Review* 72 (1981–82): 1–17.

————. *From the Maccabees to the Mishnah*. Philadelphia, 1987.

————. "The Place of the Rabbi in Jewish Society in Late Antiquity." In *The Galilee in Late Antiquity*, edited by Lee I. Levine, 157–73. New York, 1992.

————. "The Rabbinic Conversion Ceremony." *Journal of Jewish Studies* 41, no. 2 (Autumn 1990): 177–203.

————. "The Significance of Yavneh: Pharisees, Rabbis, and the End of Jewish Sectarianism." *Hebrew Union College Annual* 55 (1984): 27–53.

————. "The Temple and the Synagogue." In *The Temple in Antiquity*, edited by Truman G. Madsen, 151–74. Provo, 1984.

Cook, Arthur Bernard. "The Bee in Greek Mythology." *Journal of Hellenic Studies* 15 (1895): 1–24.

Cooper, John. *Eat and Be Satisfied: A Social History of Jewish Food*. Northvale, N.J., 1993.

Cramer, Peter. *Baptism and Change in the Early Middle Ages, c. 250–c. 1150*. Cambridge, 1993.

Crocker, J. Christopher. "My Brother the Parrot." In *The Social Use of Metaphor*, edited by J. David Sapir and J. Christopher Crocker, 164–92. Philadelphia, 1977.

Curtius, Ernst Robert. *European Literature and the Latin Middle Ages*. Princeton, 1953.

Daiches, Samuel. *Babylonian Oil Magic in the Talmud and in the Later Jewish Literature*. London, 1913.

Dan, Joseph. *Ha-Sippur ha-'Ivri Bimei ha-Beinayim*. Jerusalem, 1975.

————. "The Theophany of Sar ha-Torah: Wonderworking Story, Magic, and Mysticism in the Heikhalot and Merkavah Literature." Hebrew. *Jerusalem Studies in Jewish Folklore*, 13–14:127–57. Jerusalem, 1992.

————. *Three Types of Ancient Jewish Mysticism*. Cincinnati, 1984.

————. *Torat ha-Sod shel Ḥasidut Ashkenaz*. Jerusalem, 1968.

Daniélou, Jean. "Eucharistie et Cantique des Cantiques." *Irénikon* 23 (1950): 257–77.

Darnton, Robert. *The Great Cat Massacre and Other Episodes of French Cultural History*. New York, 1984.

————. "The Symbolic Element in History." *Journal of Modern History* 58:1 (March 1986): 218–34.

Davidson, Israel, ed. *Oẓar ha-Shirah ve-ha-Piyyuṭ*. 1924. Reprint. 4 vols. New York, 1970.

Davis, Moshe. "Moroccan Water-Feast." *American Hebrew*, May 24, 1940:4.

Davis, Natalie Zemon. *From the Archives*. Stanford, 1987.

————. *The Return of Martin Guerre*. Cambridge, Mass., 1983.

————. "The Rites of Violence." In *Society and Culture in Early Modern France*, 153–87. Stanford, 1979.

————. *Society and Culture in Early Modern France*. Stanford, 1979.

————. "Some Tasks and Themes in the Study of Popular Religion." In *The Pursuit of Holiness in Late Medieval and Renaissance Religion*, edited by Charles Trinkhaus and Heicko A. Oberman, 307–36. Leiden, 1974.

————. "Women on Top." In *Society and Culture in Early Modern France*, 124–51. Stanford, 1979.

Demaitre, Luke. "The Idea of Childhood and Child Care in Medieval Writings of the Middle Ages." *Journal of Psychohistory* 4 (1977): 461–90.

Demsky, Aaron. "Sheshakh." Hebrew. In *Enẓiqlopedia Miqra'it*, 8:267–68. Jerusalem, 1982.

————. "Writing in Ancient Israel and Early Judaism. Part One: The Biblical Period." In *Mikra: Text, Translation, Reading and Interpretation of the Hebrew Bible in Ancient Judaism and Early Christianity*, edited by Martin Jan Mulder, 1–20. Asses/Maastricht and Philadelphia, 1988.

Despres, Denise. "Cultic Anti-Judaism and Chaucer's Litel Clergeon." *Modern Philology* 91:4 (May 1994): 413–27.

Dobrinsky, Herbert C. *A Treasury of Sephardic Laws and Customs*. New York, 1986.

Dornseiff, Franz. "ABC." In *Handwörterbuch des deutschen Aberglaubens*, edited by Hanns Bächtold-Stäubli, 1:14–16. Berlin, 1927.

————. *Das Alphabet in Mystik und Magie*. Leipzig, 1925.

Douglas, Mary. *Purity and Danger*. London, 1966.

Duby, Georges, et al. "Portraits." In *A History of Private Life*, edited by Philippe Ariès and Georges Duby, 2:63–85. Cambridge, Mass., 1990.

Dyck, Cornelius J. "Anabaptists." In *The Encyclopedia of Religion*, 1:247–49. New York, 1987.

Eickelman, Dale F. "The Art of Memory: Islamic Education and Its Social Reproduction." *Comparative Studies in Society and History* 20, no. 3 (July 1978): 485–516.

Eilberg-Schwartz, Howard. *The Savage in Judaism: An Anthropology of Israelite Religion and Ancient Judaism*. Bloomington, 1990.

————. "Voyeurism, Anthropology, and the Study of Judaism." *Journal of the American Academy of Religion* 62, no. 1 (Spring 1994): 173–77.

Eilberg-Schwartz, Howard, ed. *People of the Body*. Albany, 1992.

Elbogen, Ismar. *Jewish Liturgy: A Comprehensive History*. Translated by Raymond P. Scheindlin. Philadelphia, 1993.

Eliade, Mircea. *Rites and Symbols of Initiation*. New York, 1958.

Epstein, Abraham. "Leontin und andere Namen in den 'Teʿamim shel Ḥumash,'" *Monatsschrift für Geschichte und Wissenschaft des Judentums* 49 (1900): 557–70.

————. "Studies in *Sefer Yeẓirah*." Hebrew. In Abraham Epstein, *Mi-Qadmoniyot ha-Yehudim* [*Kitvei R. Avraham Epstein*, 2], 179–203. Jerusalem, 1957.

Epstein, Marc Michael. *Dreams of Subversion: Medieval Jewish Art and Literature*. University Park: Pennsylvania State University Press, forthcoming.

————. "The Elephant and the Law: The Medieval Jewish Minority Adapts a Christian Motif." *Art Bulletin* 76, no. 3 (September 1994): 465–78.

————. "'The Ways of Truth Are Curtailed and Hidden': A Medieval Hebrew Fable as a Vehicle for Covert Polemic." *Prooftexts* 14, no. 3 (September 1994): 205–31.

Feeley-Harnik, Gillian. "Is Historical Anthropology Possible? The Case of the Runaway Slave."

In *Humanizing America's Iconic Book*, edited by Gene M. Tucker and Douglas A. Knight, 95–126. Chico, 1980.

———. *The Lord's Table: Eucharist and Passover in Early Christianity*. Philadelphia, 1981. Reprint, with a new preface. Washington, D.C., 1994.

Fernandez, James W. "The Performance of Ritual Metaphors." In *The Social Use of Metaphor*, edited by J. David Sapir and J. Christopher Crocker, 100–131. Philadelphia, 1977.

———. "Persuasions and Performances: Of the Beast in Every Body . . . and the Metaphors of Everyman." In *Myth, Symbol, and Culture*, edited by Clifford Geertz, 39–59. New York, 1971.

Fildes, Valerie. *Breasts, Bottles and Babies: A History of Infant Feeding*. Edinburgh, 1986.

Finkelstein, Louis. *Mavo le Masekhetot Avot ve-Avot de-Rabbi Natan*. New York, 1950.

Fishbane, Michael. *Biblical Interpretation in Ancient Israel*. Oxford, 1985.

———. "The Well of Living Water: A Biblical Motif and Its Ancient Transformations." In *She'arei Talmon: Studies in the Bible, Qumran, and the Ancient Near East Presented to Shemaryahu Talmon*, edited by Michael Fishbane and Emanuel Tov, 3–16. Winona Lake, Ind., 1992.

Fisher, J. D. C. *Christian Initiation: Baptism in the Medieval West*. London, 1965.

Fleisher, Ezra. "New Light on Qiliri." Hebrew. *Tarbiz* 50 (1981): 282–302.

———. *Shirat ha-Qodesh ha-'Ivrit Bimei ha-Beinayim*. Jerusalem, 1975.

Flusser, David. *Society and Religion in the Second Temple Period*. Volume 8 of *The World History of the Jewish People*, edited by Michael Avi-Yonah and Zvi Baras. Jerusalem, 1977.

Forster, Robert, and Orest Ranum, eds. *Ritual, Religion and the Sacred*. Baltimore, 1982.

Forsyth, Ilene H. "Children in Early Medieval Art: Ninth through Twelfth Centuries." *Journal of Psychohistory* 4 (1976): 31–70.

———. *The Throne of Wisdom: Wood Sculptures of the Madonna in Romanesque France*. Princeton, 1972.

Fraade, Steven D. *From Tradition to Commentary*. Albany, 1991.

———. "Interpretive Authority in the Studying Community at Qumran." *Journal of Jewish Studies* 44, no. 1 (Spring 1993): 46–69.

Freehof, Solomon B. "Ceremonial Creativity among the Ashkenazim." In *The Seventy-Fifth Anniversary Volume of* The Jewish Quarterly Review, edited by Abraham A. Neuman and Solomon Zeitlin, 210–24. Philadelphia, 1967.

Friedman, Shamma Yehudah. "The Shortest Go First." Hebrew. *Leshineinu* 35 (1971): 117–29, 192–206.

Gafni, Isaiah, ed. *Mosedot ha-Qehillah u-Ma'arekhet ha-Ḥunukh ha-Yehudi bi-Tequfat ha-Talmud*. Jerusalem, 1978.

Gaidoz, H. "Les gâteaux alphabétiques." *Paris. Ecole Pratique des Hautes Etudes. Sciences philologiques et historiques. Bibliothèque* 73 (1887): 1–8.

Galvaris, George. *Bread and the Liturgy: The Symbolism of Early Christian and Byzantine Bread Stamps*. Madison, 1970.

Gaster, Moses. *The Tittled Bible*. London, 1929.

Gaster, Theodore H., ed. *Thespis: Ritual, Myth and Drama in the Ancient Near East*. New York, 1961.

Geertz, Clifford. "Religion as a Cultural Symbol." In *Anthropological Approaches to the Study of Religion*, edited by Michael Banton, 1–46. London, 1966. Reprinted in Clifford Geertz, *The Interpretation of Cultures*, 87–125. New York, 1973.

———. "Thick Description: Towards an Interpretative Theory of Culture." In Clifford Geertz, *The Interpretation of Cultures*, 3–30. New York, 1973.

Geffen, Rela M., ed. *Celebration and Renewal: Rites of Passage in Judaism*. Philadelphia, 1993.

Giladi, Avner. "Concepts of Childhood and Attitudes towards Children in Medieval Islam." *Journal of the Economic and Social History of the Orient* 32 (1989): 121–51.

Gilat, Yitzhaq. "Age Thirteen for the Commandments." Hebrew. In *Meḥqarei Talmud*, vol. 1, edited by Yaakov Zussman and David Rosenthal. Jerusalem, 1992.

Ginsberg, H. L. "Heart." In *Encyclopedia Judaica*, 8:7–8. Jerusalem, 1971.

Ginzburg, Carlo. *The Cheese and the Worms*. Baltimore, 1980.

———. *Ecstacies: Deciphering the Witches' Sabbath*. London, 1990.

———. "High and Low: The Theme of Forbidden Knowledge in the Sixteenth and Seventeenth Centuries." *Past and Present* 73 (1976): 28–41.

———. *Night Battles*. New York, 1983.

Goitein, S. D. "Jewish Education in Yemen as an Archetype of Traditional Jewish Education." Hebrew. In S. D. Goitein, *Ha-Teimanim: Historiah, Sidrei Ḥevrah, Ḥayyei ha-Ruaḥ*, edited by Menahem Ben-Sasson, 241–68. Jerusalem, 1983.

———. *Jews and Arabs*. New York, 1957.

———. *A Mediterranean Society*. 6 vols. Berkeley, 1967–93.

———. "Moses Maimonides, Man of Action." In *Hommage à Georges Vajda: Etudes d'histoire et de pensée juives*, edited by Gérard Nahon and Charles Touati, 155–67. Louvain, 1980.

———. *Sidrei Ḥinukh*. Jerusalem, 1962.

———. *Ha-Teimanim*. Edited by Menahem Ben-Sasson. Jerusalem, 1983.

Golb, Norman. *Toledot ha-Yehudim ba-ʿIr Rouen Bimei ha-Beinayim*. Tel Aviv, 1976.

Goldberg, Harvey. "Anthropology and the Study of Traditional Jewish Societies." *Association for Jewish Studies Review* 15, no. 1 (Spring 1990): 1–22.

———. Introduction. In *Judaism Viewed from Within and from Without*, edited by Harvey Goldberg, 1–43. Albany, 1987.

———. *Jewish Life in Muslim Libya: Rivals and Relatives*. Chicago, 1990.

———. "A Jewish Wedding in Tripolitania: A Study in Cultural Sources." *Maghreb Review* 3, no. 9 (1978): 1–6.

———. "The Mimuna and the Minority Status of Moroccan Jews." *Ethnology* 17, no. 1 (January 1978): 75–87.

———. "Torah and Children: Symbolic Aspects of the Reproduction of Jews and Judaism." In *Judaism Viewed from Within and from Without*, edited by Harvey Goldberg, 107–30. Albany, 1987.

Goldin, Judah. "Several Sidelights of a Torah Education in Tannaite and Early Amoraic Times." In *Ex Orbe Religionum: Studia Geo Widengren Oblata*. Studies in the History of Religions [Supplement to *Numen*, 21–22]. 2 vols., 1:176–91. Leiden, 1972.

Goldin, Simha. "Die Beziehung der jüdischen Familie im Mittelalter zu Kind und Kindheit." *Jahrbuch der Kindheit* 6 (1989): 211–56.

Goldman, Ari. *The Search for God at Harvard*. New York, 1991.

Goldschmidt, Daniel. "The Text of the Prayers according to the Reggio Manuscript of the 'Maḥzor Vitry.'" Hebrew. *Revue des études juives* 125 (1966): 63–75. Reprinted in Daniel Goldschmidt, *Meḥqarei Tefillah u-Fiyyuṭ*, 66–79. Jerusalem, 1979.

Goodblatt, David. "The Sources on the Beginnings of Organized Jewish Education in the Land of Israel." Hebrew. *Meḥqarim be-Toledot ʿAm Yisrael be-Erez Yisrael* 5 (1980): 83–103.

Goodich, Michael. "Bartholomaeus Anglicus on Child-Rearing." *History of Childhood Quarterly* 3, no. 1 (1975): 75–84.

———. "Childhood and Adolescence among the Thirteenth-Century Saints." *History of Childhood Quarterly* 1, no. 2 (1973): 285–309.

Goody, Jack. *Literacy in Traditional Societies.* Cambridge, 1968.

Graboïs, Aryeh. "L'exégèse rabbinique." In *Le moyen âge et la Bible,* edited by Pierre Riché and G. Lobrichon. Paris, 1984.

———. "The *Hebraica Veritas* and Jewish-Christian Intellectual Relations in the Twelfth Century." *Speculum* 50, no. 4 (October 1975): 613–34.

Graetz, Heinrich. *The Structure of Jewish History and Other Essays.* Translated and edited by Ismar Schorsch. New York, 1975.

Grendler, Paul F. *Schooling in Renaissance Italy: Literacy and Learning, 1300–1600.* Baltimore, 1989.

Gross, Heinrich. "Das handschriftliche Werk Assufot." *Magazin für die Wissenschaft des Judenthums* 10 (1883): 64–87.

Grossman, Avraham. "Exile and Redemption in Rabbi Joseph Qara's Writings." Hebrew. In *Tarbut ve-Ḥevrah be-Toledot Yisrael bimei ha-Beinayim* [Haim Hillel Ben-Sasson Memorial Volume], edited by Menahem Ben-Sasson et al., 269–301. Jerusalem, 1989.

———. "Between Spain and France." Hebrew. In *Galut Aḥar Golah* [Haim Beinart Festschrift], edited by Aaron Mirsky et al., 75–101. Jerusalem, 1988.

———. *Ḥakhmei Ashkenaz ha-Rishonim.* Jerusalem, 1981.

———. "The Jewish-Christian Polemic and Jewish Biblical Exegesis in Twelfth-Century France." Hebrew. *Zion* 51, no. 1 (1985): 29–60.

Gruber, Mayer. "The Motherhood of God in Second Isaiah." *Revue Biblique* 90 (1983): 351–59.

Gruenwald, Itamar. *Apocalyptic and Merkavah Mysticism.* Leiden, 1980.

Güdemann, Mortiz. *Geschichte des Erziehungswesens und der Cultur der abendländischen Juden.* 3 vols. 1880–88. Reprint. Amsterdam, 1969.

Gutmann, Joseph. "Christian Influences on Jewish Customs." In *Spirituality and Prayer: Jewish and Christian Understandings,* edited by Leon Klenicki and Gabe Huck, 128–38. New York, 1983.

———. *The Jewish Life-Cycle.* Leiden, 1987.

Gutmann, Joseph, ed. *Beauty in Holiness: Studies in Jewish Customs and Ceremonial Art.* [New York,] 1970.

Hajdu, Helga. *Das Mnemotechnische Schriftum des Mittelalters.* Vienna, 1936.

Hallo, William W. "Isaiah 28:9–13 and the Ugaritic Abecedaries." *Journal of Biblical Literature* 77 (1958): 324–28.

Halperin, David J. *The Faces of the Chariot.* Tübingen, 1988.

———. *The Merkavah in Rabbinic Literature.* New Haven, 1980.

Haskins, Charles Homer. *The Renaissance of the Twelfth Century.* Cambridge, Mass., 1927.

Haupt, Paul. "Manna, Nectar and Ambrosia." *Proceedings of the American Philosophical Society* 61 (1922): 227–36.

Havlin, Shlomoh Z. "Hadran." In *Encyclopedia Judaica,* 7:1053–54. Jerusalem, 1971.

———. "Moshe b. Maimon." In *Encyclopedia Hebraica,* 24:536–42. Jerusalem, 1972.

Heilman, Samuel C. *Synagogue Life: A Study of Symbolic Interaction.* Chicago, 1976.

Heller, Bernard. "Le nom divin de vingt-deux lettres." *Revue des études juives* 55 (1908): 69–70.

Heschel, Abraham Joshua. *The Earth Is the Lord's.* New York, 1949.

Hidiroglou, Patricia. "Les juifs d'après la littérature historique latine, de Philippe Auguste à Philippe le Bel." *Revue des études juives* 133 (1974): 373–456.

Hirschberg, H. Z. *A History of the Jews in North Africa.* 2 vols. Leiden, 1974–81.

Horowitz, Elliott. "'And It Was Reversed': Jews and Their Enemies in the Festivities of Purim." Hebrew. *Zion* 59, nos. 2–3 (1994): 129–68.

———. "Coffee, Coffee Houses, and the Nocturnal Rituals of Early Modern Jewry." *Association for Jewish Studies Review* 14, no. 1 (1989): 17–46.

———. "'A Different Mode of Civility': Lancelot Addison on the Jews of Barbary." In *Christianity and Judaism* [Studies in Church History, 29], edited by Diane Wood, 309–25. Cambridge, Mass. 1992.

———. "The Eve of Circumcision: A Chapter in the History of Jewish Nightlife." *Journal of Social History* 23 (1989): 45–70.

———. "The Rite to Be Reckless: On the Perpetration and Interpretation of Purim Violence." *Poetics Today* 15, no. 1 (Spring 1994): 9–54.

———. "The Way We Were." *Jewish History* 1, no. 1 (Spring 1986): 75–90.

Hsia, R. Po-chia. *The Myth of Ritual Murder.* New Haven, 1988.

Hyman, Paula E. *The Emancipation of the Jews of Alsace.* New Haven, 1991.

Idel, Moshe. "Development of an Ancient Technique of a Medieval Prophetic Vision." Hebrew. *Sinai* 86 (1979–80): 1–7.

———. *Kabbalah: New Perspectives.* New Haven, 1988.

———. "On the Method of the Author of *Sefer ha-Meishiv.*" Hebrew. *Sefunot,* n.s., 2, no. 17 (1983): 185–266.

———. "The World of the Angels in the Form of Man." Hebrew. In *Meḥqarim be-Qabbalah, be-Filosofia, ve-ha-Hagut* [Isaiah Tishby Festschrift], edited by Joseph Dan and Joseph Hacker, 1–66. Jerusalem, 1986.

Immanuel, Simha. "On 'Mahzor Vitry.'" *'Alei Sefer* 12 (1985): 129–30.

Jong, Mayke de. *Kind en klooster in de vroege middeleeuwen.* English summary. Amsterdam, 1993.

Jordan, William Chester. "A travers le regard des enfants." *Provence Historique* 150 (1987): 531–43.

———. "Christian Excommunication of the Jews in the Middle Ages: A Restatement of the Issues." *Jewish History* 1, no. 1 (Spring 1986): 31–38.

———. *The French Monarchy and the Jews.* Philadelphia, 1989.

———. "Jews on Top: Women and the Availability of Consumption Loans in Northern France in the Mid-Thirteenth Century." *Journal of Jewish Studies* 29 (1978): 39–56.

Joselit, Jenna. *New York's Jewish Jews.* Bloomington, 1990.

Kafih, Joseph. *Halikhot Teiman.* Jerusalem, 1963.

"Kallir, Eleazar." In *Encyclopedia Judaica,* 7:713–15. Jerusalem, 1971.

Kamelhar, Israel. *Rabbeinu Eleazar b. Yehudah mi-Germaiza ha-Roqeah.* 1930. Reprint. New York, 1975.

Kanarfogel, Ephraim. "Attitudes toward Childhood and Children in Medieval Jewish Society." In *Approaches to Judaism in Medieval Times,* edited by David Blumenthal, 2:1–34. Chico, 1985.

———. *Jewish Education and Society in the High Middle Ages.* Detroit, 1992.

Katz, Ernst. "Torah Study on the Mountain and by the Water." Hebrew. *Yeda' 'Am* 11 (1966): 4–8.

Katz, Jacob. *Exclusiveness and Tolerance.* New York, 1961.

————. The "Shabbes Goy." Philadelphia, 1989.

————. Tradition and Crisis: Jewish Society at the End of the Middle Ages. Translated by Bernard Dov Cooperman. New York, 1993.

Keiner, Ronald C. "The Hebrew Paraphrase of Saadiah Gaon's Kitab Al-Amanat Wa'l-I'tiqadat." Association for Jewish Studies Review 9, no. 1 (Spring 1986): 1–25.

Kimelman, Reuven. "Rabbi Yohanan and Origen on the Song of Songs." Harvard Theological Review 73 (1980): 567–95.

Kirshenblatt-Gimblett. "The Cut That Binds: The Western Ashkenazic Torah Binder as Nexus between Circumcision and Torah." In Celebration: Studies in Festivity and Ritual, edited by Victor Turner, 136–46. Washington, D.C., 1982.

Klein, Isaac. A Guide to Jewish Religious Practice. New York, 1979.

Kotek, S. "On the Period of Childhood in Sefer Ḥasidim: Medicine, Psychology and Education in the Middle Ages." Hebrew. Qorot 8 (1984): 297–318.

Kraemer, David. "Images of Jewish Childhood in Talmudic Literature." In The Jewish Family: Metaphor and Memory, edited by David Kraemer, 65–80. Oxford, 1989.

Krauss, Samuel. Das Leben Jesu nach jüdischen Quellen. 1902. Reprint. Hildesheim, 1977.

————. "Note sur le nom divin de vingt-deux lettres et sur le démon de l'oubli." Revue des études juives 56 (1908): 253–54.

————. Talmudische Archäologie. 3 vols. 1912. Reprint. Hildesheim, 1966.

Kriegk, G[eorg]. L[udwig]. "Das Schulwesen." In Deutsches Bürgerthum im Mittelalter, edited by G. L. Kriegk. 1868–71. 2 vols. Reprint. 2:64–127, 357–65. Frankfurt am Main, 1969.

Ladurie, Emmanuel Le Roy. Montaillou: The Promised Land of Error. New York, 1978.

Langmuir, Gavin. "AHA Forum: Comment." American Historical Review 91, no. 3 (June 1986): 614–24.

————. Toward a Definition of Antisemitism. Berkeley, 1990.

Lasareff, V. "Studies in the Iconography of the Virgin." Art Bulletin 20 (1938): 42–65.

Latham, R. E., ed. Revised Medieval Latin Word-List. London, 1965.

Lauterbach, Jacob Z. "Tashlik: A Study in Jewish Ceremonies." Hebrew Union College Annual 11 (1936): 207–304.

Leach, Edmond R. "Ritual." In International Encyclopedia of the Social Sciences, edited by David L. Sills, 13:520–26. New York, 1968.

Lechner, Maria-Lioba. "Beichteier: Ein Beitrag zum kirchlichen Abgabenwesen und zum Ostereierbrauchtum." Rheinisches Jahrbuch für Volkskunde 9 (1958): 244–54.

Leclercq, Jean. The Love of Learning and the Desire for God. 1961. Reprint. New York, 1982.

Le Goff, Jacques. "Culture cléricale et traditions folkloriques dans la civilisation mérovingienne." Annales: ESC 22 (1967): 780–91.

————. Intellectuals in the Middle Ages. 1957. Reprint. Cambridge, Mass., 1993.

————. "Préface." In Marc Bloch, Les rois thaumaturges. Paris, 1983.

Levenson, Jon D. The Death and Resurrection of the Beloved Son: The Transformation of Child Sacrifice in Judaism and Christianity. New Haven, 1993.

Lévi, Israel. "Un commentaire biblique de Leontin le maître de R. Gershom." Revue des études juives 49 (1904): 237–38.

Levine, Lee I. "The Sages and the Synagogue in Late Antiquity." In The Galilee in Late Antiquity, edited by Lee I. Levine, 201–22. New York, 1992.

Levine, Lee I., ed. *The Rabbinic Class of Roman Palestine in Late Antiquity.* New York, 1989.

Lieberman, Saul. *Hellenism in Jewish Palestine.* 2d rev. ed., 1962. Reprinted with *Greek in Jewish Palestine.* New York, 1994.

———. "Qelas Qillusin." *'Alei 'Ayin,* 75–81. Jerusalem, 1948–52. Reprinted in Saul Lieberman, *Meḥqarim be-Torat Ereẓ Yisrael,* edited by David Rosenthal, 432–39. Jerusalem, 1991.

———. Review of *Masekhet Soferim,* edited by Michael Higger. *Qiryat Sefer* 15 (1939): 56–57.

———. *Sheqi'in.* Jerusalem, 1970.

Liebes, Yehuda. "Christian Influences on the Zohar." In Yehuda Liebes, *Studies in the Zohar,* 139–61. Albany, 1993.

———. "The Messiah of the Zohar." In Yehuda Liebes, *Studies in the Zohar,* 1–84. Albany, 1993.

Lincoln, Bruce. "Beverages." In *The Encyclopedia of Religion,* edited by Mircea Eliade, 2:119–23. New York, 1987.

Lopez, Robert S. *The Birth of Europe.* New York, 1967.

———. *The Commercial Revolution of the Middle Ages, 950–1350.* New York, 1971.

Lord, Albert B. *The Singer of Tales.* Harvard Studies in Comparative Literature, 24. Cambridge, Mass., 1960.

Löw, Leopold. *Die Lebensalter in der jüdischen Literatur.* Szegedin, 1875.

Lynch, Joseph H. *Godparents and Kinship in Early Medieval Europe.* Princeton, 1986.

McLaughlin, Mary Martin. "Survivors and Surrogates: Children and Parents from the Ninth to the Thirteenth Centuries." In *The History of Childhood,* edited by Lloyd de Mause, 101–81. New York, 1974.

Malkiel, David J. "Infanticide in Passover Iconography." *Journal of the Warburg and Courtauld Institutes* 56 (1993): 85–99.

Mann, Jacob, ed. *Texts and Studies in Jewish History and Literature.* 1931. Reprint. 2 vols. New York, 1972.

Maranda, Pierre. "The Dialectic of Metaphor: An Anthropological Essay on Hermeneutics." In *The Reader in the Text: Essays on Audience and Interpretation,* edited by Susan R. Suleiman and Inge Crosman, 183–204. Princeton, 1980.

Marcus, Ivan G. "Circumcision, Jewish." In *The Dictionary of the Middle Ages,* edited by Joseph R. Strayer, 3:410–12. New York, 1983.

———. "Une communauté pieuse et le doute: Qiddouch ha-Chem (mourir pour la sanctification du nom) chez les juifs d'Europe du Nord et l'histoire de rabbi Amnon de Mayence." *Annales: Histoire, Sciences Sociales* 5 (September–October 1994): 1031–47.

———. "The Dynamics of Ashkenaz and Its People-Centered Authority." *Proceedings of the Rabbinical Assembly* 55 (1992): 129–38.

———. "From Politics to Martyrdom: Shifting Paradigms in the Hebrew Narratives of the 1096 Crusade Riots." *Prooftexts* 2, no. 1 (January 1982): 40–52.

———. "Hierarchies, Religious Boundaries and Jewish Spirituality in Medieval Germany." *Jewish History* 1, no. 2 (Fall 1986): 7–26.

———. "The Historical Meaning of the German Pietists." In *Gershom Scholem's Major Trends in Jewish Mysticism 50 Years After,* edited by Peter Schäfer and Joseph Dan, 103–114. Tübingen, 1993.

———. "History, Story and Collective Memory: Narrativity in Early Ashkenazic Culture." *Prooftexts* 10, no. 3 (Fall 1990): 365–88.

————. "Jews and Christians Imagining the Other in Medieval Europe." *Prooftexts* 15 (September 1995): 209–26.

————. "The Jews in the Medieval World." In *The Schocken Guide to Jewish Books*, edited by Barry Holtz, 70–91. New York, 1991.

————. "The Jews in Western Europe: Fourth to Sixteenth Century." In *Bibliographical Essays in Medieval Jewish Studies*, 17–105. New York, 1976.

————. "Judeo-Latin." In *The Dictionary of the Middle Ages*, edited by Joseph R. Strayer, 7:176–77. New York, 1986.

————. "Medieval Jewish Studies: Toward an Anthropological History of the Jews." In *Jewish Studies: The State of the Field*, edited by Shaye J. D. Cohen and Ed Greenstein, 113–27. Detroit, 1990.

————. *Piety and Society: The Jewish Pietists of Medieval Germany.* Leiden, 1981.

————. "Prayer Gestures in German Ḥasidism." In *Mysticism, Magic and Kabbalah in Ashkenazi Judaism*, edited by Karl Grözinger and Joseph Dan, 44–59. Berlin, 1995.

————. "Schools, Jewish." In *The Dictionary of the Middle Ages*, edited by Joseph R. Strayer, 11:69–72. New York, 1988.

Margalit, D. "On Memory." Hebrew. *Qorot* 5 (1972): 759–72.

Marrou, Henri. *History of Education in Antiquity.* New York, 1956.

Marx, Alexander. "Moses Maimonides." In Alexander Marx, *Essays in Jewish Biography*, 87–111. Philadelphia, 1947.

Merchavia, Ch. *Ha-Talmud Bi-Re'i ha-Naẓrut.* Jerusalem, 1970.

Metzger, Thérèse and Mendel Metzger, eds. *Jewish Life in the Middle Ages.* New York, 1982.

Michaelis, Johannes. *A Compendius Syriac Dictionary.* Edited by R. Payne Smith. 1903. Reprint. Oxford, 1975.

————. *Lexicon Syriacum.* Göttingen, 1788.

Minty, Mary. "Kiddush ha-Shem in the Eyes of Christians in Germany in the Middle Ages." Hebrew. *Ẓion* 59, no. 2 (1994): 209–66.

Mintz, Alan. *Ḥurban: Responses to Catastrophe in Hebrew Literature.* New York, 1984.

Momigliano, Arnaldo. "A Medieval Jewish Autobiography." In *History and Imagination: Essays in Honour of H. R. Trevor-Roper*, edited by Hugh Lloyd-Jones et al., 30–36. Duckworth, 1981.

Moore, R. I. *The Formation of a Persecuting Society.* Oxford, 1987.

Moran, Jo Ann Hoeppner. *The Growth of English Schooling, 1340–1548.* Princeton, 1985.

Morray-Jones, C. R. A. "Heikhalot Literature and Talmudic Tradition: Alexander's Three Test Cases." *Journal for the Study of Judaism* 22, no. 1 (1991): 1–39.

Morris, Colin. *The Discovery of the Individual: 1050–1200.* New York, 1972.

Murray, Robert. *Symbols of Church and Kingdom: A Study in Early Syriac Tradition.* Cambridge, 1975.

Narkiss, Bezalel. *Hebrew Illuminated Manuscripts.* Jerusalem, 1969.

————. "The Iconography of the Illustrations." In *The Bird's Head Haggadah of the Bezalel National Art Museum in Jerusalem*, edited by M. Spitzer, 89–110. Jerusalem, 1967.

————. "Illuminated Hebrew Children's Books from Medieval Egypt." In *Studies in Jewish Art* [Scripta Hierosolymitana, 24], edited by Moshe Barasch, 58–79. Jerusalem, 1972.

————. Introduction to *Machsor Lipsiae*, edited by Elias Katz. Leipzig, 1964.

Neufeld, Edward. "Apiculture in Ancient Palestine (Early and Middle Iron Age) within the

Framework of the Ancient Near East." In *Ugarit-Forschungen*, edited by Kurt Bergerhof et al., 10:219–47. Neukirchen-Vluyn, 1978.

Neusner, Jacob. *The Memorized Torah: The Mnemonic System of the Mishnah*. Chico, 1985.

Ong, Walter. *Orality and Literacy*. London, 1982.

Parry, Milman. *L'Epithète traditionelle dans Homère*. Paris, 1928. English translation in Milman Parry, *The Making of Homeric Verse*, edited by Adam Parry, 1–190. Oxford, 1971.

Pelikan, Jaroslav. *The Christian Tradition: A History of the Development of Doctrine*. 5 vols. Vol. 1. Chicago, 1971.

Perlow, Towa. *L'Education et l'enseignement chez les juifs à l'époque talmudique*. Paris, 1931.

Pilgram, Beate-Cornelia. "Geschenke an Schulanfänger." *Rheinisch-Westfälische Zeitschrift für Volkskunde* 21 (1974): 56–69.

Pines, Shlomo. Introduction to Moses Maimonides, *The Guide of the Perplexed*. Chicago, 1963.

Pollack, Herman. *Jewish Folkways in Germanic Lands (1648–1806): Studies in Aspects of Daily Life*. Cambridge, Mass., 1971.

Pope, Marvin, ed. *The Anchor Bible Song of Songs*. New York, 1977.

Poznanski, Samuel. Introduction [Hebrew] to his *Kommentar zu Ezechiel und den XII kleinen Propheten von Eliezer aus Beaugency*. 1913. Reprint. Jerusalem, 1968.

Price, S. R. F. *Rituals and Power: The Roman Imperial Cult in Asia Minor*. Cambridge, 1984.

Quinn, Patricia A. *Benedictine Oblation: A Study of the Rearing of Boys in Monasteries in the Early Middle Ages*. Ph.D. diss., State University of New York, Binghamton, 1985.

Rabinowitz, Louis I. "Tefillin." In *Encyclopedia Judaica* 15:898–904. Jerusalem, 1976.

Radding, Charles M. *A World Made by Men: Cognition and Society, 400–1200*. Chapel Hill, 1985.

Riché, Pierre. *Education and Culture in the Barbarian West from the Sixth through the Eighth Century*. Columbia, S.C., 1976.

———. "L'enfant dans la société monastique au XIIe siècle." In *Pierre Abélard, Pierre le Vénérable*. Actes et mémoires du colloque international, Abbaye de Cluny, 2–9 July 1972, 689–701. Paris, 1975.

———. "Le Psautier, livre de lecture élémentaire d'après les vies des saints mérovingiens." In *Etudes mérovingiennes*, 253–56. Paris, 1953.

Riché, Pierre, and Danièle Alexandre-Bidon, eds. *L'enfance au moyen âge*. Paris, 1994.

Riley-Smith, Jonathan. *The Crusades: A Short History*. New Haven, 1987.

Rivkind, Isaac. *Le-Ot u-le-Zikkaron: Toledot Bar-Mitzvah . . .* New York, 1942.

Rosenthal, Erwin I. J. "The Study of the Bible in Medieval Judaism." In *The Cambridge History of the Bible*, edited by G. W. H. Lampe, 2:252–79. Cambridge, 1969.

Roskies, Diane. "Alphabet Instruction in the East European Heder: Some Comparative and Historical Notes." *Yivo Annual of Jewish Social Science* 17 (1978): 21–53.

Roth, Cecil. *A History of the Jews in England*. 3d ed. Oxford, 1964.

———. *The Jews in the Renaissance*. 1959. Reprint. Philadelphia, 1977.

Roth, Ernst. "Educating Jewish Children on Shavuot." Hebrew. *Yeda' 'Am* 11 (1966): 9–12.

Rubin, Miri. *Corpus Christi: The Eucharist in Late Medieval Culture*. Cambridge, 1991.

Safrai, Shmuel. "Elementary Education: Its Religious and Social Significance in the Talmudic Period." In *Jewish Society through the Ages*, edited by H. H. Ben-Sasson and Shmuel Ettinger, 148–69. New York, 1971.

Sanday, Peggy Reeves. *Divine Hungar: Cannibalism as a Cultural System*. Cambridge, 1986.

Schäfer, Peter. *Hekhalot-Studien*. Tübingen, 1988.

———. *The Hidden and Manifest God*. Albany, 1992.

———. "Jewish Magic Literature in Late Antiquity and Early Middle Ages." *Journal of Jewish Studies* 41, no. 1 (Spring 1990): 75–91.

Schäfer, Peter, ed. *Synopse zur Hekhalot-Literatur*. Tübingen, 1981.

Schauss, Hayyim. *The Lifetime of a Jew throughout the Ages of Jewish History*. New York, 1950.

Schechter, Solomon. "The Child in Jewish Literature." 1889. Reprinted in Solomon Schechter, *Studies in Judaism*, 1st ser., 282–312. Philadelphia, 1920.

———. "Nachmanides." 1896. In Solomon Schechter, *Studies in Judaism*, 1st ser., 99–141. Philadelphia, 1920.

Schirmann, Jefim. "Samuel the Nagid, the Man, the Soldier, the Politician." *Jewish Social Studies* 13, no. 2 (April 1951): 99–126.

Schmidt, Leopold. *Volksglaube und Volksbrauch*. Berlin, 1966.

Schmitt, Jean-Claude. "Introduction and General Bibliography." *History and Anthropology* 1, no. 1 (November 1984): 1–28.

———. *La raison des gestes dans l'occident médiéval*. Paris, 1990.

Scholem, Gershom. *Catalogus Codicum Cabbalisticorum Hebraicorum*. Jerusalem, 1930.

———. *Jewish Gnosticism, Merkabah Mysticism, and Talmudic Tradition*. 1960. 2d improved ed. New York, 1965.

———. *Kabbalah*. New York, 1974.

———. *Major Trends in Jewish Mysticism*. New York, 1941.

———. *Origins of the Kabbalah*. Edited by R. J. Zwi Werblowsky. Princeton, 1987.

———. "Sidrei de-Shimmusha Rabba." Hebrew. *Tarbiẕ* 16 (1945): 196–209.

———. "Tradition and New Creation in the Ritual of the Kabbalists." In Gershom Scholem, *On the Kabbalah and Its Symbolism*, 118–57. New York, 1965.

Schorsch, Ismar. "From Wolfenbüttel to Wissenschaft: The Divergent Paths of Isaak Markus Jost and Leopold Zunz." *Leo Baeck Yearbook* 22 (1977): 109–28.

———. "Moritz Güdemann: Rabbi, Historian, Apologist." *Leo Baeck Year Book* 11 (1966): 42–66.

———. "The Myth of Sephardic Supremacy." *Leo Baeck Year Book* 34 (1989): 47–66.

Schultz, Magdalene. "The Blood Libel—A Motif in the History of Childhood." *Proceedings of the Ninth World Congress of Jewish Studies*, Division B, 1: 55–60. Jerusalem, 1986.

———. "Kindermotive in jüdischen Handschriften aus dem Mittelalter." *Jahrbuch der Kindheit* 2 (1985): 181–203, 267–69.

Schwabe, Moïse. "Jewish and Greco-Roman Schools in the Period of the Mishnah and the Talmud." Hebrew. *Tarbiẕ* 21 (1950): 112–23.

Scribner, Bob. "Is a History of Popular Culture Possible?" *History of European Ideas* 10, no. 2 (1989): 175–91.

Sears, Elizabeth. *The Ages of Man: Medieval Interpretations of the Life Cycle*. Princeton, 1986.

Seiferth, Wolfgang. *Synagogue and Church in the Middle Ages: Two Symbols in Art and Literature*. Translated from the German by Lee Chadeayne and Paul Gottwald. New York, 1970.

Sermoneta, Giuseppe. "Aspetti del pensiero moderno nell'ebraismo italiano tra rinascimento e età barocca." *Italia Judaica* 2 (1986): 17–35.

Shahar, Shulamit. *Childhood in the Middle Ages*. London, 1990.

Shamgar-Handelman, Lea, and Don Handelman. "Celebrations of Bureaucracy: Birthday Parties in Israeli Kindergartens." *Ethnology* 30, no. 4 (1991): 293–312.

Shereshevsky, Ezra. "Hebrew Traditions in Peter Comestor's *Historia Scholastica I, Genesis*." *Jewish Quarterly Review* 59 (1968–69): 268–89.

———. *Rashi the Man and His World.* New York, 1982.

Sinanoglou, Leah. "The Christ Child as Sacrifice: A Medieval Tradition and the Corpus Christi Plays." *Speculum* 48, no. 3 (July 1973): 491–509.

Smalley, Beryl. *The Study of the Bible in the Middle Ages.* Oxford, 1952.

Smith, Jonathan Z. "I Am a Parrot (Red)." In Jonathan Z. Smith, *Map Is Not Territory*, 265–88. Leiden, 1978.

———. *To Take Place: Toward Theory in Ritual.* Chicago, 1987.

Smith, Robert Payne. *Catalogi codd. MSS. Bodleianae, pars IV. cod. syr.* Oxford, 1864.

Soloveitchik, Haym. "Can Halakhic Texts Talk History?" *Association for Jewish Studies Review* 3 (1978): 152–96.

———. *Halakhah, Kalkalah ve-Dimui 'Aẓmi: Ha-Mashkanta'ut bimei ha-Beinayim.* Jerusalem, 1986.

———. "Religious Law and Change: The Medieval Ashkenazic Example." *Association for Jewish Studies Review* 12 (1987): 205–21.

———. *She'eilot u-Teshuvot ke-Maqor Histori.* Jerusalem, 1990.

———. "Three Themes in the *Sefer Ḥasidim*." *Association for Jewish Studies Review* 1 (1976): 311–57.

Southern, R. W. *The Making of the Middle Ages.* New Haven, 1953.

———. *Medieval Humanism.* Oxford, 1970.

Spamer, Adolf. "Sitte und Brauch." In *Handbuch der deutschen Volkskunde*, edited by Wilhelm Pessler, 2:165–66, 225–31. 3 vols. Potsdam, 1935–38.

Specht, Franz Anton. *Geschichte des Unterrichtswesens in Deutschland.* Stuttgart, 1885.

Spence, Jonathan D. *The Memory Palace of Matteo Ricci.* New York, 1984.

Sperber, Dan. *Rethinking Symbolism.* Cambridge, 1974.

Sperber, Daniel. *Minhagei Yisrael.* Jerusalem, 1989.

———. "Mourning Customs in the Period of Counting the Omer." Hebrew. In *Yad Le-Heiman* [Abraham Habermann Memorial Volume], edited by Zvi Malakhi, 361–69. Jerusalem, 1983.

Spiegel, Shalom. "The Legend of Isaac's Slaying and Resurrection." Hebrew. In *Alexander Marx Jubilee Volume*, edited by Saul Lieberman, Hebrew section, 471–547. New York, 1950. Translated by Judah Goldin as *The Last Trial*. Philadelphia, 1967.

Steinschneider, Moritz, ed. *Catalog der hebräischen Handschriften in der Stadtbibliothek zu Hamburg.* Hamburg, 1878.

Stern, S. M. "Life of Shmuel ha-Nagid." Hebrew. *Zion* 15 (1950): 135–45.

Stern, Shmuel Eliezer. "The Torah Education Rite among German Rabbis." Hebrew. *Zefunot* 1, no. 1 (Fall 1988): 15–21.

Stock, Brian. *The Implications of Literacy.* Princeton, 1983.

Stow, Kenneth R. "Agobard of Lyons and the Medieval Concept of the Jews." *Conservative Judaism* 29 (1974): 58–65.

———. "The Jewish Family in the Rhineland." *American Historical Review* 92 (1987): 1085–1110.

Swartz, Michael. "'Like the Ministering Angels': Ritual and Purity in Early Jewish Mysticism and Magic." *Association for Jewish Studies Review* 19, no. 2 (1994): 135–67.

Tal, Shlomo. "Isserles, Moses ben Israel." In *Encyclopedia Judaica*, 11:1081–85. Jerusalem, 1971.

Tambiah, S. J. "The Magical Power of Words." *Man* 3 (1968): 175–208.

Ta-Shema, Israel. "Havdalah." In *Encyclopedia Judaica*, 7:1481–82. Jerusalem, 1971.

———. *Minhag Ashkenaz ha-Qadmon*. Jerusalem, 1992.

———. "On Some Aspects of 'Mahzor Vitry.'" Hebrew. *'Alei Sefer* 11 (1984): 81–89.

———. "Some Matters Relating to Mourners' Qaddish and Its Customs." Hebrew. *Tarbiz* 53 (1984): 559–68.

Thomas, Keith. *Religion and the Decline of Magic*. New York, 1971.

Thurston, Herbert. "The Alphabet and the Consecration of Churches." *The Month* 115 (1910): 621–31.

Touitou, E. "Quelques aspects de l'exégèse biblique juive en France." *Archives juives* 21 (1985): 35–39.

Trachtenberg, Joshua. *The Devil and the Jews*. 1943. Reprint. Philadelphia, 1961.

———. *Jewish Magic and Superstition*. 1939. Reprint. New York, 1961.

Trexler, Charles C. *The Christian at Prayer*. Binghamton, 1987.

Turner, Terrence. " 'We are Parrots,' 'Twins Are Birds': Play of Tropes as Operational Structure." In *Beyond Metaphor: The Theory of Tropes in Anthropology*, edited by James W. Fernandez, 121–58. Stanford, 1991.

Turner, Victor. "Betwixt and Between: The Liminal Period in *Rites de Passage*." In *The Forest of Symbols*, 93–111. Ithaca, 1967.

———. *Dramas, Fields, and Metaphors*. Ithaca, 1974.

———. *The Ritual Process*. Chicago, 1969.

Twersky, Isadore. *Introduction to the Code of Maimonides (Mishneh Torah)*. New Haven, 1980.

———. "Jewish Education in Medieval Europe." Hebrew. In *Enziqlopedia Hinukhit*, edited by Aaron Kleinberger et al., 4:251–64. Jerusalem, 1964.

Urbach, Ephraim E. *Ba'alei ha-Tosafot*. 4th ed. 2 vols. Jerusalem, 1980.

———. "The Homiletical Interpretations of the Sages and the Expositions of Origen on Canticles, and the Jewish-Christian Disputation." In *Studies in Aggadah and Folk-Literature* [Scripta Hierosolymitana, 22], edited by Joseph Heinemann and Dov Noy, 247–75. Jerusalem, 1971.

Urbach, Ephraim, E., ed. *The Sages*. Jerusalem., 1979.

Van Gennep, Arnold. *Rites of Passage*. Chicago, 1960.

Vermes, Geza. "Redemption and Genesis xxii—the Binding of Isaac and the Sacrifice of Jesus." In *Scripture and Tradition: Haggadic Studies*, 193–227. Leiden, 1973.

Walter, Christopher. *Art and Ritual in the Byzantine Church*. London, 1982.

Wasserteil, David. *Minhagei Yisrael*. Jerusalem, 1980.

Waszink, Jan Hendrik. "Biene und Honig als Symbol des Dichters und der Dichtung in der griechisch-römischen Antike." *Rheinisch-Westfälische Akademie der Wissenschaften, Vorträge*, G 196, 5–38. Obladen, 1974.

Weckman, George. "Understanding Initiation." *History of Religions* 10 (1970–71): 62–79.

Weill, Shalva. "The Language and Ritual of Socialization: Birthday Parties in a Kindergarten Context." *Man* 21 (1986): 329–41.

Weinstein, Roni. *"Ad Ya'avor Za'am ha-Na'arut": Yaldut, Na'arut ve-Hitbagrut ba-Hevrah ha-Yehudit be-Italiyah ba-Me'ah ha-16*. Master's thesis, Department of Jewish History, Hebrew University. Jerusalem, 1989.

————. "Rites of Passage in Sixteenth-Century Italy: The Bar-Mitzvah Ceremony and Its Sociological Implications." Hebrew. *Italia* 11 (1994): 77–98.

Wells, David A. "Attitudes to the Jews in Early Middle High German Religious Literature and Sermons." *London German Studies* 4 (Institute of Germanic Studies, 1992): 27–69.

Werner, Marina. *Alone of All Her Sex.* New York, 1976.

Westermarck, Edward. *Ritual and Belief in Morocco.* 1926. Reprint. 2 vols. New Hyde Park, 1968.

Williman, Daniel. "Schools, Grammar." In *Dictionary of the Middle Ages,* edited by Joseph R. Strayer, 11:63–64. New York, 1988.

Wolfson, Elliot R. "Circumcision and the Divine Name: A Study in the Transmission of Esoteric Doctrine." *Jewish Quarterly Review* 78, nos. 1–2 (July-October 1987): 77–112.

Wuttke, Adolph. *Der deutsche Volksaberglaube der Gegenwart.* 2d ed. Berlin, 1869.

Yassif, Eli. "Exempla in Sefer Ḥasidim." Hebrew. *Tarbiz* 57, no. 2 (1988): 217–55.

————. "Hebrew Narrative in Eastern Lands." Hebrew. *Peʿamim* 26 (1986): 53–70.

Yates, Frances A. *The Art of Memory.* Chicago, 1966.

Yudlov, Yizḥaq. "Italian Alphabet Charts." Hebrew. *Qiryat Sefer* 62, nos. 3–4 (1987): 930–32.

Yuval, Israel. *Ḥakhamim be-Doram.* Jerusalem, 1989.

————. "'The Lord Will Take Vengeance, Vengeance for His Temple.'" Hebrew. *Zion* 59, nos. 2–3 (1994): 351–414.

————. "On Some Publications of the Journal 'Moriah' and the 'Ashkenazic Torah Project.'" Hebrew. *Qiryat Sefer* 61 (1986): 349–59.

————. "Vengeance and Curses, Blood and Libel." Hebrew. *Zion* 58, no. 1 (1993): 70–90.

Zafrani, Ḥaim. "Traditional Jewish Education in Morocco." Hebrew. In *Zakhur le-Avraham* [Studies in Memory of Abraham Elameliach], edited by H. Z. Hirschberg, 123–39. Jerusalem, 1972.

Zfatman, Sara. *Bein Ashkenaz ve-Zarfat: Le-Toledot ha-Sippur ha-Yehudi bimei ha-Beinayim.* Jerusalem, 1993.

Zimmer, Eric. "Body Gestures During Prayer." Hebrew. *Sidra* 5 (1989): 89–130.

————. "R. David b. Isaac of Fulda: The Trials and Tribulations of a Sixteenth-Century German Rabbi." *Jewish Social Studies* 45, no. 23 (Spring 1983): 217–32.

Zlotnick, Dov. *The Iron Pillar—Mishnah.* Jerusalem, 1988.

————. "Memory and the Integrity of the Oral Tradition." *Journal of the Ancient Near Eastern Society* 16–17 (1984–85): 229–41.

Zuesse, Evan M. "Meditation on Ritual." *Journal of the American Academy of Religion* 43, no. 3 (1975): 517–30.

————. "Ritual." In *Encyclopedia of Religion,* edited by Mircea Eliade, 12:405–22. New York, 1987.

Zunz, Leopold. "Salomon b. Isaac genannt Raschi." *Zeitschrift für die Wissenschaft des Judentums* (1822–23): 277–385.

————. *Zur Geschichte und Literatur.* Berlin, 1845.

Index

Aaron, 90, 98

Aaron b. Jacob ha-Kohen of Lunel, 33, 114, 122–23

Abaye, 142n37

Abbahu, 51

Abelard, Peter, 103

Abraham: and circumcision, 106; sacrifice of Isaac by, 6–7, 97

Abraham b. Moses Maimuni, 19, 21

Acculturation: Ashkenazic model of, 8–13, 103–5, 111; definition of, 9, 11; inward (premodern), 11–13, 102, 104, 111, 154n84; of Muslim and Christian elements into Judaism, 11; outward (modern), 11, 12; of Renaissance-period Italian Jews, 11, 12; Sephardic model of, 8–12

Addison, Lancelot, 20–25

Age: at bar mitzvah, 13, 17, 119–26; at circumcision, 44; at life-cycle events, 43–44; and mother's authority over child, 43; at oblation into Christian monasteries, 17, 117–18, 125; of religious majority, 17, 103, 105, 118–19, 124, 125–26; at school initiation, 1, 13–14, 15, 16, 25–26, 33, 42–46, 108, 113, 129n1

Akiva, 35, 36, 38, 49, 58, 68, 72

Alexander, Philip, 39

Algeria, initiation ceremonies in, 22–23

Alphabet, Hebrew. See Letters, Hebrew

'Amei ha-arez, 52

Ami, 37

'Amram b. Sheshna, 68–69

Anabaptists, 107

Angels: candy thrown down by, 18; and mnemonic devices, 50

Arba'ah Turim (The Four Pillars), 69

Ariès, Philippe, 123, 126

'Arukh (Arrangement), 59, 62, 63, 64

Ashkenazic culture: importance of Shavuot for initiation rituals in, 1, 14, 16, 25–27, 31, 32, 42–46, 79, 102, 104, 105, 108, 113, 115; model of acculturation in, 8–13, 103–5, 111; rabbinic elites in, 8–10, 12–13; ritualization of metaphors in, 5–7

Assimilation. See Acculturation; Cultural adaptation

At-b(a)sh method of learning letters, 36, 39, 109

Augustine (saint), 106

Avot de-Rabbi Natan, 38, 44

AYQ BKHR, 39

Bandinelli, Roland (later Pope Alexander III), 114

Baptism, Christian, 106–7

Bar, Shlomo, 23

Baraita de-Niddah, 70

Barhadbsabba (Nestorian bishop), 61

Bar mitzvah: age at, 13, 17, 119–26; development of, 13, 16, 17, 101, 103, 105–6, 113, 118–26; feast at, 122, 123, 125; use of wimpel at, 77, 124

Bava Batra 21a, 43, 44

Bede, 117

Benedictines, 117

Benei Makhir, 112